AF688541

DITCH THE BILLABLE HOUR!

Implementing Value-Based Pricing in a Law Firm

Shaun Jardine

BENNION KEARNY

First published 2024 by Bennion Kearny

Woodside, Oakamoor, ST10 3AE

www.BennionKearny.com

ISBN: 978-1-915855-23-7

Shaun Jardine has asserted his right under the Copyright, Designs and Patents Act 1988, to be identified as the author of this book.

Copyright Shaun Jardine 2024. All Rights Reserved.

No part of this publication may be reproduced, stored in a retrieval system, or transmitted in any form or by any means, electronic, mechanical, photocopying, recording or otherwise, without the prior permission of the publisher.

A CIP catalogue record for this book is available from the British Library.

This book is sold subject to the condition that it shall not, by way of trade or otherwise, be lent, re-sold, hired out or otherwise circulated without the publisher's prior consent in any form of binding or cover other than that in which it is published and without a similar condition including this condition being imposed on the subsequent purchaser.

Bennion Kearny has endeavoured to provide trademark information about all the companies and products mentioned in this book by the appropriate use of capitals. However, Bennion Kearny cannot guarantee the accuracy of this information.

Bennion Kearny Limited, 6 Woodside, Churnet View Road, Oakamoor, ST10 3AE, United Kingdom.

Cover design by Hannah Powell

To the three other members of *Team Jardine* – my wife Debbie and daughters Alex and Rebecca – who, without doubt, are the three most important people in my life. Thank you for putting up with me while I have been writing this. Also, a mention of another great woman – my mum Gwen Jardine – who confided to my daughter Rebecca, when she heard I was writing this book, *"I don't imagine that will be a bestseller..."* My mum may well be right, to be honest; she has been most of my life, but I hope she is not entirely correct on this occasion!

ABOUT THE AUTHOR

Shaun Jardine is a solicitor (non-practicing) and law firm owner/CEO with experience leading large legal teams.

Shaun likes to change and is unapologetically a disruptor. He has spoken about change management at numerous conferences in the UK, USA, and South Africa. He is one of the few current law firm management consultants who has "been there and done that" when it comes to actually implementing value-based pricing.

Shaun retired from his law firm in 2021 and created Big Yellow Penguin. He has since presented to thousands of lawyers in the UK and worldwide about the merits of value-based pricing through various conference appearances, webinars, and podcasts. He is much in demand as a conference keynote speaker and – without fear of contradiction – believes he is the only speaker ever to have addressed lawyer conferences dressed as a penguin!

Shaun has developed the 8 P Point Plan™, a value-based pricing process that is easy to understand and follow. The 8 PPP was inspired by the methodology and teachings of Professor John Kotter of the Harvard Business School. Kotter is a global authority on change management and, with Holger Rathgeber, wrote the fable *Our Iceberg Is Melting* – a story about a group of penguins who had to change their behaviours or perish.

ACKNOWLEDGEMENTS

This book has been both a labour of love and a real challenge. There is so much to say and be excited about, and trying to condense it has been a struggle. Much of what you will read here has been informed by existing books about value-based pricing. I have read many books, taken bits that resonated with me, and added my own spin and experience gained whilst working with many law firms over the past few years.

I was first introduced to the concept of value-based pricing by an old friend – law firm marketer Simon White. I regularly had lunch with Simon, and the deal was that whoever got the most out of having the meeting paid for lunch. I nearly always paid. One day, Simon waved a book at me and said, *"You have to read this book"*. It was a pithy novel/parable called *Avoiding Extinction: Reimagining Legal Services for the 21st Century* by a Canadian lawyer called Mitch Kowalski. It featured a reference to value-based pricing, which is when I first came across the topic. I am delighted to say, after reading Mitch's book, that I got in touch with him when he visited the UK and we met up. I even managed to entice him to speak at an event I put on at Coventry University for law students, which also attracted some of the great and the good of the legal profession.

At about the same time, I came across a Melbourne-based lawyer – John Chisholm – via social media. John describes himself as a recovering lawyer and is passionate about the benefits of value-based pricing for the legal profession. John and I exchanged many messages, most of which initially discussed Australia's dominance at cricket and the joys of law firm management. Some years later, John and I met up in the UK. John, in fact, conducted a workshop for some of our proactive, curious lawyers and a few other selected law firms.

In 2017, after being nagged by John, I attended two conferences, both held in a town called Allen on the outskirts of Dallas, Texas. The first event was the *Art of Value Conference,* organized by Kirk Bowman and Ed Kless, followed by a VeraSage meeting chaired by Ron Baker. VeraSage is a pricing think-tank created by Ron Baker and some other forward-thinking professionals who believed that the professional services charging model needed to move away from the billable hour. At the two events, I met lots of lawyers from all over the world who either had or were in the process of changing their professional services pricing models. I was slightly surprised to be the only British lawyer at both events.

Ron Baker deserves a special mention. As you read this book, you will see that Ron features a lot… and for good reason! He is undoubtedly one of the leading thinkers when it comes to value-based pricing and has been so for over 20 years. If this book ignites a thirst for knowledge in VBP and you want to learn more, read Ron's books and/or listen to him on the *Soul of Enterprise* – a radio station/podcast he records with his good friend and VeraSage Fellow Ed Kless. There is a wealth of Ron's knowledge and wisdom out there in books, podcasts, and blog posts. You will find that most books on the subject of pricing professional services mention Ron's wisdom somewhere in them. Even Lord Neuberger – the then-Master of the Rolls – quoted Ron Baker in a speech he gave in 2012. So, if Ron is good enough for Neuberger, he is good enough for me!

Also, whilst on the subject of VBP knowledge and good books, a big nod to another VeraSage Fellow – Tim Williams – from Ignition Consulting who wrote *Positioning for Professionals.* The book explains how professional knowledge firms can differentiate their way to success. It's a good read. Tim is also a formidable blogger, and I recommend you read as much of his material as you can.

A special thank you and second mention to Simon White, who cleared out his extensive library when he moved home and allowed me to have over 35 books on leadership, marketing, law firm management, and pricing. He even had some rare Ron Baker first editions! Simon's generosity allowed me to read many books I would never have otherwise read, and one or two I wish I never had read!

If you want to embark on the knowledge-gathering trail, have a listen to Kirk Bowman's podcast, *The Art of Value.* As I mentioned, Kirk Bowman and Ed Kless designed and delivered the *Art of Value Conference* that I attended in 2017 and that was a career-changing event for me. Not only did I learn a huge amount about VBP, but I also met some great, inspiring lawyers, including Steve and Jacqui Brown, Chris

Marston, Peter Carayiannis, Matthew Burgess, and Thomas Bowden, who inspired me to think differently about pricing and value and take the plunge into introducing VBP at my own firm. They have also kindly let me pick their brains as part of my research efforts. You will see some of Greg Kyte's artwork in this book. Thank you, Greg, for letting me use it. Milton at his computer makes me smile every time I do a presentation.

Thank you also to those who allowed me to interview them as part of my research for the Words with the Wise feature. The interviews were great fun (well, they were for me), and I learned so much. Thank you Nicola Jones, David Gilroy, Graham Moore, Kirsty Pappin, Paul Roberts, Robin Dicks, Simon Tupman, Matthew Burgess, Leanne Bentley-French, Thomas Bowden, Christopher Marston, Karen Finch, Will Whawell, Melissa Lyon, Terri Mottershead, Katherine Thomas, and Jon Whittle. A special thank you to Dr Jacqui Rigby, who has forgotten more about legal project management than I will ever know. Jacqui assisted me with the design of some materials I use at a VBP Masterclass for law firm leaders, which I hold from time to time. Many of the operational tips, exercises, and template plans that you will read in this book were created by Jacqui.

Thank you also to my publisher, James Lumsden-Cook of Bennion Kearny, for believing in this book so much he even paid me an advance! I hope his confidence is repaid with sales… notwithstanding my mum's comment above. Thanks also to Hannah Powell for the cover design.

Finally, a last and heartfelt thank you to John Chisholm for introducing me to your network of pricing buddies from all over the world, for nagging me to attend the *Art of Value* and *VeraSage* Conference, and for answering what may have seemed (at times) endless questions – this book is mainly your fault!

> If I read a book that cost me $20 and I get one good idea, I've gotten one of the greatest bargains of all time.
>
> **Tom Peters**

CONTENTS

INTRODUCTION

If there is one way you can change how people think about lawyers, it's by changing the way you charge for the service. Relationships are not built on charging for time. In fact, the only 'time' clients are interested in, is *how long* it will take to deliver the result.

Everyone dislikes paying open-ended hourly rates. When clients are told an hourly rate is £x hundred per hour, their immediate concern is, 'How long will this take?'

The lawyer's fallback position is typically… 'We don't know. We will charge an hourly rate, and we will book the time.'

I have not found one lawyer who would engage a builder to build an extension to their home and pay them at a day rate, so why do we expect clients to do the same with lawyers every single day? With the billable hour, the slowest horse wins the race. Clients are wising up, finding their voices, and the model must change.

Value-based pricing (VBP) seeks to disregard time as an input. My definition of VBP is: 'agreeing a price that is fair to both the client and the law firm; a price that reflects value for both parties.' It's not a time-based measure.

Put it another way. 'It's not the 6 minutes it takes me to tell you the answer to a problem. It's six minutes plus the 36 years of experience that allows me to know the answer and convey it in six minutes.'

VALUE-BASED PRICING, WHY NOW?

1. It's never easier to start a law firm; there are disruptors in the market.
2. Pressure on fees.
3. Pressure on costs.
4. Battle for talent.
5. Clients don't believe the billable hour gives good value for money.
6. Technology, particularly GenAI, has changed the game.
7. Geography is no longer a factor for clients to instruct lawyers, or for lawyers to work for employers. Agile working is here to stay.
8. Erroneous assumptions continue to be made by many professionals, including:
    a. Our clients know the pricing of our competitors.
    b. Our competitors' pricing is aligned to the price the client would pay.
    c. Our clients are able to, and have, undertaken price comparisons.

Let's face it, legal services are, in the main, a distressed purchase. Clients contact lawyers either to stop a pain or achieve a gain.

Clients want:

1. Results.
2. Certainty.
3. Transparency.
4. No surprises.
5. Availability.
6. 'Got my Back' – Reassurance.
7. Clarity.
8. Comfort.
9. No extras.
10. And value.

With all this in mind, the aim of this book is simple. It's to give practical advice and guidance to help lawyers understand the value they create and how to implement VBP in their businesses.

HOW THIS BOOK WORKS

Some years ago, I remember reading a white paper put out by an AI legal tech company. I won't name the company to spare their blushes. It was a beautifully designed and presented paper. A total of eight lawyers were interviewed. One said he liked the hourly rate. One sat on the fence. Six said they would like to ditch it… but it was too hard to do so. End of white paper.

I sent a copy to my friend, John Chisholm, and we had a rant for a while. The paper has niggled me for several years. Just because something is hard does not mean it shouldn't be changed, especially if the advantages of changing are beneficial to all. This book is partly a product of my reaction to that white paper.

I have, as you will see, developed and set out what I call the 8 P Point Plan™ (8PPP), a VBP implementation process. I hope it is easy to understand and follow. I hope by adopting various aspects of a framework, it can be replicated, amended, developed and some parts incorporated into your businesses.

Obviously, I don't know your business or its people. So please treat the book as 'food for thought.' I do criticise some lawyers and their approach to doing things, but this is not aimed at you, the reader… although I am sure you will have come across individuals where the criticism cap would fit! I also mention what 'you' should do as well as 'your firm'. Obviously, I have no idea who will read this book and no idea what your firm is like, so please don't take any of my comments to heart.

When writing, you will see I use customer and client interchangeably. I personally prefer to use customer. I know some lawyers dislike intensely describing their clients as customers. Some lawyers have told me so to my face! So, to keep you all happy, I use both interchangeably.

I also flit between calling the legal business a firm, law firm, your firm, and company. I call owners of the businesses, Partners, Equity Partners, directors, stakeholders, and shareholders. I also mention CEOs and Managing Partners, and CFOs and Heads of Finance.

When I talk about management teams, I use a number of words interchangeably, including Board, Executive Board, EXCO, and your management team.

When referring to law firm owners, I mention Equity Partners, EPs, Shareholders, and owners.

When I refer to the person likely to lead a VBP project, I refer to Change Manager, Project Sponsor, Chief Pricing Officer, and Project Leader. The chances are, if you are reading this book, you may play one of those roles.

I will also be mentioning how you need to document and create systems within your business to create a pricing process. This is where the journey is taking you. You will need to capture data and learnings and store them somewhere, develop processes and communicate them to your staff. My shorthand for this will be a reference to a Big Book of Usefulness – a *BBU*. It may be that a BBU becomes a manual at your firm. It may be that your operations team develop processes and systems that are integrated into your Practice Management System. BBU covers it all.

The 8 P Point Plan, which you will be reading about, is inspired by the methodology and teachings of Professor John Kotter of the Harvard Business School. John Kotter is a global authority on change management, and he and Holger Rathgeber wrote the fable 'Our iceberg is melting', a story about a group of penguins who had to change their behaviours or perish. I read this book as part of my preparation for carrying out a large change management exercise in 2015/16.

In my opinion, 'Our Iceberg is melting' is a book that is perfect for lawyers. It takes an hour and a quarter to read, it has large print, there are coloured pictures of penguins, and one of them even has a briefcase! The lessons are clear and easy to remember.

One of the exercises (see page 78) invites you to listen to John Kotter himself explain the story. It is worth watching. Kotter will introduce you to a number of penguins, including an inquisitive penguin called Fred, a get-stuff-done penguin called Alice, and a 'Naysayer' penguin called NoNo. You will have Naysayers in your organisation; we all have.

WHY ARE YOU READING THIS BOOK?

I suspect the answer is because you are inquisitive, forward-thinking, and perhaps have a notion and desire to bring about change in your business. You may even be a proactive, inquisitive penguin. I suspect you are not a Naysayer!

You will appreciate it is the leader's job is to lead, and you will also know that the leaders in an organisation can come from anywhere in an organisation, and all are not always necessarily Partners/owners or members of the Board. I spoke at a large legal conference in London in 2023. After my session, I was approached by a Trainee Solicitor, who was frustrated that his Head of Department wouldn't let him seek to increase his prices. He wanted some advice. That Trainee Solicitor was a leader in the making. You will need support on the VBP journey and find like-minded colleagues within Practice Area teams who will support you on your journey.

The important thing to understand as you prepare to go on a change management journey is that change is difficult. Change takes time to embed and ingrain. People dislike change.

In my experience, lawyers – in particular – dislike change. They are naturally conservative, risk-averse, pay attention to detail, are experts at filibustering and are argumentative. Many lawyers who are prepared to talk about change usually believe it is something that should happen to everybody else other than them.

You will know the technical term for keeping things the same is called preserving the status quo. This should not be confused with Status Quo, the 70s rock band who opened the global fund-raising concert Live Aid at Wembley in 1984.

Status quo bias is a cognitive prejudice that refers to the tendency of people to prefer things to stay the same by default. Those afflicted by status quo bias are resistant to change and have a preference for the current or existing situation, even when making a change might be advantageous or necessary.

This book aims to help you move away from the status quo you may be experiencing and help your lawyers unlearn practices they have been implementing for years. In the chapters coming up, we will *get down, deeper and down* (*#if you know, you know*) into the detail.

You will, as you embark on this project, face objections from Naysayer penguins in your firm. In fact, I have listed – in the Appendices – 50 reasons you will be confronted with as to why you should not do this project; 50 reasons why you should not change, just retain the status quo. I saw this list posted on Facebook… it had a lot of likes! One of the jobs of those leading the VBP change is to overcome these 50 objections.

So, dear reader, this book is my attempt to get you started on your VBP journey. It's not a blueprint that will immediately work in your organisation, but it will hopefully work like a road map and point you in the right direction.

INTRODUCING THE 8 P POINT PLAN

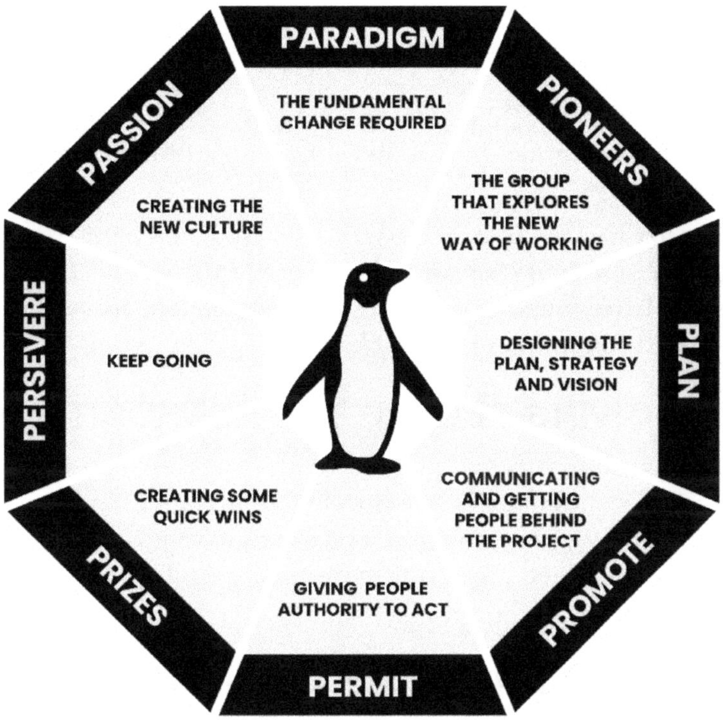

P#1 PARADIGM – THE FUNDAMENTAL CHANGE REQUIRED

Why the change is necessary. What the benefits and risks are. Why change should be part of the Strategy. Why people should get onboard.

P#2 PIONEERS – THE GROUP THAT EXPLORES THE NEW WAY OF WORKING

You need help. A pilot group of Pioneer penguins who will support, deliver, and champion the change that needs to happen in your firm. It's important that you identify key influencers and proactive members of staff who can help you plan and execute the change. You don't want Naysayer penguins in this group. You are aiming for an enthusiastic group of change agents who can inspire and persuade others in your organisation.

P#3 PLAN – DESIGNING THE PLAN, STRATEGY AND VISION

In this step, you are planning to create a Strategic Vision to help deliver the change. A picture of the future state, the benefits to your firm, your customers and your staff and

– crucially – how it looks different from your current way of doing things. Ideally, you will be able to link your Vision to your values and mission.

P#4 PROMOTE – COMMUNICATING AND GETTING PEOPLE BEHIND THE PROJECT

A crucial step is to communicate the Vision to the whole firm and stakeholders. This is where many Plans fail.

Depending on the size of your firm, you will use a variety of channels to engage with your audience. The Vision in P#3 must be reinforced by both the leadership/Pioneer Group's actions and behaviours. By effective communication, you will get buy-in and create enthusiasm and commitment to the change.

P#5 PERMIT – GIVING PEOPLE THE AUTHORITY TO ACT

The fifth step is to give authority and permission to your team and stakeholders. Any barriers, policies, or behaviours impeding the change which has to happen, need to be removed. Resources and support need to be provided to the team to facilitate the change. You need to enable the team to take ownership and responsibility for the change.

P#6 PRIZES – CREATING SOME QUICK WINS

It's fundamentally important to celebrate and generate quick wins that demonstrate the value of the change and that it is being successful.

Conscious efforts will have to be made to celebrate milestones, plus recognise and reward team members; this will help build momentum and confidence in the change occurring.

P#7 PERSEVERE – KEEP GOING

The seventh step is to build on the success of the changes you have implemented. It is looking at gaps and the opportunities for improvement. The changes you have designed and undertaken need to become embedded into your systems and processes.

P#8 PASSION – CREATING THE NEW CULTURE

The eighth and final step is to embed the change into your business.

By the time you get to this stage, you may need to align and integrate the changes with your Vision, Goals, and Values and embed them. Your leadership and management need to have totally bought into the process and be leading by example.

*

It perhaps won't surprise you to learn that the majority of this book focuses on P#3 Plan. This section is by far the largest and is broken down into four subsections: Knowledge, Tools, Vision, and Plan.

As we start out on this journey, I probably need to point out there are numerous ways that legal services can be priced. This book is **not** an analysis of Alternative Fee Arrangements and competing pricing methodologies. It's about one methodology, value-based pricing.

This book does not take an in-depth look at project management either. I do give some planning and project management guidance, but it is not hugely detailed. I have tried to limit my thoughts to what I know can work in the value-based pricing space of a typical law firm. By typical firm, I mean something outside the Top 50, by size, in the UK. I don't profess to know or understand how Magic Circle global law firms work. I imagine that they are very well run and have sophisticated pricing teams and systems which, in many cases, I suspect will be wedded to the billable hour.

In all law firms, regardless of size, there will be lawyers and managers who will be struggling with the logic of the billable hour and looking for an alternative. I hope this book provides the insight and motivation to change.

UNUSUAL FEATURES OF THE BOOK!

Let's face it, we all learn in different ways. I have sought to deliver the content and information to take into account the different ways in which people learn. Some of us are audible learners, others visual, and some like to learn by doing.

Throughout the book, various images and boxes will crop up. They are explained below.

BRACE YOURSELF FOR SOME HOME TRUTHS!

BRACE YOURSELF…
incoming provocative statement

In some cases, you may think I am stating the obvious. In other cases, they may give you food for thought. But the comments may help you with your thinking.

QUOTES

Here is a self-explanatory quote!
Shaun Jardine

Dotted around each chapter, I have included quotes from a variety of individuals. Hopefully, one or two will strike a chord with you, and you can use them in any presentations/Business Cases you have to make in the future.

Why are there many quotes in this book, you may ask? It's because lawyers are always looking for proof – 'Who said that?', 'What support do you have for your proposition?'

You can, where appropriate, quote Ron Baker, Jurgen Klopp, Pele, Tim Williams, Nelson Mandela, Gandhi, and my next-door neighbour!

POSSIBILITY THINKING

POSSIBILITY THINKING

I am a great fan of trying to enhance the power of a crowd and get groups of people thinking about how to solve a problem. Many brains make light work!

Some years ago, I attended a two-day leadership course organised by Andy Gilbert of MAD (Make a Difference) training. Andy led a session on what he called Possibility Thinking. You will see, in this book, that I refer to Possibility Thinking on many occasions.

HOW IT WORKS

1. To adopt a Possibility Thinking mindset, you basically write down the problem, e.g., 'I don't have enough time to do x' and then turn the problem into a solution-focused question containing the word 'possibly' or 'might' or 'could'.
    a. How can I possibly make more time to enable me to do X?
    b. What could I possibly do to free up more time to do X?
    c. Who could possibly help me with X?
2. Then, create a table on a piece of paper of, say, 30 lines (can be more), and in a timed session, answer the question you have posed with a group of like-minded people.

    The crucial thing is to treat **anything** as a possibility. Do not evaluate the answers as you write them. Do not have a conversation with yourself. Set a timer for, say, four minutes. Then start frantically writing!

    If you take the example 'How could I possibly get home from work', you will start with obvious answers – car, bike, taxi, walk – but as time goes on, the answers become a little more extreme and interesting. Some of those answers become really inventive and interesting. I have led Possibility Thinking sessions many times. I get groups to give me over 50 ways on the 'How do I get home from work?' question, and every single time I do it, someone dreams up an answer that I have never heard before. It's amazing!

3. Once you have a list of possibility answers, you will find you have a readymade list of new creative ideas. Simply highlight the 'possibles', explore them, and create some goals.

You will find examples of possibility questions throughout this book. They are real-life examples of questions I have posed to groups of lawyers. I strongly recommend that you practise Possibility Thinking. You will get answers from your people, and involving them in the process will help you immeasurably.

THE BIG SURVEY QUESTIONS

BIG SURVEY QUESTIONS

I asked this question in a poll of 80 different law firms.

The answer is not unusual! Sad, but not unusual.

Q: I believe that some of the clients my firm acts for should be dismissed as they are too painful and/or unprofitable to act for.

A: 76%.

Some of the comments which were given to the question.

Q: What prevents your firm deselecting clients?

A: Included 'Worry about our reputation', 'Inertia', and 'Partners'.

Your staff know which clients they would like to see the back of.

I regularly conduct what I call Pricing Confidence Surveys with the law firms and lawyers I work with. I have been fortunate enough to survey many law firms and groups of law firms – most recently, the members of the BOLD Legal Group (a group which has 670 law firm members).

The surveys I conduct are always anonymous, and the data always comes directly to me, not the firm/organisations asking for the survey to be conducted. As a result, the answers I get are very honest and powerful. At the time of writing this book, I have received data from over 165 law firms.

Where appropriate, and to provide you with reassurance and proof – which may be useful in your own journey – I have extracted some of the survey data and posted it in the text.

You may well find that many of the questions would receive similar answers from your employees. Be brave and ask the questions.

WORDS WITH THE WISE

WORDS WITH THE WISE

Melissa Lyon, Hive Legal

Value-based pricing plays to people's strengths. If you take away the notion that the billable hour is only about providing technical advice, everyone in the firm can contribute in some way to the value that you're providing the client. So, everyone feels a lot more invested in the business.

When you see the image of a person at a lectern, you are going to hear from some wise people. People who have been there and done it, and have a view about VBP and its implementation. I have really enjoyed speaking with the 'wise' and hope that you enjoy reading their wisdom as well.

Thank you to the following wise people who provided information and generously gave me time to interview them as part of my preparation and research.

Jacqueline Brown
Graham Moore
Kirsty Pappin
Robin Dicks
Will Whawell
David Gilroy

Nicola Jones
Dr Jacqui Rigby
Paul Roberts
Thomas Bowden
Katherine Thomas
Matthew Burgess

Christopher Marston
John Chisholm
Karen Finch
Simon Tupman
Melissa Lyon
Terri Mottershead

Jon Whittle

Leanne Bentley

Steven Brown

Tim Williams

8 PPP PENGUIN LOGIC

8 PPP PENGUIN LOGIC

If you see this symbol, you will read what I call Penguin Logic... a tip or a thought from me that I hope will help with your learning, understanding and implementation.

SHINGLES LOGIC

SHINGLES LOGIC

I have created a fictional firm called Shingles and Co., which crops up in the book. I called the firm Shingles as the disease is a painful condition, most common in older people. Beware when you see the dinosaur image – we know that dinosaurs belong in the past. Shingles thinking is not a good thing!

GOLDEN RULES

When you see blocks of gold, I am seeking to highlight a rule that I think is important. There are not too many of them, but bearing them in mind will certainly help you on the VBP journey.

Here is the first golden rule. Well, to be honest, it is more of a golden tome!

GOLDEN RULE #1

The management of your business must be 100% onboard with this project. Otherwise, it won't be fully implemented.

- They must become engaged and be involved in championing the change in culture that needs to happen.
- They must help define the objectives and then implement them.
- Resources must be made available.
- Staff must be made available to participate in the project.
- Obstacles will need to be removed.
- Funds and expertise will need to be made available.
- It will need to be made clear – across the business – that this is a serious initiative and vital for the firm's success.

Lots of carefully considered communications will be required.

CRIB SHEETS

And finally, at the end of each chapter/major section, there is a crib sheet packed full of what I hope you will find to be useful material to help you deliver the VBP project. Some of the sections have lots of links to blogs and exercises. The aim of the crib sheet is to identify materials, reading, and exercises, and basically give you a steer on how to implement VBP. My aim is to help cut down on some of the research and legwork that you would otherwise have to do.

Many of the exercises in the crib sheet can be allocated to members of the Pioneer Penguin Group to get them engaged in the process early on.

CRIB SHEET

READING & VIEWING

There are some recommended reading sections. These are relatively short YouTube clips, Ted Talks, podcasts, blogs, articles, and white papers that may help with your understanding. Some of them are even funny!

Some of the links to documents may well be taken down from the websites that they were on at the time I wrote this book. Apologies if that happens, but it is beyond my control.

TIPS/CHECKLISTS

Some words of wisdom.

EXERCISES

These are exercises which you may wish to carry out with some of your team and Pioneer Penguin Groups as you work through the process.

I have marked some of these as **COMPULSORY** if I think that they are sufficiently important.

POSSIBILITY THINKING QUESTIONS TO POSE

As you already know, I am a great fan of Possibility Thinking.

Some of the questions appearing in the text and the crib sheets may help you in the VBP process if you assemble your troops and ask the questions of them.

THE VBP COLONY

I have created an online community called the VBP Colony which you can access via my website www.bigyellowpenguin.co.uk

As I have mentioned, I am a great believer in the power of the crowd, and all of the areas of the 8PPP appear on the colony website as separate chat rooms. Some of the planning documents and templates you will come across in the book are available in the colony for download, too.

The thinking behind the colony is to provide a forum where all those looking for new VBP icebergs can meet in a relaxed online atmosphere and exchange views, thoughts, information, business-orientated ideas and updates about value-based pricing. Who knows, members of the colony may even form and build business connections.

I do, however, hope that the conversations blatantly, unashamedly, unreservedly, without fear or favour relate to the legal profession and its future! Our iceberg is melting. I hope you will register to join the colony, pose questions, network, and give support to others on their VBP journey.

APPENDICES TEMPLATES

The appendices contain useful templates and materials that you can use, including a rather long task list. I have created the list and set it out in subsections of each area of the Plan. You may well think of additional tasks as you read this book.

A Word version of the detailed RACI task template, plus electronic versions of the templates you see in the book, are available on the Colony website.

Now, let's get started!

P#1 PARADIGM

THE FUNDAMENTAL CHANGE REQUIRED

CREATE A SENSE OF URGENCY

> 'Paradigm shifts require us to challenge our assumptions and question our beliefs.'
>
> **Albert Einstein**

Welcome to the first P in the 8P Point Plan: P#1 for Paradigm.

I am delighted you are considering going on a VBP journey, but a note of caution first. To implement VBP successfully, you must accept that you will need a paradigm shift and change how you have been pricing and doing things to date.

You will need to:

- Create a sense of urgency to make this change happen.
- Grab people's attention.
- Sell the need for change and point out the consequences of not changing.

- Immerse people in information about the need to change.
- Discuss ways to solve the issues and problems that people will identify with change.
- Empower people to help them play a part in solving the problems.
- Ensure urgency is maintained is crucial for generating change.

GOLDEN RULE #2

If complacency is allowed to settle in,
then the change won't happen.

DEFINE THE CHANGE GOAL

Later, not now, you will have to consider what outcome you are seeking to achieve. You can't write that outcome now, as you haven't read the book! But if you are contemplating making a paradigm shift in your business, you need to define what that means; what is the Goal?

One of the key drivers should be that you want to develop a better business by embracing VBP.

> Speed is the ultimate competitive weapon. Be the first in the field. Do it now.
>
> **Richard Branson, Screw It, Let's Do It**

Implementing VBP is not creating a few hints and tips. It requires a change of mindset and an understanding that all aspects of the business will be involved at some stage – from lawyers, the operations teams, BD and marketing, compliance, finance and, crucially, the whole management/ownership team.

Profit maximisation is not the sole driver for this change. Don't get me wrong, I believe profit optimisation is important. But it's not the only reason to embark on this project.

Implementing VBP can give your business a clear advantage. It differentiates it. It has benefits for clients, employees, and law firm owners. There are huge benefits for all when it comes to value-based pricing.

1. You focus on what customers actually want, and that is *results*, *outcomes*, and *solutions*. Customers are not interested in time and inputs.

   Customers do not really care who delivers their work as long as they get the outcome they want. Spoiler alert… they don't care how long your firm has been in business, for example. They don't even care that much if you are qualified to do the work. They will assume you are, as you work at an organisation that describes itself as a law firm. They assume that you are competent to deliver a high-quality and compliant legal service. In 36 years of practising law, no one ever asked me to show them my practising certificate. I suspect you never ask to see your dentist's qualifications, either. Competence is table stakes, not a differentiator.
2. You won't treat all clients equally. Simply because not all clients are the same. We know some are prepared to pay for a better service level than others, and those that pay more should receive a better service level.
3. You will work for customers who really value what you do.
4. Your number of customer complaints should fall. How many current complaints relate to fees and clients not being updated regarding costs?
5. Your customers will become a referral source.
6. Your cash flow will improve.
7. Aged debt will reduce.
8. You will stop doing work for free.
9. Your administration costs will reduce.
10. Your lawyers will work smarter, not harder.
11. Your lawyers will have a better work-life balance.
12. Your business will become more profitable as you dispense with an artificial cap on its income-earning potential (hourly rates x annual chargeable hours = lawyer target).
13. You may even choose to free yourself from the tyranny of the billable hour. The only 'time' our clients are interested in, is how long it takes to get the result. Lawyers know and understand that the concept of chargeable and non-chargeable time gets in the way of this.

Do not underestimate that implementing VBP takes time, commitment, and stamina. Whilst there will be quick wins, the real returns will take some years to realise as your business processes, procedures, know-how, and capabilities improve.

GOLDEN RULE #3

Every lawyer knows that real, meaningful relationships with clients are not built on charging for time.

WHAT IS A VALUE-BASED PRICE?

As laid out in the Introduction, 'A value-based price is one which is fair to the client, and also fair to the lawyer who created the valuable solution', or – to put it another way in my case – it's not the 12 minutes it takes me to tell you a solution to your problem, it's the 12 minutes plus 36 years' experience.

Take a lawyer who charges £300 an hour and can answer a client's question in 15 minutes and save a client £200,000. Is the correct price for the advice £75 (being the 15 minutes it took to deal with the issue)? It is if you charge by the hour. But the value-based price would and should be much higher… why not 15/20% of the value created… or even more?

You probably know the old joke where a mechanical engineer gets called out to fix a mission-critical, expensive machine that has broken down at a factory.

The engineer arrives and gets taken to the machine. He puts his ear to the machine and listens, then places his hand into a little tool bag and brings out a hammer. He taps the machine, and it starts running. He is in and out of the plant in 15 minutes.

The engineer sends in a bill for £1,000, whereupon the managing director demands a full breakdown of the bill. He receives an invoice which reads £5 for the use of the hammer and £995 for knowing where to tap. The joke is VBP in action!

> A journey of a thousand miles begins with a single step.
>
> **Chinese proverb**

WHAT ARE YOUR REASONS FOR THE PARADIGM SHIFT?

You must have a reason to change. Whatever the reason is, it is important that implementing VBP needs to be broadcast and publicised as a strategic objective at your firm. To be fair, it probably needs to be your number one strategic objective above all others while you get the project underway. You are embarking on a process that should be a priority and should remain high on agendas until such time as the exercise is completed.

Your reasons for implementing VBP may be many. Let's take a look at some of the likely ones:

1. No one owns pricing at your firm, and your price setting policies are flawed.
2. The current practice of setting budgets is illogical and frustrating.
3. Financial issues. Your business is not making enough money, or you think it has the potential to earn more revenue or a better margin.
4. You are not capturing the value you create.
5. You have succession planning issues and need to make your business more attractive to lawyers to remain with the business.
6. You want to improve your relationships with clients or get new ones.
7. You may feel that the billable hours' days are numbered and would like to get ahead of the curve.

Let's look at these areas in a little more detail.

1. WHO OWNS PRICING?

Pricing is the number one profit lever if used correctly. Yet, in most law firms, it is totally neglected.

The arrows of the pricing function in most firms are not going in the same direction. In fact, some of the arrows are not even arrows… they may even just be sticks! It's a confusing mess; it's a free for all.

And one of the problems with pricing is that it is not a science. It is an art. Don't believe me; read these quotes below.

> Pricing is guesswork. It is usually assumed that marketers use scientific methods to determine the price of their products. Nothing could be further from the truth.
>
> **David Ogilvy, Ogilvy on Advertising**

I like the Ogilvy quote, but I like the next one more. In his book *Smarter Pricing*, Tony Cram references a quotation from Mark Ritson of the London Business School who reportedly said:

> Pricing is the worst managed of all marketing areas. How prices are decided is often a mixture of voodoo and bingo.
>
> **Mark Ritson, Former Professor of the London Business School**

I would have paid good money to sit in on that lecture with Mark Ritson.

The sad thing is Ritson is not wrong. In the numerous surveys I have undertaken with law firms, many lawyers tell me there is very little ownership and oversight in their businesses when it comes to the pricing of their services. But we know that pricing is the number 1 profit lever if used correctly. What is going on?

What currently happens in the pricing space in many law firms is a combination of:

1. Hourly rate setting and time recording.
2. Standard fixed prices set for services such as conveyancing, simple will drafting, and lasting powers of attorney, plus low-priced fixed-fee matrimonial products.
3. Debt recovery litigation with fixed prices for letters before action and fixed cost recovery from courts.
4. Fixed prices for other work, looked at on a case-by-case basis.

In each of the scenarios outlined above, the price setting process within teams is pretty much left to the lawyers, Partners or Team Leaders, with little or no oversight and input from the management team as to how those prices are set, communicated, and reviewed. There is no structure and no discipline.

If a sale is lost by a lawyer, it is usually assumed that the price was too high, not that the offer was wrong. Does this sound familiar?

Pricing is not something you do once and then ignore for the next 12 months. Pricing is an ongoing transformative process. To implement a process, you need to first design the framework, design documentation for the structure, communicate rules, create boundaries, and then train people how to use it all.

At present, in many law firms, there is no clearly defined and regulated pricing process, and there needs to be.

BRACE YOURSELF…
incoming provocative statement

Do you remember when the UK Government introduced a stamp duty tax holiday in 2020/2021, and every residential conveyancing transaction had to be completed by a certain date so that clients avoided the increase in stamp duty tax?

Do you remember the pressure on your people?

Do you remember the workloads?

Did you increase your prices by a huge amount (and I am talking about a minimum doubling or trebling of the prices charged) to try to capture some of that value and not burn out your staff? Most firms didn't.

Your conveyancing staff remember, and that may account for the fact that 50% of them would leave the profession if they could wave a magic wand. Firms lost control of their pricing, and many have lost employees as a result.

BIG SURVEY QUESTIONS

Q: When someone joins your team, how is pricing training undertaken?

A: The answers that come back are usually mixed. 'A Partner tells them what to do', 'bill an hourly rate', and the vast majority of people say, 'it isn't.'

Q: How are your pricing policies currently documented?

A: Predominantly, the answers are 'they are not' or, sometimes, 'we put them in a client Engagement Letter.'

Very few firms respond, saying they have a Practice Area-specific policy document.

Q: How is pricing set and reviewed at your firm?

A. Answers are usually negative, with many respondents confirming 'I have no idea.'

*

If you were to ask these questions of your staff, your lawyers, and your Partners, what responses would you get?

BASE COSTS

Call it whatever you want – base costs, reserve price, bottom line, or walk away price to create effective pricing decisions – you have to have some idea and understanding of the base costs for doing the work.

Once you have an idea of what it costs to deliver a service, the important thing is not to go below that base cost (unless there is a gold-plated strategic reason for doing so). If you do work at less than cost, guess what? You make a loss.

How are base prices currently calculated at your firm?

1. Is it 'hourly rates in drag', by which I mean a lawyer will guess how long a piece of work will take and multiply it by their hourly rate?
2. Made up on the fly/gut feel/best endeavours (delete as appropriate).
3. They follow what your competitors do.
4. They rely on what the lawyer learned at their old firm and let them carry on doing that at yours.
5. By allowing lawyers to learn from each other via trial, error, and osmosis!
6. They rely on the time recording data booked to a similar matter.
7. No idea.

Quite often, it is all of these in one form or another.

Ron Baker talks about three prices.

1. **Reservation price.** Below this price, the firm would turn down the work. It must get this price as a minimum. It will generate a normal profit.
2. **Hope-for price**. A firm should get this price more often than not. It will generate an increased profit margin for the firm.
3. **Pump fist price**. This is an aspirational price for when the firm is adding extraordinary value. It will generate a substantial/windfall profit.

8 PPP PENGUIN LOGIC

Commercial property – a pump fist price

A commercial property lawyer met with a Value Officer (VO) and originally proposed a quote of £14,000 for amending a defective leasehold title and then dealing with the subsequent sale of a property. The matter was somewhat complicated, and six titles would be involved.

After discussing the matter with the VO, reflecting on how complicated the matter was likely to be, and discovering that the client proposed to sell the properties for circa £6m if the titles could be sorted, the lawyer agreed to ask for a price of £57,500. The client accepted by return.

You will see that I talk about pump fist pricing often. It's what we deserve.

SHINGLES LOGIC

'It's better to have a small fee than no fee' or 'We have capacity in my team.'

These are usually the same lawyers who follow their competitors' pricing and seek to undercut them.

I suspect that many people reading this book will maintain that they rely on the time recording financial data of historical matters. The problem is the historical financial data you have in your PMS probably cannot always be relied upon.

In order to understand what the real costs are, you may need to actually do some detailed 'time and motion' studies to really learn what the work you do actually costs.

In her book *Pricing Value,* Rhondalynn Korolak summed up the situation ably in my view:

> There's only one proven and reliable way to find out what clients think about your prices and that is to sell them things.
>
> **Rhondalynn Korolak, Pricing Value**

The Vision of Change you create in P#3 must be compelling and aspirational.

A pricing policy is more than just tweaking hourly rates at the beginning of a new financial year or encouraging an increase in hourly rates.

It is interesting/depressing (delete as appropriate) that pricing seldom features in a law firm's Vision and strategic planning process. When was the last time (if ever) the management team of your business looked at the pricing of individual Practice Areas, other than talking about raising hourly rates?

The Pricing Confidence Surveys I have undertaken with many firms show it is simply not thought about, and therefore, it's not surprising it never gets on management agendas.

WORDS WITH THE WISE

David Falzani, Nottingham University

Double Your Price: The Strategy and Tactics of Smart Pricing

In his book, *Double Your Price*, David Falzani of Nottingham University identified two large UK businesses which had ceased trading. He looked at their accounts filed with Companies House.

Thomas Cook – the travel company – ceased trading in 2019. It had 21,000 staff, as well as 600,000 stranded customers around the world. It had final year losses of £163 million.

The question is what the average transaction price increase, as a percentage of the booking value, would needed to have been added to every holiday sold, to have enabled Thomas Cook to have broken even.

The second example is **British Home Stores**. A national high street store chain which made 11,000 staff redundant, its 2013 accounts showed a loss of £887,000 at the gross profit level.

Same question. What was the average transaction price increase, as a percentage, which would have allowed BHS to have broken even?

Answers

Thomas Cook average price increase: 1.7%.

BHS average price increase: 0.13%.

Now, assuming that these price increases alone could have saved these businesses, it does beg the question – how was pricing being monitored?

If pricing is not making it on to any agenda of your management team, hopefully this will encourage you to add it.

BIG SURVEY QUESTIONS

In May 2022, I presented a webinar for the Law Society of England and Wales, which explored how law firms win, deliver and price work. During the webinar, the following two poll questions were posed:

Q: Which of these statements is closest to the truth?

We have a pricing strategy and policy that is consistently applied.

Individual matters are priced by individuals on a best-efforts basis.

Q: What currently stops you from setting fees based on value to the client?

We don't know the value of our work to clients.

Partners are uncomfortable with it.

We don't have the skill sets.

Our IT systems don't allow us to do it.

How would *you* answer these questions?

The first poll results were:

We have a pricing strategy and policy that is consistently applied: 39.4%.

Individual matters are priced by individuals on a best-efforts basis: 60.6%.

What this tells me is that 40% of firms probably have a menu price of some kind. Not unexpected in the conveyancing/wills sector. And, in many cases, 60% of firms let their staff make prices up as they go along. I have repeated these questions with other groups and surveys and the 60/40% split is common.

The answers to the second poll were:

We don't know the value of our work to clients: 74.2%.

Partners are uncomfortable with it: 7.6%.

We don't have the skill sets: 13.6%.

Our IT systems don't allow us to do it: 4.5%.

The second poll question highlighted a widespread problem. Lawyers don't know the value of the work they provide to their clients.

GET A GRIP!

Law firm management teams have to take control of pricing in their businesses and stop what – in many firms – is a free-for-all, where lawyers continue to do what they've always done, completely unchallenged. This can include lawyers who have recently joined your firm.

8 PPP PENGUIN LOGIC

- What procedures can be put in place for communicating and approving pricing?
- How can you exchange pricing information and ensure teams know what is going on in the department?
- How can you train your people to understand more about pricing?

- Can you create a departmental manual/BBU of some description backed by internal policies and templates, which all lawyers can refer to and contribute to? This could become:
    - A document where examples of best practice are documented.
    - Where templates of Fixed-Price Agreements containing options can be stored, reviewed, amended, and recycled.
    - Where there are sections dealing with Frequently Asked Questions covering topics such as:
        - How to have a value conversation.
        - What you should ask.
        - How a Fixed-Price Agreement should be completed.
        - How to deal with price objections.

You need to take back control and ownership of your pricing, and soon!

2. LAW FIRM BUDGET SETTING IS ILLOGICAL

Chances are, many of the people reading this book work at law firms that are implementing some kind of cost-plus pricing that hasn't changed for years.

Many firms will adopt the 1/3, 1/3, 1/3 target setting model. A third covers the cost of hiring the individual lawyer, a third covers a share/contribution of the overheads, and a third covers a contribution to profit. It's simple. But very few firms stick to the formula they espouse; the first two 1/3s are always incurred, the third for profit often fails to materialise in full or at all.

What currently happens in your firm when it comes to setting financial budgets and targets?

Let's have a look at what happens in Shingles & Co. Do any of the scenarios set out here sound familiar?

SHINGLES LOGIC

At the beginning of the financial year, Betty Rex, Shingles' CFO, sets a date for the Equity Partners' meeting at which they will discuss the first version of the budget. One item on the agenda will be the hourly rates to be charged in the next financial year. As is often the case, not all the Partners will have looked at the draft budget, which was sent before the meeting.

Once Betty explains the proposed charging rates, the excuses start. The research undertaken by Partners into the prevailing hourly rates ranges from zero to some. Many Partners are reluctant to charge more than they currently do and say so. The in-depth reasoning given by some Partners about the hourly rates set is usually along the lines of:

- 'Our competition charges far less than that. I can't charge more.'
- 'The court scale rate for a lawyer of my grade is £X, and I have to charge that, as that is all we will recover if we win.'
- 'My clients won't pay that at all.'
- 'We need to keep rates low to keep clients happy.'
- 'It's unrealistic to charge a city rate as we don't have those overheads.'
- 'You can't charge out a trainee solicitor at that rate…' (even though Partners agree the trainee concerned is more productive than the Head of Department).
- 'You can't charge out that lawyer at that rate as it would upset another member of the team' (who is useless by comparison).
- 'I can't go above £300; the current market won't wear it' (insert any figure you like here. No research is undertaken into whatever market we are talking about).

- 'There is a recession, and our clients are hard up…has anyone thought about reducing the charges?'

The Partners at Shingles usually try to convince each other that other Practice Areas (not their own, of course) should charge more. The proceedings are concluded when one Partner (usually someone senior) will forcefully say, 'I am not charging my team out at that, and that is final. Shall we move on?' and then the subject is changed.

The outcome is usually a hotchpotch, which results in the hourly rates going up very slightly.

Betty returns to her office. She can't understand why this hourly rate dance has to happen at all. The Partners essentially set their rates based on a combination of vanity and their own perception of how competent they believe they and others are. They also seek to maintain a pecking order within their silos which is illogical. Betty thinks differently; surely, isn't it the client's perception of competence that is key when it comes to paying anything?

I am sure you can add many more to the above. The reasoning/excuses are often a combination of poor leadership, blissful ignorance, low confidence, fear (especially when it relates to having conversations with clients), a lack of understanding of the finances of the business, an illogical fear of the competition (which, when translated, usually means any of the other firms within a 50-mile radius regardless of how good they are), and a refusal even to try to charge what someone might actually be willing to pay. You may be thinking this is Status Quo Bias in action. It is.

SHINGLES LOGIC

Once the hourly rates are meticulously calculated (not), Betty – now a little ashen-faced – moves on to address the billable hours targets to be set for each lawyer. Betty is armed with details of actual hours worked from last year, along with various benchmarking studies that usually show that their firm has got to make significant improvements to get anywhere near the upper quartile of the benchmarking survey.

Betty is secretly thinking, 'I wonder if this is the year we can get to a decent (higher number) and improve our utilisation and realisation rates?'

Betty has meticulously calculated the number of working days along the following lines:

- 52 weeks in a year, multiplied by 5 working days = 260 working days.
- Subtract the eight UK bank holidays = 252 working days.
- Less, say, 25 days holiday = 227 working days.
- Knocked off a couple of sickness days… say 225 working days.

So, a full-time lawyer has 225 days available.

And then begins the debate about the number of chargeable hours per day that should be multiplied by 225.

Again, the Shingles Partners give their detailed well-researched reasoning (not) in support of the hours they propose for the members of their silos/teams (delete as appropriate, but you know at this stage they are well and truly silos; perhaps at this meeting better to describe them as bunkers!).

The Shingles Partners know the budget setting game is to keep your team target low so that if you exceed the artificially low figure at the end of the year, you can claim your team is supremely profitable as a result of your wonderful leadership.

The Partners' reasons are usually something like:

- 'I had a good year last year, but that was because we got that one big case concluded and don't think it will happen again.'
- 'If X wants to be considered for equity partnership, they will just have to do more.'
- 'I have more people in my team now, and that takes more management time, so I need a lower chargeable figure.'
- 'I have taken on a new management role overseeing technology implementation (insert any

implementation), and that reduces my fee-earning capability.'

- 'I have part-timers in my team, can you allow for that please? Also, don't forget many of the part-timers in my team don't work Mondays and most bank holidays fall on Mondays, so they still have a disproportionate amount of holiday available, which reduces their hours, so take that into account when setting targets please.'
- 'Lawyer Y is a work horse; they are great at time recording – so put their target up.'
- 'Lawyer Z sits around dreaming most of the day, only showing two chargeable hours – put theirs up and give them a wakeup call.'
- 'Give the Associates 7 hours a day – if they want to be Partners, they have to earn it.'
- 'Don't forget X is working their notice and their replacement doesn't start until three months after they have left and the replacement will take time to bed in, so don't expect them to bill anything for at least three months.'
- 'I am hoping X will leave the team. So, don't budget for them at all.'

And so on and so on.

Betty grimaces. All she wants from this meeting is an annualised chargeable hours/fee target worked out along the lines of the link to lawyer overhead (salary) so she can work out a lawyer/team gross profit target figure.

Betty leaves the meeting. She will eventually end up with at least three or four versions of a budget.

A week or so later, two of the Partners that were unable to attend the first finance meeting (which had been in the diary for two months) will have a one-to-one with Betty and ask that their detailed research (not)/totally off-the-cuff views are incorporated into the revised fifth version of the budget.

The hours to be worked in the year are usually fudged with Betty setting a target which – more often than not – can easily be renegotiated by a Partner at a later date, uttering the magic phrase, 'There is no way I can do that… can we revisit the numbers later?'

CHARGEABLE HOURS PER DAY TARGET

When it comes to the number of lawyer hours per day to be worked, you will know how – in many firms – the full-time lawyer target could be anything between 1,100 or 1,400 hours per annum if your lawyers bill in 6-minute units. This could increase to an eyewatering 2,400 hours if your lawyers bill in 15/20-minute units (at this point, we welcome our US readers).

I know one Managing Partner who used to set a target of 1,100 hours for each full-time lawyer and then secretly hoped the lawyers would bill 850 hours and set a firm budget based on the 850. To complicate matters further, the lawyers were given budgets based on 1,100 hours, so they thought they were being stretched. So much for one version of the truth!

HOW MANY HOURS A DAY ARE CHARGEABLE?

Let's do the math. (NB, the letter 's' has been deliberately left off the word math in case any US lawyers are actually reading this book. Welcome again.). In a typical UK law firm, it is this:

1,400 hours divided by 225days = 6.2 hours per day.

1,100 hours divided by 225 days = 4.8 hours a day.

850 hours divided by 225 days = 3.7 hours a day.

At all times, remember that we are talking about lawyer **chargeable** hours.

Let's get back to Shingles…

SHINGLES LOGIC

Chargeable Hours Per Day Target

Somewhat battle-weary, Betty has also been dragged into debates with one team about the thresholds that should apply on the red, amber, and green lights that populate the financial management dashboard the lawyers see.

One Partner agrees that the dashboard will go green at 4.8 hours, but doesn't want their staff to be demotivated by the dashboard too much, as red is a horrible, aggressive colour, so she insists it goes amber when two chargeable hours are recorded. Betty knows that the numbers will rarely go green, and that Partner will spend ridiculous sums buying chocolate to try to motivate her team members when the dashboard would actually do that far more effectively without the additional calories.

Betty sighs and agrees. She makes a note that the non-chargeable and write-off time codes are something to discuss in the future. Having said that, she knows that none of this data ever gets analysed at future Partners' meetings in any event, and if she ever sought to raise it, it would be another rod for her own back.

Betty decides that the benchmarking reports that take hours to complete and submit and then get studied by the Partners for maybe a whole 20 minutes (if that) can also get postponed to another meeting. She knows that the benchmarking data is pretty meaningless anyway as it is impossible to know what the definition of a lawyer/fee-earner is in her firm (it changes most years), and that that conversation will only open another can of worms as to whether 'non-lawyers' should be regarded as fee-earners when they ring the barrister's chambers to book a barrister for a court hearing date, and what figure should they charge the client for doing that.

So that's the annual targets set at Shingles… next stop for Betty is the Staff Bonus Scheme, which she knows is just another title for Partner patronage. At least she doesn't have to work out which of the 40 lawyers gets one of the 21 office car parking spaces. That's the COO's job!

BRACE YOURSELF…
incoming provocative statement

If you are an aspiring law firm owner/salaried Partner or associate reading this book, please put it down and have a cup of tea with two sugars. You may be suffering from shock. This stuff outlined in Shingles really does go on!

Does any of this ring true with you? I suspect it does. I kid you not, I have seen one firm have a version 11 budget, which was still being finessed four months after the financial year had started. I have seen another firm that – eight months after a budget had been set – had not communicated **any targets** to their lawyers as they didn't want to demotivate them. And one firm that doesn't bother with a formal budget at all. Status Quo Bonkers Bias.

Let's ask ourselves, why does this happen? It's simple: the management structure is usually such that the finance team members don't have the necessary permission or power to say to the Partners/owners, 'Stop! You are all doing this wrong!'

So why do we persist with this? Why do the finance budget setting dance every year? The reason why is that law firm owners don't really know anything any different; after all, they wanted to be lawyers, not accountants. They know what they know, and they understand the hourly rate and annual hours target model.

This wonderful budget setting system is perhaps best summed up by US lawyer Tom Bowden. I met Tom in Dallas in 2017. Tom's take on the process outlined above is this.

WORDS FROM THE WISE

Thomas L. Bowden, Sr., Timeless Counsel, Plc

So, you take an arbitrary segment of your staff, assign them an arbitrary number of hours to record and/or work each year, then take an arbitrary portion of your overhead and add it to the salaries of the arbitrarily selected staff, add to that an arbitrary figure for your desired profit and divide by the arbitrarily chosen number of hours, and voilà, that's your ever so precisely determined 'costs' per hour.

Now measure your actual hours very precisely or all those completely arbitrary choices will be completely useless. Of course, they're useless anyway, because no matter how precisely you measure the wrong thing, it's still wrong.

When you consider the method of budget setting outlined above, it is not at all surprising that many external operators have moved into the legal market in England and Wales.

3. FINANCIAL ISSUES

One reason for your sense of urgency and desire to make a paradigm shift could be the business needs to make more money. It may not be realising its full potential.

One of the reasons that law firms don't make sufficient profit is because, in many cases, the lawyers who own the business (in the main) do not understand the business's finances and how the decisions they make impact profitability.

The chances are that the starting point for your VBP journey is going to involve an analysis of the financial data that you have at your disposal. Your firm probably spends a huge amount of money each year on a Practice Management System (PMS) that deals with the finances of the business, records time, and keeps client money in tip-top order. I imagine your PMS creates numerous reports. Your accounts teams may prepare these financial reports, distribute them to Partners, and – more often than not – get little or no feedback, then repeat the same cycle the following month. Or you may rely on Partners to look at the financial data on the system and interpret it themselves.

In the main, the reports are not going to be read by lawyer Partners. Why? Often, they are too lengthy; lawyers don't like or understand the numbers and the data may well be out of date by the time the Partners get to see them at the scheduled Partner's meeting.

Most law firm CFOs and auditors will privately confirm that many lawyers who look at the financial data presented do not understand what it is telling them.

The area of the accounts that most owners/Equity Partners are interested in is the PEP figure (Profit per Equity Partner), as this impacts the drawings you get on a monthly basis and where you can book to go on holiday! It's not surprising, really. The Equity Partners/Owners want to know, 'What is in this for me?'

If you analyse your firm's training budget to ascertain what percentage is spent on providing financial training for your lawyers/Partners, I suspect the figure is a small one.

I am sorry if you think I am painting a bleak picture. In reality, though, it may even be worse than this. Do your lawyers even regularly look at the financial dashboards you paid for as part of your PMS? Do they know what the data on the dashboard is telling them? Ask your PMS provider to provide you with a report that identifies – from the back end of the system – who actually looks at the financial information which is readily available from their desktops. You may well find that not enough do.

So, for whatever reason you want to change, reviewing and understanding the financial management information and the data available from your PMS is usually a good place to start. There may be some training required to explain to people what it means.

4. TO CAPTURE MORE VALUE

The reason you bought this book is to learn more about value-based pricing. You will immediately realise that the cost plus or 1/3, 1/3, 1/3 model, or any combination of chargeable hours multiplied by days worked, fails to take into account any value that has been created for the client or the price that the customer is prepared to pay.

Value is never mentioned in the process outlined above. Why is this? In short, it's never been something lawyers have been told about or taught to consider as part of the process of being a lawyer. As a result, when we join firms, we do what they have always done. We adopt a flawed model, and we don't even attempt to find out what that value is. It's not something that we ever think about… until now.

Curiously, we know from our own lives, when we consume or purchase anything, that we instinctively realise whether we have received value. It is the same with our customers. They make the same call every time we send a bill, and they question the value they received.

Value is something that is not easy to define and is very subjective, so it is no wonder that many law firms shy away from trying to get their heads around it.

Value-based pricing is an art, not a science, and that troubles lawyers, who like things to be certain. It is a mindset and attitude. In the same way, all of our clients are different, so are our lawyers. It is not a formula you can roll out and apply.

BRACE YOURSELF…
incoming provocative statement

I am sorry to break it to you, but to implement VBP we need to adopt the thinking of John Maynard Keynes and take the view that when it comes to our policies regarding VBP, 'It is better to be roughly right than precisely wrong.'

YOUR CURRENT FIXED PRICES

Now, I know that many of you reading this will maintain that your firms provide perfectly adequate fixed prices already, and that is pretty much the same as value-based pricing, so you don't need to worry too much... well, I am afraid you are wrong.

Often, the way law firms calculate their fixed rates is by adopting what my aforementioned friend John Chisholm calls 'billable hours in drag'. Lawyers look at the issue before them, think about how long it's going to take to deliver the service, and give the client a fixed price to do the job based on the hours multiplied by their hourly rate. Again, in this calculation, there is no factoring in the value generated for the client, the impact on the lawyer's workload, the degree of urgency, etc.

In most cases, the fixed fee given woefully underestimates the time actually taken because it's human nature to underestimate the time it takes us to do something. Often, the fixed fee is wrong seconds after it's been communicated.

If you don't believe me, find out the work in progress (WIP) write-offs you have against closed matters at your firm, where a fixed fee was given. It will scare you.

8 PPP PENGUIN LOGIC

It is curious that, sometimes, if pushed, law firms will give a fixed price to clients when asked.

Is it really up to our clients to suggest that their lawyers change their business model, or should we just get on with offering them what they want, which is choice?

When you stand back and look at pricing happening around you in the real world, you will realise there are thousands of examples of non-cost plus and non-time-based pricing.

If you think about it logically, when airlines are selling tickets, the closer it gets to a departure date, the cheaper the available tickets should be, as the airlines' flight costs are already covered. They are not though, are they? They are more expensive. Why? Because airlines embrace dynamic pricing and know they can charge more for a seat the closer it gets to take off as client choice is severely limited.

Luxury brands charge premium prices. They're not at all related to the cost of production.

Zero-alcohol gin is charged at the same price as normal gin, even though there is no duty paid on it.

You don't know how many hours it took to make your car. You might have never even considered that question until now.

Some printer companies practically give away printers knowing that they're going to make their margin on the inkjet cartridges they sell, as they recognise their customers dislike chopping and changing printer setups.

Car wash machines offer different prices for different services delivered. The same is true concerning mobile phone data/call and text plans.

We are frequently exposed to add-on pricing. It's very common. Think back to the airlines, the add-ons that we pay to either select a seat next to our partner, opt for extra legroom, or check our luggage into the hold.

Think about the fixed-price subscriptions you pay in the operation of *your* business.

You probably pay per user for the PMS Case Management Systems and the library facilities your lawyers look at daily. They are all subscription/user based. They are not based on usage. If you check the contracts you have signed, you will probably see that there are provisions in the contract that require **you** to keep the prices you pay to the supplier confidential. Why? Because you have been value-priced, my friend, and others in the sector will be paying more, and others will be paying less.

GOLDEN RULE #4

One of the golden rules of VBP that you have to accept is that it is an art, not a science.

NB. This will be repeated often!

5. SUCCESSION PLANNING

Another driver for this project of yours may be that your business is not attractive to other lawyers for succession purposes. Associates might not want to buy into the business that has been created and currently provides them with gainful employment. Shingles' owners are stunned that the Associates don't seem to want to adopt the traditional model of coming onboard, getting their heads down for a few years and waiting for a tap on the shoulder. They may not be enthusiastic about borrowing money to invest in the business as their capital contribution. The knock-on effect is, of course, that your existing owners do not have an exit strategy. Who is going to buy them out and let them depart gracefully into retirement with their capital if there are no incoming Partners to take their places?

Look at it from your rising stars' points of view, those lawyers who you think will be able to join the equity/ownership of the firm. No one wants to buy into a business if it isn't making any money, not realising its full potential, is not well run, is riddled with Partner patronage examples, isn't proactive or forward-thinking, and doesn't create sufficient income to provide the lifestyle that they aspire to.

6. WRONG TYPE OF CLIENTS

Your client base could be the problem and the motivation for the change to VBP. You may be going after the wrong kind of work.

8 PPP PENGUIN LOGIC

This book is not about branding or positioning. If you want to read a great book on this subject, I recommend you read Tim Williams' *Positioning for Professionals*.

You may be doing lots of work for free. You may have clients who don't pay your bills. Some clients won't even have paid you for the disbursements you have shelled out on their behalf!

Client selection is important to successfully implementing VBP. We will look at client selection later in the book. One thing is for sure, your lawyers know who your bad clients are.

A BIG SURVEY QUESTION

Q: Do you believe that some of the clients your firm acts for should be dismissed as they are too painful and or unprofitable to act for?

A: The responses from lawyers always contain many yes answers; positive responses (sack particular clients) range from 53% to 96%!

What's stopping you from asking the question?

I have read numerous books and seen LinkedIn posts from people who refer to the wrong types of clients as BMWs (Bitches, Moaners and Whiners). I have read one other UK-based trainer refer to them as PIA clients (Pain in the Arse). However, to be honest, I think that it is misconceived, rude, and quite frankly disrespectful to call clients PIAs or BMWs for a number of reasons.

1. You choose the clients you currently act for.
2. You set the pricing you charge.
3. You chose to deliver work that was out of scope and do more than you envisaged.
4. You drafted the bill (even if it wrote off WIP that you didn't want to ask to be included in the bill).
5. You took their money when they paid.
6. You decided to ignore difficult conversations with clients when bills became overdue.
7. You decided to take no action when matters went out of scope or put matters on stop until clients paid.
8. You moan about the clients to colleagues when you put the phone down after having a conversation with them, but do nothing to make the situation better.
9. You stop credit control chasing the client for payment as 'They are a good client and will pay… eventually.'
10. You take on the next matter from the same client without addressing any of the points above.

Rant over!

8 PPP PENGUIN LOGIC

If you have lawyers moaning about your clients, they are *part* of the problem. In fact, they may have caused it!

TRUSTED ADVISOR STATUS

Most law firm websites will talk about how they perceive themselves to be their clients' 'trusted advisor', putting clients at 'the centre of everything we do'. I can totally get why lawyers would want this Trusted Advisor title. We want to help clients, and there is great kudos in the trusted advisor label. From a profit perspective, it makes sense as well, as people will often pay a premium where trust is high. What's not to like?

But guess what? In the main, lawyers are never going to achieve trusted advisor status. Let's demonstrate this. Think about one of your best clients. Now answer the following:

- Who is their partner/spouse? Can you name them?
- What football team do they support?
- What hobbies do they pursue?
- What faith, if any, do they practise?
- If they have a faith, when did you last send them a card on a religious holiday?
- When is their birthday?
- When did you last wish them happy birthday?
- Where did they go on holiday last year?
- If they have children, what are their schooling aims?
- Do you know anything about their immediate family, children, and parents?
- Are they a carer for a family member?
- What do they know about you?
- What have they ever confided in you about?
- Do they confide in you about the strategy and finances of their businesses?
- If they are shareholders in a business, do you know if they have a shareholders' agreement?
- Have you ever even asked what their exit strategy is?
- Do you know if they have made a will, and if so, where the original is?
- Have you ever visited their business?
- When did you last proactively call them when you *did not* have a current piece of work to talk about?
- Do you start calls with 'I am sorry I have not got back to you…'? (Which, by the way, the client hears as 'My matter is not that high on your list of priorities.')

The chances are you can't answer many of the above questions positively, except perhaps for the last one, and that's not a good thing.

8 PPP PENGUIN LOGIC

I am afraid, in the vast majority of cases, lawyers are a supplier – someone who does their legal work. Often, we are not trusted advisers as we have not earned the right to be trusted.

Most law firms do not put the client at the centre of everything they do, even though they profess so on their websites and marketing collateral.

If lawyers were trusted advisers, why would some mystery shopping reports show that law firms' website chatbots perform better than some lawyers who took a call in-person?!

BRACE YOURSELF…
incoming provocative statement

Do not believe the propaganda on your website and marketing collateral.

It is not a privilege for clients to meet you or your lawyers. Don't act like it is.

One of the reasons lawyers are not regarded as trusted advisors or experts is that many cannot even give a price for their work, day-in, day-out!

Chances are, your law firm might have a database detailing tens of thousands of clients who have instructed your firm over the years. I have news for you: they are not clients. Most of them will be 'former clients', and they will have instructed other firms who wanted their business and who kept in touch, or who they felt were better equipped and more aligned to their journey.

Most clients view lawyers as professional suppliers who can help them with a transaction on a journey from A to B. We are dispensable. The cost of changing from one law firm to another is usually zero.

If you can embrace the change to VBP, you can give clients fixed, agreed prices and choice. Your change in mindset will encourage you and your lawyers to do the work efficiently without cutting corners. You will have time to become genuinely interested in clients' lives, outcomes, and goals, and you can give your clients the results they want more quickly. You can possibly become a trusted advisor if – and only if – your clients think you have earned the right to be one.

A BIG SURVEY QUESTION

Q: Think about the most profitable matters you have had in the past. What influenced this profitability?

Type of client was – by far – the top featured answer. Many lawyers have clients whom they like and regard as great to deal with. You have just got to get more of them.

Other factors included:

- Type of transaction.
- Value pricing.
- Property value.
- Cooperation from clients and lawyers.
- Fixed price.
- Value/Risk/Complexity.
- Fluke/Luck.
- Good lawyers on the *other* side.

7. THE HOURLY RATE - ARE ITS DAYS NUMBERED?

I know that some lawyers will disagree that the hourly rate needs to die. You will, in your VBP journey, come across this; those who believe you cannot run a law business without your people clocking their hours and accounting for their lives in 6-minute units. I think they are mistaken.

WHY TIME RECORDING MAY BE USEFUL

I have heard Ron Baker say, 'The problem with the billable hour is, it's hard to tell a room full of multi-millionaires their business model is wrong.' Now, I agree with Ron that this might be the case for Equity Partners of, say, the Top 50 law firms, but what about regional law firms, high-street firms, solopreneurs and startups? The owners are not multi-millionaires and probably never will be.

If you are starting a VBP project, my view on continuing to time record is this, if it helps get buy-in from others, keep time recording going for the pilot project. It's a battle you can fight later, once you have generated some wins and successes. Scrapping time recording can be polarizing, so if you need to keep time recording going, that is fine – just don't use it to price the work. If your VBP project takes off and is successful, you will (I suspect) ditch time recording completely in the fullness of time. Most firms that embrace VBP do.

If you are going to continue time recording, it is important to get the culture right so that staff feel that they can record all of their time without any adverse consequences. Fee-earner utilisation is easily distorted by underreported time.

Reasons you may want to continue some aspects of time recording include:

1. Helping to track KPIs that are aligned with business objectives.
2. Helping to track team and individual lawyer performance KPIs.
3. Helping to track the allocation of work across teams.
4. Helping to identify lawyers who may not have enough work to do.
5. Helping to calculate base costs by tracking what labour costs may be required to deliver a service. Tracking and calculating an average time cost of a repeatable transaction.
6. Identifying possible scope creep and cases with a financial risk. It may be that the lack of time posted between two milestones can identify bottlenecks. Exception reporting may identify live files with no activity being undertaken.
7. Helping to track and monitor Service Level Agreement achievements.
8. Calculating client profitability by using cost of time spent working for a client.
9. To track investment time and business development activities, cost of inquiry, cost of acquisition, and conversion rates linked to KPIs. This could include identifying specific market segments, types of business, etc.

I will concede that one good reason to have all matter time recorded diligently and accurately is so you know exactly what your base costs are – when you have captured all of the time it takes to resolve a matter. However, if you are honest, you will know time recording doesn't really work like that in the real world, does it?

Chances are that, in your firm, the time recording data is completely wrong and is not currently an accurate measure for base costs. I say this because:

1. Not all lawyers time record the work undertaken on a matter accurately. Some will leave their time recording for days or weeks. One of my old Partners, 15 years ago, used to leave it for months before filling in timesheets. People forget what they have done. Can you say that your firm's time recording policy is

adhered to by all your staff? Do you even have a coherent, detailed written policy? Not all firms do.

2. Not all time recorded is genuine.

BRACE YOURSELF…
incoming provocative statement

Some lawyers lie/fib/can't recall/use their best endeavours to book (delete as appropriate) their actual time, and pad their timesheets.

In her compelling autobiography, *(Out)Law: From Teenage Mum to Legal Trailblazer*, lawyer Alice Stephenson records, 'Cheating came in countless guises… I heard of one senior Partner who thought it reasonable to include his Sunday afternoon rounds of golf with a client's CEO, and another who clocked time spent at a charity dinner he attended with his wife because it was sponsored by an important client.'

Sorry to burst your bubble here, but some lawyers fudge their figures because they are worried or (in fact) told if they don't account for all of their time or hit their targets, they will be fired. They can't remember what they did, but know they did something, so they make something up and use their best endeavours to populate the timesheet.

One firm I have come across has a policy of requiring lawyers to do free, fixed-fee interviews, and it then threatens to discipline staff if they don't hit fee income targets. Targets which don't take into account the free work/pro bono marketing they are compelled to do!

One US firm recently sued their own lawyers for not hitting time recording targets.

Faced with fines, litigation, disciplinary proceedings, being singled out at a Partners' meeting, or career-limiting appraisals, lawyers will put down time which does not exist and give time recording their best shot. In many cases, they underbook the time they actually spent, not inflate it.

Inaccurate time recording can be a symptom of a culture problem within the business, and in some cases, it's a culture problem caused, ignored, and perpetuated by the leadership team.

1. Lawyers don't work the same. Some lawyers type their own work. Others dictate work, get it transcribed, and then check and amend it again. It may take Lawyer A more time to dictate a document, proof the draft, amend the draft,

and then sign it off than Lawyer B, who can type accurately and quickly, or who uses a digital transcription app on their phone. Lawyer A is more profitable.

2. Not all lawyers use their technology effectively. If you don't believe me, speak to any Legal IT trainer. Many CTOs will secretly tell you they wish their workforce would learn to use all of the features of the technology and Case/Practice Management Systems they already have in their businesses before demanding shiny, new systems.

   Some efficient lawyers will use macros, hot docs, and shortcuts on their systems. Others think a macro is a lovely pasta dish covered with cheese. Yet the macaroni-eating luddites can – in the world of the hourly rate – bill more. In fact, where is the incentive to embrace and use technology at all when you charge by the hour? Why seek to spend money on new systems that speed up a process? You only have lawyers producing more work in fewer hours, so it costs you money! So, instead of making more money, the expenditure on technology can decrease your margin.

3. Some lawyers don't believe they are worth their own hourly rate and, as a result, discount what they do. Discounting is common.

   Phil Wedgwood, in his book *Timeshift*, coined the phrase 'Quintuple discounting'. This is where:

   a. Lawyers just didn't time record at all.
   b. When a lawyer time recorded but got it wrong, or chose to under- or over-record time.
   c. A lawyer discounted time when posting or collating for billing.
   d. The Partners – when presented with the draft bill – discounted it again.
   e. The point-of-sale discount when the client says it is too much.

   Does this sound familiar?

   Many CFOs know huge amounts of time don't even get on a timesheet. Common discounting reasons you have probably heard include:

   - 'I was exploring a theory and went down a few dead ends. So, I haven't charged for that.'
   - 'I was training a lawyer.'
   - 'I was amending the drafting of another lawyer, and they had already booked huge amounts of time – so I didn't bother booking mine on.'

   And what is curious here, is that by uttering these statements, the lawyers are identifying one thing… not all work that gets booked under the billable hour model can be considered as having created value for the client. That is why they shied away from posting it at all.

8 PPP PENGUIN LOGIC

When have you ever heard a lawyer look at a WIP ledger and say, 'We should have charged more…' It's a statement as rare as hens' teeth. Why? Because such a question requires the lawyer to make a subjective assessment about value, and lawyers don't like being subjective.

A BIG SURVEY QUESTION

Q: What is your view about your firm's time recording policy? Tick the boxes which you think apply to you.

I like time recording. I am good at it. I can account for my time and hit my target: 15.38%.

I struggle to hit my daily target: 6.41%.

I think our policy is not detailed enough: 5.13%.

I think our policy is too detailed: 1.28%.

I think that teams should receive more training to help us time record more effectively: 11.54%.

I don't time record: 61.54%.

I would rather not have to time record if the firm can design a suitable alternative system: 8.97%.

I do get concerned about booking all of my time to a matter as I don't want to have to face questions about writing off WIP that is booked: 5.13%.

I think time recording on conveyancing matters is pointless: 24.36%.

*

I also once asked a Private Client lawyer, in a one-to-one, whether she complied with her firm's time recording policy.

She told me that she did not charge for emails, both in and out, in accordance with the practice's official time recording policy. Her logic was if she rang the client, it would only be one unit of her time. So, she charged one unit for the work (for reading *and* sending an email, and not calling the client at all) even though her time spent was more than one unit. On the one hand, a breach of the policy, on the other, a fully justified policy she had created in her head to keep her clients' costs down.

Lots of lawyers won't time record all conversations with clients as they are worried about the bill increasing. Clients also have similar worries, and that prevents them from calling or limits the time that they spend having conversations with their lawyers.

4. Some lawyers who give fixed fees and estimates will stop time recording once the estimated fee level is reached. They do this for a number of reasons. Firstly, to avoid having a conversation with the client and explaining the original estimate was wrong and that the client will have to pay more. Secondly, so that the lawyer won't have to write off any work in progress (WIP) that may be on the ledger when the file is closed. If there is, their Team Leader/Partner will give them a hard time and not approve the write-off.

   The result of this practice is that the utilisation rate of that lawyer looks awful, and the Head of Finance and Team Leader jump to the wrong conclusion that the lawyer only works three hours a day… or even less.

   One Managing Partner who retained me to help his firm told me he wanted to address the poor utilisation rates of some of his lawyers. I asked him if the Heads of those teams were the kind of people who would berate staff and give them a hard time if they tried to write off any time. He thought about it for a moment and said, 'Yes… you have a point.' Problem not solved, but at least it was identified in less than one chargeable unit!

8 PPP PENGUIN LOGIC

In 2022, I spoke at a meeting in Manchester to a group of law firm CFOs where the turnovers of the 25 firms present ranged from £40 million to over £100 million. I asked the

WIP question re: write-offs – 'Are you writing off between 10/20% of your WIP?'

Many heads nodded.

Tens of millions of pounds getting written off because the model utilised just isn't good enough.

5. Some lawyers will do more work on a file for a client even though the hourly rate penalises them for doing this. This is scope creep – doing more than you are paid to do. The time may or may not be booked at all. The lawyer usually has no intention of billing it.
6. Some lawyers are really good at project and case planning; others are not. There is usually no system. Many years ago, I did some work for a law firm that was running five very heavyweight matters on one single file number, and posting all documents onto a single treasury tag that was the size of a tug-of-war rope! They were a large city firm. The lack of efficiency led to an increased bill, so from the lawyers' perspective, what was not to like? Basic project management and file hygiene would have saved thousands of pounds of costs.
7. You have no incentive to have fewer lawyers on a case. You may as well bring a colleague to sit on a meeting… the client is paying. The slowest horse will win the race. All the charges can get logged to the lawyers' timesheets.

   The argument (if any) that will ensue about what time – from which lawyer – gets billed to the client, and what time gets written off, can be postponed for a month or two. In some cases, the time will just get billed anyway. In other cases, the Partner – when preparing the bill – writes off the junior lawyer's time. All of a sudden, a lawyer who thought they had worked ten chargeable hours on a matter have nothing to show on a fee income target.

SHINGLES LOGIC

Controlling what gets billed and what gets written off can be divisive, especially if bonuses are at stake. In Shingles-type organisations, Partner patronage can result in fee-earner favouritism. It's not a collegiate way to run a team, pitching lawyer against lawyer.

8. Dealing with time recording is expensive. VeraSage Fellow, Tim Williams, believes that advertising agencies can benefit from an immediate 10-20% cost

reduction by eliminating the tracking and billing of time. I would love to give you a comparison for the legal the legal sector, but there isn't one as no one measures it. Tim is fond of saying, 'Think of the costs you incur as a 'complexity tax'…'

Maybe a quote from the management guru Peter Drucker can clarify the situation…

> There is nothing so useless as doing efficiently that which should not be done at all.
>
> **Peter Drucker**

9. The impact of Artificial Intelligence (GenAI) on the hourly rate and time recording will be immense. Let's face it, we haven't even begun to address the issues that will arise in the future with the impact of time recording and AI. This book won't do so, either.

   I can say that AI scares the living daylights out of me. Not because of the technology, I think it's great. What scares me is that many law firms are not thinking about how their businesses and charging models will have to change.

The last Words With The Wise interview I carried out, as I prepared this book, was with Terri Mottershead from The Centre for Legal Innovation (Australia, New Zealand, and Asia-Pacific). The topics we discussed below will – I am sure – be of interest to you. Don't have nightmares…

WORDS FROM THE WISE

Terri Mottershead, Executive Director – Centre for Legal Innovation (Australia, New Zealand, and Asia-Pacific)

Lawyers are not the gatekeepers of knowledge anymore. It will become harder to charge by the hour for knowledge identification, acquisition, collation, analysis, and summaries because that will all be done in seconds by AI. What lawyers will charge for is their experience – the human-centred, trusted advisor role – that's where their value will increasingly be focused, and that aligns with value-based pricing.

The world of legal work has changed. How we charge for it must change. We must be focused on outcomes, and we can't be focused on pricing by the hour. The billable hour was never a good measure of the value-add of legal professionals, and it's certainly not going to continue to be an acceptable measure in a tech/AI fuelled, data-driven and customer-centric legal world. In the next short while, we are going to see the legal world focus more on the application of AI, experimentation, continuous improvement, and agility. It will be coupled with more sophisticated clients doing the same thing. This will place significant pressure on the legal industry to transform their billing practices from hours to outcomes, or risk losing work to those who do.

Documents of all types are being dropped into different sorts of generative AI functionality to produce summaries of all the major points. You can also ask for a more detailed explanation of a clause. This can be done in multiple languages. And you're not confined to text. You can also ask for an image or video to explain what a clause means. All of this, generously, takes minutes. It has dramatically expanded access to and understanding of this information. This is the new world in which lawyers have to ask and know the answer to 'What value do we add?'.

The Centre for Legal Innovation at the College of Law recently conducted some roundtables on the awareness/use of generative AI in all sectors of the legal ecosystem. From those, and additional research we undertook, we found five alternative approaches identified for those seeking to defend the billable hour:

1. GenAI saves time; cost savings should be passed on to the client – better, cheaper, and faster – less hours spent means less billable time.
2. GenAI with private cloud access is drawing on a firm's own knowledge and collective experience, so it may take less time to retrieve/arrive at the solution, but that should not be cheaper (i.e., value billing may be the best option here to fully reflect that knowledge/experience).
3. GenAI responses have accuracy issues. It hallucinates, it's biased, it doesn't attribute things, and it takes time to verify. These things are being worked on, but right now, we still need to thoroughly check everything, so nothing's going to be cheaper. We should still bill by the hour.

4. GenAI is a knowledge worker. It's like an intern. So, we should be able to work out an hourly rate for the work that GenAI does, and bill it by the hour.
5. GenAI allows us to now offer different levels of service at different price points. The options both involve GenAI generating the response, but differ as:
    - We then do a light review, and we'll charge a lower price for the work.
    - We then undertake a thorough review; we check everything, and we charge a higher price.

   The problem with this solution is that lawyers retain a professional responsibility and liability for the quality and accuracy of their advice, so unless/until laws/regulations are changed, in most places, this solution won't work.

The overriding issue for each of these solutions is that we needed the answers yesterday. That doesn't mean we should be making bad decisions in haste. But it does mean we will have to approach the solutions as iterative – guidance/guidelines we develop today will continuously change. If we do nothing, it will not stop a whole bunch of other people (not necessarily lawyers) from bridging the huge gap between consumers' need/demand and availability.

The compelling question that every legal business should be asking now is, 'What value do we add?' and 'How do we redefine risk?' GenAI has changed the work we do, how we do it, who does it, when, where, and why. It's changed not just the practice of law but the business of law, too. This sort of systemic change cannot be reconciled, nor can new, different, better solutions be found by defending the status quo. And that applies as much to billing as it does to every other aspect of the legal world.

Right now, law firms have identified an internal and external value for GenAI:

- The internal value is around increased efficiency, being able to pull out data-driven insights and trends, accessibility, scalability and – in time – accuracy and consistency. That's probably where most law firms are at, right now, in terms of generative AI experiments.
- The external value is where the more interesting opportunities arise. That's about sharing information and democratizing knowledge, creating opportunities for clients to self-serve, customising services/products/solutions, and

doubling down on the human-centred trust advisor role. It's what AI can't replace.

We're in an experimentation phase with GenAI in legal, right now, but some schools of thought have emerged around risk for corporate clients and consumers and what they are willing to pay for:

1. For corporate clients who are not investing heavily in the tech themselves (or not right now), they are looking for increased integration with law firms and will rely on these firms' choices/decisions about the tech and its outputs OR will share that risk.
2. Other corporate clients are using the tech themselves, but when it comes to the more complex or 'bet the company' work, they still send it to their law firms and rely on the firm's sign-off/insurance/liability/risk for the final product.
3. For consumers, they have a similar approach. Some will rely on the law firm entirely. Others, especially those for whom the only other alternative is no access to legal advice at all, may be willing to share the risk if they know exactly what they are sharing. If current laws/regulations make access to legal advice impossible, consumers will go to the next best alternative, and that may not be a lawyer or law firm!

I've spoken with lawyers who are experimenting with GenAI by asking it to respond to prompts they think a client is likely to ask. The lawyers can then see, assess, and pre-empt issues (e.g., the kind of questions, document summaries, and preliminary advice their clients will bring to them when they meet).

An already identified, an ethical question for lawyers is whether you need to disclose to clients that you've used GenAI. Your insurer is going to want to know that as well. And, after the now infamous cases from the United States, the courts are going to want to know, too!

GenAI has fundamentally changed what lawyers do; it is redefining our value, where we add it and what, how, who, when, and why we charge for it.

SHINGLES LOGIC

How much effort is spent at firms like Shingles doing the following?

- Training people to book time.
- Booking time.
- Reviewing the time booked when it comes to creating a bill.
- Writing off time booked against a series of write-off codes.
- Having finance teams log those write-offs against the codes.
- Panicking towards the end of the financial year to get the WIP that will never get billed written off to avoid paying tax on it.
- Running off matter sheets and asking lawyers to highlight the time to be written off.
- Having the finance team write off the time to get it off the ledger.
- Explaining to the bank manager why £x thousand of WIP has been removed from the management accounts without any payments having come in.
- Debating with Partners about whether they will bill the WIP on their matters, and if so, when.
- Debating with auditors what percentages of booked time should remain in the accounts for tax purposes.

BRACE YOURSELF…

incoming provocative statement

It's a fiction that hours booked are a measure of value.

8 PPP PENGUIN LOGIC

Q: How will we know if we are making or losing money if we don't record billable hours?

A: The short answer is *in the same way* that the rest of the world manages to do so, even though they don't time record. It's a non-question.

The more diplomatic answer I tend to give is 'gross profitability of teams'. You know what the salary costs are per month. You know what they bill per month, and they can provide you with actual numbers of fixed-prices accepted.

Consider these ten rules about the billable hour, created by US lawyer Matt Homann.

WORDS FROM THE WISE

Matt Homann, The (Non) Billable Hour

Matt Homann has a great website which features a section called '10 Rules'. He created a list of ten rules about the billable hour, which I have repeated here.

1. Ask your clients what they buy from you. If it isn't time, stop selling something they don't buy!
2. Imagine a world where your clients know each month how much your bill will be so they could plan for it. They do.
3. If you don't agree on fees at the beginning of a case, you'll be begging for them at the end of it.
4. Sophisticated clients who insist on hourly billing do so because they're smarter than you are, not because they want you to be paid fairly.

5. When you bill by the hour, your once-in-a-lifetime flash of brilliant insight that saves your client millions of dollars has the same contribution to your bottom line as the six minutes you just spent opening the mail.
6. Businesses succeed when their people work better. Law firms succeed when their people work longer. Your clients understand this – and resent you for it.
7. Every time your clients jokingly ask you, 'Are you going to charge me for this?' they aren't joking – and they'll check next month's bill to be sure.
8. The hardest thing to measure is talent. The easiest thing to measure is time. The two have absolutely no relationship to one another. Your law firm measures talent, right?
9. Would you shop at a store where the cost of your purchase isn't set until after you've agreed to buy it? You ask your clients to.
10. There are 1,440 minutes each day. How many did you make matter? How many did you bill for? Were they the same minutes? Didn't think so.

I thought I would offer some Big Yellow Penguin additions to Matt's list:

11. We make pricing mistakes all the time; let's accept this. They are called WIP write-offs! See above.
12. Why do people laugh at lawyer jokes? It's not because they think they are funny. It's because they think they are true… and that's not funny if you are a lawyer.
13. Some people believe the hourly rate is fair because:
    - Everyone pays the same rate.
    - It's fair because it's simple and can be delegated as an administrative task.
    - It reflects the work and costs incurred.
    - It's easier to set hourly rates with profit margins.
    - It's in clients' best interests.

Don't believe your own propaganda!

> A billable rate and an estimate of hours is not a price — it's a non-binding estimate. Nobody prefers non-binding estimates over a set price, including lawyers. The legal market is now filling up with providers willing and able to offer a set price at the outset. They're going to take business away from providers who can't.
>
> **Jordan Furlong**

BRACE YOURSELF…
incoming corny joke

A lawyer dies and goes to Heaven. 'There must be some mistake,' the lawyer argues, 'I'm too young to die. I'm only 55.'

'Fifty-five?' says Saint Peter. 'Not, according to our calculations. You're 82.'

'How'd you get that?' the lawyer asks.

Answers St. Peter: 'We added up your timesheets.'

Whilst on the subject of jokes, you may enjoy this cartoon from Greg Kyte, an accountant, stand-up comic, cartoonist, and podcaster. I met Greg at the Dallas VeraSage conference in 2017, and he has kindly allowed me to publish his take on the realisation rate here. You can tell Greg is American, he spells Realisation with a Z!

> In law, the most exciting possibilities lie not in swapping machines and lawyers but in using AI to deliver client outcomes in entirely new ways – for example, through online dispute resolution rather than physical courts and, more fundamentally, through dispute avoidance rather than dispute resolution.
>
> **Richard Susskind**

If you can wean yourself off the billable hour, you can create a better business. The benefits are many:

- Your lawyers will work better as a team.
- The team will develop a more collegiate culture. They have time to help each other and will delegate willingly.
- There is time to work pro bono for organisations and charities your employees care about. The hourly rate discourages this.
- To scope the work properly, you must take time to plan the work. It becomes investment time.
- An efficient lawyer is not penalised; they can be incentivised.
- Lawyers are motivated to engage with technology and put aside the time to learn how to use it.
- Clients' and lawyers' interests are aligned. Under the hourly rate, the lawyer will want to do more to get paid more. The client wants the lawyer to do less, so they pay less.

CLIENTS DISLIKE HOURLY RATES

When clients are told that an hourly rate is £300 plus an extra 20% VAT, their immediate concern is (naturally), 'Wow, that sounds a lot! £360 per hour… how long is this going to take?' The lawyer's fallback position is usually, 'We don't know. We will charge an hourly rate, and we will book the time.'

Even the worst-performing lawyer can make money if a client agrees to pay an hourly rate.

As lawyers, we know the law. However, there is one law many lawyers will be unfamiliar with, and that is Parkinson's Law – the law that work *expands* to fill the time allotted for its completion. Sound familiar?

Parkinson's law is practised every day in law firms as – under the billable hour model – lawyers can only make money if they are doing something. The term Parkinson's Law was apparently first coined by Cyril Northcote Parkinson in a humorous essay he wrote for 'The Economist' in 1955. With current hourly rates and timesheets, I suspect Cyril would not find things so funny. Our clients certainly don't.

When you think about the way consumers operate, the way we buy anything outside of the legal world, most buyers of anything (including those who buy legal services) want:

- Price transparency.
- Certainty.
- Results.
- No extras.
- Value.

And it's the last bullet point – **value** – that is hard to get our heads around, for the simple reason that everybody is different and so are their needs. Let's look at what clients want.

WHAT DO CLIENTS WANT?

To properly embrace VBP, lawyers need to understand that clients usually fall into one of two types, a client who is in pain and wants to have assistance in alleviating the pain, or a client who has something to gain and needs legal assistance to help realise that gain. I will refer to pain and gain quite a lot throughout the book.

Examples of a client in pain can include the following:

- A client that wants a divorce.
- A client arguing over custody of the children.
- A client that needs help in sorting out their deceased father's probate so that the mother can have some income.
- A client that needs legal assistance to bring a personal injury claim.

- A client that has been unfairly treated at work.
- A client that needs to commence or defend litigation.
- A client involved in a breach of contract case.

Examples of a client seeking gain can include the following:

- A client wanting to buy their dream home.
- A client wanting their late father's probate sorted so they, as beneficiaries, can start a new chapter in their life.
- A client wanting to purchase a commercial unit for the expansion of a business.
- A client wanting to secure their immigration status and have the right to remain in a certain country and start a new life.

Most lawyers incorrectly assume they know what clients want and need.

8 PPP PENGUIN LOGIC

Never assume you know what is important to the client

Remember, 'Assume' makes an Ass out of U and Me.

How often do lawyers ask the crucial question, 'What do you want to achieve by instructing me?'

The answer is not enough.

In 2023, as part of a training conference I organised, I interviewed Jon Whittle, who was the author of a brilliant research report called *The Riddle of Perception,* published by LexisNexis. The report, first authored in 2016, explored the legal landscape and contained a section dealing with client perceptions and what clients wanted from lawyers.

One of the highlights (at least for me) in the report was a list of 14 features that lawyers were asked to list in order of importance to clients. The researchers also asked clients what was most important to them. Guess what? They were dramatically different.

The report found: 'Lawyers also seem to have a skewed sense of what their clients actually care about when it comes to service. When we asked lawyers what their clients value most, they put 'clear cost/fixed fees' at the top of the list. But when we asked clients, they put 'a clear understanding of my particular needs' above everything else.'

	Lawyer Perceptions	Client Perceptions
1	Provides Clear Indication of Costs/Fixed Fees	Clear Understanding of My Particular Needs
2	Clear Understanding of My Particular Needs	Efficient
3	Provides Good Customer Service	Keeps To Timetable/Avoids Case Dragging On
4	Easy To Get in Touch With	Keeps Me Informed Along the Way
5	Keeps Me Informed Along the Way	Provides Clear Indication of Costs/Fixed Fee
6	Keeps To Timetable /Avoids Case Dragging On	Easy To Get in Touch With
7	Makes Me Feel Valued as A Client	Provides Good Customer Service
8	Speaks Plainly, Not Too Much Jargon	Value For Money
9	Efficient	Does not Overcomplicate
10	Value For Money	Speaks Plainly, Not Too Much Jargon
11	Delivers Added Value	Makes Me Feel Valued as A Client
12	Does not Overcomplicate	Choice Of Pricing/Service Level
13	Choice Of Pricing/Service Level	Delivers Added Value
14	Lower Prices Than Others	Lower Prices Than Others

I often use this list when training lawyers and play a 'Guess what clients want game'. When I mix up the list and ask lawyers to put them into the order that they think clients value, would you be shocked to learn they get it wrong? In fact, the best that a lawyer has ever done is get the first three in order.

As the interview with Jon Whittle at my conference was so powerful, I had the session transcribed.

WORDS FROM THE WISE

Jon Whittle, Jon Whittle Consulting Ltd

One of the reasons LexisNexis decided to compile the report was because, whilst we were specialists in providing law firms with comprehensive legal research and legal productivity tools, we thought it would be illuminating to have a better understanding of how lawyers interacted with their own clients.

If we understood the needs of Law Firm clients, it would help LexisNexis improve the quality of the services it provided to law firms. So, we did some market research to help LexisNexis with their understanding of how law firms worked with their clients – to get under the bonnet of what law firms actually did!

When we started the work, we began to unearth a huge disconnect between what a client thought a good relationship with their law firm looked like, and what lawyers thought made up a good lawyer-client relationship.

We were working with 122 law firms, and got access to 108 clients and really drilled into both parties' respective perceptions of value. The client's perception and the lawyer's perception. It immediately became apparent that there was a problem – 77% of lawyers thought the legal service they gave represented good or excellent value for money. However, only 26% of clients thought they got good or excellent value in the service they received from their lawyers. This was one of the widest gaps in perception of value between a provider and a customer that I have seen in any of the professions.

As a follow-up piece, when we asked if lawyers worked in a service industry, all of those surveyed said yes, but caveated their answer by saying that they did not think their colleagues did. This translated into a statistic which states that 77% of other lawyers did not believe they were in a service industry. If 77% of lawyers are not in a service industry, what industry are they in? I think this mindset is a crucial window into the mindset that causes so many challenges in the relationship between lawyers and their clients.

The question I wanted to explore as a consequence of these research results was to understand why lawyers' perceptions of value were so different from those of their clients. My conclusion was that its roots lie in a very simple observation: which is that the whole point of being a lawyer is to deliver high-quality, robust, secure, dependable legal advice. The fundamental requirement to deliver good law trumps all other considerations.

Furthermore, everything the law firm does is driven by that objective. It's critical. The rule of law matters more than anything else. Which is why law firms invest, first and foremost, in legal processes, technology, systems and information, all of which are designed to support the delivery of that high-quality advice. Customer care and customer service will, by definition, always come second to the delivery of good quality advice.

If you talk to law firms about improving their law firms, it usually revolves around getting more lawyers – good ones – then it's about process, technology, information and how they can make their law firm better at delivering law.

This then tips over into how law firms choose to promote themselves and their service. The focus is all about the quality of law.

If you look at any law firm's website, there will be a lot of information about what they do (their legal offering), who their people are, how many of them there are, how many of them have over 30 years' experience. It's all about them. Law Firms seem compelled to talk about what they do rather than how it helps their clients. To demonstrate this, I took the 'about us' page from ten different law firm websites, removed all the identifiers (names, locations, etc.) and showed them all to the Managing Partners of those ten law firms. Not one could pick out their own website. If a solicitor can't spot their own firm from what they're saying about their own business, then how would they expect a prospective client to choose to work with them?

So, why do clients have such a poor perception of value from law firms? It's because clients start from a very different place when they engage a law firm. They make an assumption that the legal advice they're going to get will be good. They assume this because the law firm is regulated, the law firm is trading, and the solicitor they're briefing is qualified and certified. Why, in the client's mind, would they not get good law? The client is only interested in outcomes – and that is because they are on a journey. They start at Point A with an issue, and their only objective – when going to a law firm – is to get to Point B where there is a solution to their issue. If a lawyer, when taking that matter on, does not know what Point B looks like, or why Point B matters, then you can get the disconnect regarding value. What lawyers forget is that Point B has nothing to do with the law. For example, Point B can be:

- Getting into the new house before the baby is born.
- Getting probate sorted so Granny has some money to live on.
- Getting the new factory premises bought before the machinery we've bought arrives from Germany.

So, if the lawyers have not got their heads around what matters to the client, then there is a real danger that the matter becomes just about legal process and not about real-life human issues. Lawyers are, rightly, obsessed with inputs, whereas clients, reasonably, only care about outputs. Lawyers who forget the crushing importance of the output are the ones who find themselves at the wrong end of the value perception.

If you go to the dentist with terrible toothache, you don't ask the dentist to prove their successful track record in teeth extractions. You assume because they are a dentist, because it says 'dentist' above the door, and because there is a big chair with a light on it, that the dentist knows what he/she is doing and will be able to take away the pain. As a patient of a dentist, you are in real, actual pain. You will know you are in pain because you are eating porridge, and you want to eat steak! The value is all about the pain relief, and at that point, most people will pay whatever it costs to have that pain alleviated.

It's the same with the law – it's only about the money if the value is missing.

And that final point is important. In all the research we did, we found that price was rarely important to clients. Price was at the bottom of their list. Value was what was important. To demonstrate this, we asked clients who had fixed-price engagements to express their sense of value. We found that 89% of clients on fixed-price engagements were satisfied with the outcomes, whilst clients who were on open-ended hourly rates only recorded a 26% satisfied rating. Price does matter. Value matters more.

If lawyers can focus on what really drives value in a lawyer-client relationship, and can learn to take away questions about price, then you will have happy and repeat clients.

VBP IS A MINDSET CHANGE

> Unlike other firms, we don't sell time; we sell intellectual capital and business results. In fact, we believe the traditional ways most firms charge works against the best interests of both parties. Hours and time of staff are focused on efficiency, and we don't believe you're buying efficiency. You're buying effectiveness.
>
> **Tim Williams, Ignition Consulting**
>
> Hell, there are no rules here – we're trying to accomplish something.
>
> **Thomas Edison**

Make no mistake, to successfully implement VBP, you must change the way you think about pricing and how you generate fees.

SOME HOME TRUTHS AND CRITICAL SUCCESS FACTORS

1. VBP needs to be led, sanctioned and supported from the top of your firm (Read Golden Rule #1 again).
2. You will need to involve others in the process. VBP cannot be delivered by one person.
3. You will need to identify and/or create leaders and get people to buy into and pull in the same direction. Some won't, and they may have to go.
4. Your Pioneer penguin pilot team will make mistakes.
5. You will need to think about your strategic objectives. Implementing VBP needs to be one of them if this project is to succeed.
6. Implementing VBP is not an e-mail or an internal memo from the CEO/Managing Partner to a Head of Department. Or, as I read in Macdivitt and Wilkinson's book *Value-Based Pricing,* it is not Jean-Luc Picard Syndrome, where the CEO says 'Make it so' with no Strategy or support provided.
7. Implementation is not an away day training course or webinar with a template circulated at the end.
8. You will need to call out the bad habits of lawyers and Partners and deal with Naysayer penguins who seek to undermine the process.

9. You need to look at your firm's culture and seek to embed VBP principles into it.
10. You will need to look at the way you incentivise, pay, and reward your lawyers and legal teams.
11. Your recruitment policies and processes will need to change.
12. Implementing VBP is not ordering some technology that the IT department will install.
13. VBP is time-consuming in its initial stages.
14. VBP is difficult, but then again, so is riding a bike when you don't know how to do it. It can be done.
15. You will create and amend policies and templates many times.
16. You will have to test and trial assumptions.
17. You will need to adopt a no-blame culture and create an environment of psychological safety; something that does not come naturally to many law firms.

BRACE YOURSELF...
incoming provocative statement

Some of the many hours of work that your lawyers do for their customers is of no value whatsoever, but one brilliant idea that flashed into their minds could be hugely valuable.

WORDS FROM THE WISE

Kevin Pratt, If Airlines Operated Like Law Firms

The following humorous story is attributed to Denver Attorney Kevin B. Pratt. As far as I can establish, the article first appeared in *Billing Innovations: New Win-Win Ways to End Hourly Billing* by Richard C Reed.

The Denver lawyer stepped up to the airline ticket counter and asked to buy a ticket for a flight to Chicago.

'No problem,' said the clerk, 'but before I issue the ticket, I should remind you of the new way we charge for tickets. This year, we have adopted a 'basic rate' of three dollars a minute for our flights. The clock starts when you check in at the gate and stops when you pick up your luggage. We mail you a bill about two months after the flight.'

'Well, I guess that's okay,' commented the lawyer.

The clerk continued, 'Remember, we call it a 'basic rate' because we sometimes adjust that rate up or down if the flight is very empty or very full. Too, we may multiply that rate if our expert pilot finds a tailwind. We also adjust the rate according to what you will be doing in Chicago. You look like a lawyer, so I'll assume it's very important that you get there by plane, so we quadruple the basic rate. Another thing, how much is your annual income? You see, if you earn a great deal and it turns out the plane crashes, we will have to pay more on your spouse's damage claim, and we have, of course, to consider that increased risk of the airline.'

The astounded lawyer choked, 'But how much will this trip cost me? How do I know you don't slow down on purpose? How do I know your bill will be correct?'

The clerk stared down over the end of his nose. 'I can see you're not familiar with the complexities of airline work. There are so many things we just can't know in advance – the winds, traffic delays, the weather, the routing. Airlines are a business, and we have to make a profit to stay in business. Now don't worry, we're very honest and sensitive about all this billing business and I am sure you'll be pleased with our fully itemized bill when you get it. If there's any question, just call.' Then the clerk whispered, 'But just so we understand each other, if you don't pay the bill in full and promptly, you'll never fly on this airline again.'

'Oh,' grunted the Denver lawyer, 'is there anything else I should know?'

The clerk smiled thoughtfully and murmured, 'On your flight, there is a new copilot in training, and we charge an additional 50 cents a mile. Copilots are really very important, you know, to carry the pilot's charts, to fly on clear, calm days, even to land the plane if the pilot is busy with other matters. Too, if you fly with us again, your copilot may have become your pilot. Wouldn't that be great? One other thing, if the copilot uses computerized flight routing, there will be an additional $75 charge. But of course, computerized flight routing is almost a standard charge with technologically advanced airlines.'

'But I just wanted to get to my meeting in Chicago and come home. Now I don't even know if I should fly at all,' groaned the lawyer. The clerk smiled again. 'Mature passengers come to understand that flying is just a cost of doing business. They never know how much it costs 'til we bill them. But then, there's really no choice, is there?'

'No,' conceded the lawyer, 'I guess not.'

And then the lawyer tried again. 'Why can't you just give me a fixed price and I'll decide if I'll go or not?'

The clerk frowned. 'But we can't do that. That wouldn't be fair to you. We might overcharge you and then you'd be unhappy. Or we might underestimate and then the airline would lose money and couldn't maintain the planes, and we certainly don't want that.'

And so, the Denver lawyer came to hate airlines and took his revenge by regaling acquaintances at cocktail parties about the new pitfalls of airline travel.

*

And Kevin finished his story with the comment 'Fortunately, none of you readers run an airline, so you won't feel defensive.'

THE MANAGEMENT TEAM'S ROLE

> Too many companies think they have a strategy problem when they actually have a leadership problem.
>
> **Jon Cobb**

Introducing a paradigm shift is not simply a matter of showing members of your business various statistics about how you may be struggling, the need to generate more fees, or talking about increased competition. You will need to initiate an open, honest and convincing dialogue about what's happening in the marketplace. If many people start listening and talking about the changes you propose, the urgency can build and feed on itself.

Your management team needs to 'buy into' the change. They need to be prepared to get involved and make some tough decisions as this process proceeds. You have to really work hard on P#1, and spend significant time and energy building urgency, before moving onto the next steps. Managing change isn't enough – your leaders have to lead it.

8 PPP PENGUIN LOGIC

Remember, you can find effective change leaders throughout your organisation – they don't necessarily follow the traditional company hierarchy.

A decision that will need to be taken early on, is a commitment to deal with dissent in the leadership team. The details of disagreements amongst the Board and Partners will spread like wildfire throughout your business.

- Some customers will have to be let go.
- Some customers will push back when prices are increased.
- Some customers who have paid a low price but received a gold-plated first-class service may be unhappy with a perceived demotivation to a lower service level which is commensurate to what they pay.
- The Board may decide to pull out of work areas altogether.

If the Board are not of one mind and voice, the project will fail, and your lawyers will retreat into their silos which will be built with stronger doors and thicker walls. Golden Rule #1 is repeated here.

GOLDEN RULE #1 (again)

The management of your business must be 100% onboard with this project. Otherwise, it won't be fully implemented.

- They must become engaged and be involved in championing the change in culture that needs to happen.
- They must help define the objectives and then implement them.
- Resources must be made available.
- Staff must be made available to participate in the project.

- Obstacles will need to be removed.
- Funds and expertise will need to be made available.
- It will need to be made clear – across the business – that this is a serious initiative and vital for the firm's success.

Lots of carefully considered communications will be required.

HINDERING THOUGHTS

It is normal to have hindering thoughts about embarking upon a change management project. Let's face it, there's a lot to do, and you will have concerns about how you can muster the troops and keep the project on track.

> Do not be afraid to give up the good
> to go for the great.
>
> **John Rockefeller**

Implementing VBP is emphatically not all about creating more Equity Partners' cash. It is about increasing cash into the business and not leaving value on the table, and this cash can be used for rewarding staff, expanding the business, and investing in its people.

Here are some thoughts to help you get through not only this book but also the project that may await:

- By not relying on an hourly rate, you pretty much have a unique selling point (USP). You are different. If a client asks you how you have arrived at the figure quoted, you don't have to confirm it's an hourly rate because you don't have one. If you are asked how you arrived at the figure, you can genuinely say it's based on your experience of dealing with similar cases.
- Clients are aware they are not buying your effort. They are buying the outcomes you discussed with them. For those that charge an hourly rate, the slowest horse wins the race. You are different.
- Brands that are perceived to be different can charge more.
- Your lawyers do not have targets of annual hours multiplied by an hourly rate. Team targets are easy to create. Hourly rates limit income. By moving off the

hourly right, you move away from the artificial ceiling that is imposed on your earnings.

- Suddenly, your lawyers can delegate work appropriately to other members of the team and support teamwork. There is no hoarding of work as they are no longer worried about making their timesheets look good.
- You lose the fear of clients deserting your firm. Why? Because you're going to charge them differently. Why would a client leave your firm if you're giving them choices, fixed prices, and delivering value?
- You may fear clients leaving your firm because they don't want to pay more at all. This may happen. However, if you are asking them to pay more, they may be unprofitable already.
- You will have fears about how you deal with price resistance not only from clients but also from your lawyers. These can be overcome.
- You may be concerned that your staff are not good at selling. Allay their fears. You don't want them to sell… you just want them to learn to have structured conversations with clients when taking an enquiry, using their judgment, creating some solutions, and onboarding them. You are not creating a firm of sales professionals.
- You may have fears that clients are ringing around getting lots of quotes. They are not. Not all of them. The genuinely price-sensitive clients (as opposed to value-sensitive) may not be your target market anyway.
- You may fear that all clients are interested in is a low price, but they are not. Read the LexisNexis report summary again. Even better, read the whole report.
- You may have fears about how the process can be implemented. Hopefully, the purchase of this book and what you have read so far, allays some of those fears. Implementing VBP is achievable.

If you need any more convincing, and I hope you don't, I'll give you another anecdotal example, again from Australia. You may recall I mentioned Steve and Jacqui Brown in the acknowledgements for this book.

8 PPP PENGUIN LOGIC

Steve and Jacqui Brown abandoned time recording in their law firm in 2017. Every year, Steve, on the anniversary of their last timesheet, posts about it on LinkedIn.

His post from 2023 follows.

On 1 June 2017, Lynn & Brown Lawyers stopped charging clients by time and transformed our business forever to provide our clients services on a value-based pricing model. VBP v Time recording.

1. Clients hate the uncertainty of time billing. VBP provides a fixed, agreed upfront fee and a guarantee of no hidden extras.
2. VBP focuses on outcomes, time billing focuses on inputs and time spent.
3. VBP encourages innovation, time billing encourages taking more time to perform the work, thus discouraging innovation.
4. Time billing rewards busyness, VBP rewards effectiveness (I know which one as a client I would prefer).
5. Time billing places all the risk with the client, VBP shares the risk.
6. VBP aligns the client and lawyers' interests in both wanting to achieve an effective result in the quickest possible way; time billing creates a conflict: the client wants it done in the least possible time, the lawyer takes however long they feel is necessary.
7. Time billing fosters a production mindset rather than an entrepreneurial spirit. VBP promotes problem-solving and value-adding.

This ends the sermon and a photo of our annual burning of the timesheet.

Steve contacted me a couple of days after this post appeared on LinkedIn and told me a business based in the UK had contacted him to see if they would act for them and prepare a shareholder's agreement, as they liked what Steve was saying. He asked if I could recommend a firm. I did. UK-based businesses are seeking legal advice from lawyers in Perth, Western Australia!

POSITIVE THOUGHTS

When lawyers work in a value-based pricing environment, they engage with clients differently.

Think about how it may play out in your firm in the future. Could it look like this?

- On a new matter, your firm might have two or three lawyers in the initial meeting with a prospect discussing a new commercial transaction.
- The prospect would meet and hear from lawyers from the company's commercial, commercial property, and employment teams, etc. It makes sense to get people involved.
- The prospect is impressed. The prospect may think, 'Wow, these people are really trying to understand my case.' If it was an hourly rate, only one person would be involved, simply because the client wouldn't want to pay for the others.
- If the prospect agrees to a fixed value-based price, they don't care how many lawyers are working on the matter. However, if they are paying hourly, they will think that the lawyers are running up a bill.
- Value-based pricing lawyers can allocate resources more effectively and accomplish more.
- Your lawyers know working as a team can be more effective in producing the work. Teams work more collegiately. They will spot opportunities to create more work or even be more effective. They will brainstorm. They will strategise.
- The prospect, now a client, feels they are being looked after.
- For many clients, having a value-based price, which is agreed upon, means that they do not even have to incur further costs of tracking and checking the hours that lawyers say they have worked and going through lines of spreadsheets to see whether or not their records tally with the lawyers. Guess what…they trust each other.

People change because they are shown a version of the truth that influences their feelings. When changing behaviours, both thinking and feeling are essential. Change will happen if it involves both the head and the heart.

WORDS FROM THE WISE

Dr Jacqui Rigby, Rigby Pollitt Associates

Build a compelling 3D picture that brings your goal to life. How the firm will look. How it feels to work there. What the customer will experience in practical terms and how they will feel about working with your firm. Emotions are an essential part of every powerful story, building buy-in and the passion for change.

Ensure your goal articulates the 'why'. Why are you making the change? Why now? Why will it benefit your people, your customers, and the firm?

Don't set the goal alone. Work as a small team to build and review the goal. Bring in at least one person who is visionary and who won't get tied up in 'how' the change will happen at this stage.

Robin Dicks, Thriving Consultancy

One very specific example that sticks in my mind is a firm that had one client that represented about 30% of the revenue of that biggest practice. I interviewed the key decision-maker at that client. The client said, 'At the moment, we use six firms.'

The key decision-maker at the client said, 'This firm, they do what it says on the tin, its client service is fine. It's reliable, and we quite like the people. But we're looking to reduce the number of firms we use from six to four. As things stand, they will be a casualty of that, because at no point do they ever ask us what we're trying to do strategically. At no point do they ever ask us what we really want, what we're aiming for, how we want to work. The way they communicate with our staff just doesn't feel right.'

The repercussions for the firm – if they had lost that major client – would have been close to seismic. As it was, by understanding and reacting to what the client said, they saved the relationship.

That was an absolute trigger for the firm to think, 'We can't make these assumptions.

'We've got to think about what we have. We've got to think about how we manage relationships. We need to have a better understanding of what value is represented by.'

Graham Moore, Katchr

Law firm financial data processes are often slow, clunky, and inefficient.

Often, the motivation for urgent change is when somebody has come in from outside the legal sector, and they look at what the firm is doing and they say, 'I have no idea how this firm is operating. I have no idea what's going on. I can't believe this is the way it's been managed.'

The vast majority of management information that law firm Partners see focuses on the firm-wide P&L, the balance sheet, with questions raised such as 'Is there enough cash in the bank'? and 'What was the billing figure for last month?' What this data doesn't tell you is which part of the firm is profitable. Which teams are effective and which are not.

If you are recording time, irrespective of what your pricing model is, you've got to get your time recording under control. You've got to deal with the triple discounting. You've got to remove any concept that it's a bad thing to record time and not bill it. That's probably a five-year project in itself. You've got to capture that time accurately if you're time recording; otherwise, you're just deluding yourself, which a lot of law firms are a lot of the time.

There needs to be a change of attitude and culture. A firm should aspire to develop a culture of being inquisitive, and secondly, a culture of wanting to use and be provided with quality data. In many cases, the scenario is people won't trust that data even if they extract it from their Practice Management Systems because the data entry was unreliable. But the data entry is unreliable because nobody's ever used the data, so people don't understand why they should be entering this data in the first place, let alone caring whether it is being entered correctly.

Katherine Thomas, Free Range Lawyers

I think, fundamentally, any law firm that is using artificial intelligence to do its work will find that the billable hour becomes untenable. Then, any law firm that is not using artificial intelligence and/or is not still using the billable hour will also find their position untenable. I think it's going to change law firms' propositions whether they like it or not. The question really is whether a firm is going to drive that change and have it within their control, or are they going to have those changes made to them due to competitive forces?

Will Whawell, Excelo Consulting

Point the Partners at the number of law firm failures in recent years and say, 'Why have they all failed?' And the reason why they've all failed is that they believe in this mythical figure called WIP, that everyone's billing out at 500 pounds an hour, that every single matter they've got in their office is worth £X. And it turns out not to be true. The Naysayers aren't listened to.

What is sad is the culture of the billable hour stops lawyers from admitting they know how much something is worth.

Melissa Lyon, Hive Legal

When people don't have individual budgets, they'll work together. They won't hold the work to do what they want to do. They'll bring in work for other people because they know it's all for the greater good.

Value-based pricing plays to people's strengths. If you take away the notion that the billable hour is only about providing technical advice, everyone in the firm can contribute in some way to the value that you're providing the client. So, everyone feels a lot more invested in the business.

I am often asked how I know if value-based pricing is working.

How do you trust your people to work? How do you know you're making money?

I reply there's money going out, and there's money coming in.

There are no write-offs because we've actually agreed the price with the clients, and they pay on time. We don't have bad debts.

Chris Marston, Exemplar Companies Pbc

My best advice to those contemplating VBP is you better be ready to jump in the pool all the way, because you won't succeed unless you're all-in this game. It is a game that requires belief and full faith. It doesn't reward hedging. You won't innovate properly if you're not all in this game. You must be very clear about what a win looks like. Leadership starts at the top, always.

Simon Tupman, Simon Tupman Consulting

The impact of pricing, and the extent to which it is strategic, has huge implications for the way the firm actually does business, interacts with the client, and provides value. Ultimately, I think it can make life so much easier for lawyers who are buried under timesheets and are probably lying through their teeth just to make sure that they submit a timesheet instead of focusing on creating the value. Time recording is a classic example of focusing more on the scoreboard and not on the ball.

Matthew Burgess, View Legal

Looking back, I was a very slow learner. I was regularly booking 2,500 to 3,000 chargeable hours a year. All legitimately recorded. I would work, on average, 12-to-16-hour days, six days a week, and then I'd do 12 hours on a Sunday. And I did that every single week for 51 weeks of the year. I'd take off the week after Christmas. I kept going up the levels and got to full Equity Partner and a partnership. I remember my eight-year-old daughter said, 'Dad, I never want to work at your firm.' I can remember thinking, well, if my daughter can work it out – that she would never want to do it – then it's probably obvious that no one else would want to do it either.

Karen Finch, Legally Yours

Clients will drive the pricing revolution. Clients have been so institutionalised in terms of accepting poor customer service from lawyers, they almost assume they're going to get ripped off. There's an assumption that that's the way it must be. I've spent the last eight years speaking to clients and saying you actually have the power to change the way lawyers deliver their legal services.

I think, within the next 24 months, all of the legal technology that was previously being utilised by law firms will be accessible direct to clients. Once clients have their hands on these legal tech solutions, the question will then be, 'What is the value of lawyers?' layered on top of these platforms.

John Chisholm, John Chisholm Consulting

I remain optimistic that there will be a genuine change. I just don't think there is one single thing at the moment that has created a burning platform for a paradigm shift. I do, however, think that a combination of factors, including increasing client resistance to the billable hour, the advent of GenAI (investing in tech to make things happen quicker yet still continuing to bill by the hour can only lead to a downward spiral), and the unwellness and mental health challenges in our profession will be key factors in creating a sense of urgency.

Often, the partnership structure is a barrier to any major change. If everyone's a leader, no one is. The partnership structure and the need for compromise and consensus often lead to the lowest common denominator winning out.

Nicola Jones, Athena Professional

The billable hour and learning are antithetical.

If you're driving behaviour by the billable hour, you're not driving anyone towards learning and motivation to learn.

CRIB SHEET
READING & VIEWING

WATCH (COMPULSORY)

Watch this YouTube video of The Bar and Grill Singers – a group of lawyers singing about Time Recording. When you listen to it, first listen as a lawyer, it may make you smile. Then listen to it again from the perspective of a client. It may make you weep.

By The Bar and Grill Singers

https://www.youtube.com/watch?v=UVX1zxdQaN4

WATCH (COMPULSORY)

Leading Change: Establish a Sense of Urgency

By John Kotter

https://youtu.be/2Yfrj2Y9IlI?si=vv9mP0SvVi1DW9gC

WATCH (COMPULSORY)

Angry People Make Change

Tom Peters explains the single source of innovation is angry people.

https://youtu.be/A2EdCl-CX4Q?si=3zmK7f2vZnDIdi2H

WATCH

Is your Current Pricing Set Up like Bob's Barbecue?

https://youtu.be/OJv5xIFcRXU

NB. The Hushpuppies in this YouTube clip refer to a fried potato dish… not suede shoes… it did flummox me for a while until I Googled it!

WATCH

The Impact of Changes in the Legal Services Market

Professor Stephen Mayson

Legal Procurement Conference 2012

https://youtu.be/t_tkXGe31KQ

WATCH

Cometh the Hour

This film highlights the daily struggles between general counsel and finance directors trying to manage their budgets and law firms trying to hit their billing targets.

By Riverview Law

https://youtu.be/BfXhn3tf_vE?si=lwQpq0peIKzlrxlX

READ

Our Iceberg is Melting

By John Kotter and Holger Rathgeber

WATCH

Don't Fear Failure

Tom Peters tells a story about a man who was unafraid to fail, and why that makes him an excellent role model.

https://youtu.be/73e1Hhkb0Oo

WATCH

John Kotter Himself Explains what Our Iceberg is Melting is About.

By John Kotter

https://youtu.be/tFnsLRp1VUw?si=Dy5H5bajoBxTGxKf

WATCH

Our Iceberg is Melting

YouTube clip explaining the lessons of the book.

https://www.youtube.com/watch?v=hB-c3pJR0qU&t=67s

READ

Managing Price, Gaining Profit

By Michael V. Marn and Robert L. Rosiello

To learn what a 1% improvement in price can do to profit.

https://hbr.org/1992/09/managing-price-gaining-profit

READ

The Impact of GenAI on Billable Hour Approach in UK Law Firms

By Today's Esquire

https://www.todaysesquire.com/the-impact-of-genai-on-billable-hour-approach-in-uk-law-firms/

READ

Your Self-Imposed Profit Ceiling

By Tim Williams

https://www.linkedin.com/pulse/your-self-imposed-profit-ceiling-tim-williams/

READ

For the Agency Business to Live, the Billable Hour Must Die

By Tim Williams

https://www.ignitiongroup.com/propulsion-blog/for-the-agency-business-model-to-live-the-billable-hour-must-die

TIPS/CHECKLISTS

1. Do not overthink pricing. There is no formula.
2. You can create a sense of urgency by looking at your financial data and conducting an 'as is' analysis.
3. Most lawyers are very bad when it comes to understanding accounting information and calculating profit. They won't ask for training as they don't want to admit they don't know. Train them.

EXERCISES

EXERCISE 1

Strengths and challenges

What strengths do we have as a firm that will help us deliver successful change?

What are the biggest challenges when managing change in our firm?

How might we overcome these challenges to drive success?

EXERCISE 2

Time recording

Are the time recording policies adhered to by all in your firm?

Is the data from your PMS accurate?

What do firm benchmarking studies tell you about the firm's lawyer-level performance?

EXERCISE 3 (COMPULSORY)

Complete this Maths Question

	Legal Matter
Fee	£100
Profit	£30

Questions

1. Work out the impact on profit when the client asks for – and is given – a 10% discount on the fee. Answer in the Appendices.
2. What would a 5% increase in your turnover do for your profit figures? Answer… not in the appendices!

EXERCISE 4

How is pricing currently set in your firm?

1. Ask each Practice Area to explain their methodology, and send you the calculators and spreadsheets they have.
2. Speak with lawyers who have joined your firm in the last 12 months and ask them to explain how the pricing induction was dealt with.
3. What lists and materials are currently used by your teams to get initial information and help calculate fees? Get hold of them.
4. Are there documents in your firm that could be collated into a centralised departmental 'Big Book of Usefulness' (BBU) that explains the department's pricing policies? This will need to include the induction process.
5. Review what level of pricing autonomy is accorded to individuals and teams, and what is done to encourage pricing collaboration.

EXERCISE 5

What strengths do you have, as a firm, that will help you deliver successful change?

What are the biggest challenges when managing change in your firm?

How might you overcome these challenges to drive success?

Where in your firm have you lost control of pricing?

Who is setting the prices? Lawyers? Clients? Referrers?

POSSIBILITY THINKING QUESTIONS TO POSE

1. What information can we possibly get that will support the paradigm shift?
2. How can we possibly create an environment of psychological safety?

> [In the UK] The IT and telecommunications sector has the highest AI adoption rate at 29.5%, closely followed by the legal sector at 29.2%. The hospitality, health, and retail sectors have the lowest adoption rates, at around 11.5%.
>
> **UK Artificial Intelligence (AI) Statistics and Trends in 2023, Forbes Advisor**

EXPOSURE DRAFTS
BY GREG KYTE
LEGAL SERVICES TREADMILL 8000
DISTANCE
4.1m
TIME
34:18
SPEED
7.2mph
BILLABLE OPPORTUNITY COST
£114.34

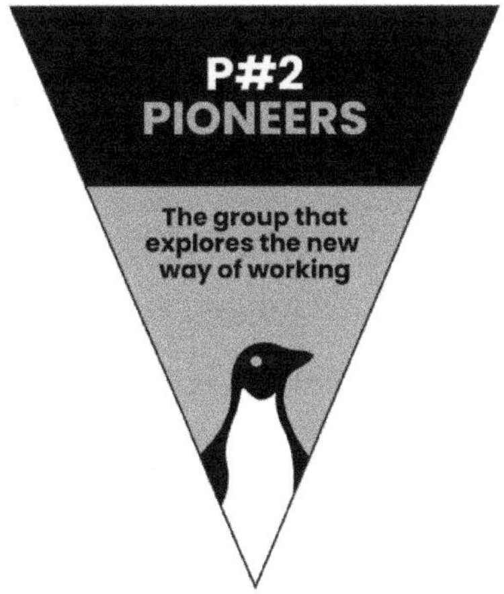

P#2 PIONEERS

THE GROUP THAT EXPLORES THE NEW WAY OF WORKING

> It is not easy to be a pioneer –
> but oh, it is fascinating!
>
> **Elizabeth Blackwell**

Now that we have decided to make a paradigm shift, thought needs to be given to those Pioneer penguins who will be part of the guiding coalition. The Pioneer Group will need to know *why* they were selected, *why* the business is undertaking this project, and *what* they are moving towards. Purpose is crucial.

The successful candidates will become part of a powerful group that guides the change. They will need to understand what they are being asked to do and why. They should be able to lead, have credibility, communicate, plus be given authority and appreciate the sense of urgency.

WORDS FROM THE WISE

Nicola Jones, Athena Professional

The Pioneer Group need to be capable, which means we need to understand what they're capable of now and look at what we need them to be able to do.

Are they motivated? They must have the opportunity to practise something they've learned, or they will forget it.

THE PIONEER GROUP

THE BOARD

Before selecting any Pioneer penguins, the Executive Board must agree that this VBP project is strategically important and communicate that this is the case. There needs to be a distinct, believable reason for the commencement of the project. The benefits must be crystal clear.

The Board will need to make it known that the Plan outcomes are not set in stone, and that the outcomes will form and develop over time. This is a new journey for everyone. It's a test for a VBP project that will be rolled out in the future.

The Board should also ensure that managers and Equity Partner owners are not only aligned with the aim of carrying out the VBP project but also that intolerable behaviours – which may derail it – will not be accepted.

The Board must ensure that the Pioneers are provided with their full support. The pilot objectives and targets are important and should be treated as such. There must be a commitment that the pilot will be resourced with management funding, support and reductions in fee-earning targets if required. The Board must make it clear that there is a real opportunity which exists, and it can be advanced by participating and supporting the project.

The Pioneer penguins will be participating in:

- The creation of knowledge-sharing tools and templates, and helping to design the methodology that will be used.
- They will be instrumental in helping create the knowledge for pricing teams to operate within Practice Areas, which will influence pricing decisions in the wider firm.

- They will prove the concept that VBP can be successful, as has been shown in other firms.
- They will help identify and design changes to be implemented by the Operations, HR, Finance, and Marketing teams.
- They will be seen as leading the pricing function. Pioneer roles and contributions will need to be recognised and appreciated by the leadership. It is worth the hard yards.

The Board must also commit to making and supporting frequent and consistent communications.

HOW MANY IN THE PIONEER GROUP?

It depends. You won't be surprised to learn that the size of a group is influenced by the size of your firm. I have worked with groups of between 1 (a solopreneur) and 12. The key thing is having the right *calibre* of Pioneer penguin. Choose key players, ideally from a number of Practice Areas.

The following will be affected (eventually):

- Lawyers doing the work day-to-day.
- Finance Team.
- Operations/Support Staff.
- IT Staff.
- Compliance Officers.
- Marketers.
- HR.

In fact, everyone in the business will eventually be impacted by the new way of working and will have to adjust their processes in the future.

I am often asked whether a business should select a small pilot group first or just go 'big bang' and roll out VBP across the whole firm in one go. My advice is always the same. Start small, seek to prove your concept and that the Pilot Plan works, and then roll it out.

PIONEER CHARACTERISTICS

You need to create a team that has more hands to do, more brainpower to think and contemplate, and more eyes to see what needs to be changed in the business. Remember, teaching is the best way to learn, so try to select patient people who can explain concepts clearly.

Pioneers must:

1. Want to be part of the project and look to change the way that pricing is undertaken.
2. Be keen to provide great customer service and create value. Customer-facing members are required in this group.
3. Have a desire and the ability to teach others. Teaching is the best way to learn.
4. Work hard. They cannot give the project lip service.
5. Enthusiastically back the project.
6. Be willing to try new things and approaches. Be 'out-of-the-box' thinkers.
7. Be part of a group wanting to create a brave new world.

The Pioneers need to know, and have it confirmed, that the project is an absolute place of psychological safety. Participating in the pilot will *not* have a career-limiting impact if the project does not pan out as expected.

It is important to try to create a small team of individuals across various Practice Areas, ideally with different levels of experience. You may need Pioneers from different geographic locations and offices, too. You want to select candidates who can influence others, those who will lead and make the change happen. Remember, those who can lead may not be current Heads of Departments or those with a title of leader. You will soon find that some of your best ideas will come from your most junior people. What is crucial is the ability for the team to work as a team and for there to be no hierarchy.

Be proactive and ask who in your firm knows anything about VBP. In one firm I worked with, I asked the question of their Marketer. She told me, 'Yes, I did a huge VBP project ten years ago when I worked for an estate agency.' No one in her current firm had known about her expertise, as she had never been asked.

In another firm, I discovered a lawyer who had been with the firm for two months and was still in her probationary period. She had received extensive VBP training at her former firm. She was delighted to learn her new employers were embarking on VBP training as she had previously been able to charge double for the work she was doing currently, and thought that her current employers were charging far too little. Ask your troops what they know.

CHANGE MANAGER AND PROJECT SPONSOR

Every change management project should have a **Sponsor** from the leadership team who should have a vested interest in the outcome and be able to support and influence the big decisions, including identifying risks and overcoming key stumbling blocks.

The **Change Manager** who will be leading the Pioneer penguins should be a person from the business who is charged with overseeing the initial pilot and also embedding change in the organisation.

The Change Manager will work closely with the Sponsor and will need to try to keep all of these people in the loop, even if they are not going to be part of the Pioneer Team itself.

It is important that the Change Manager is able to do the following:

- Explain clearly why the change is needed, desirable and feasible.
- Establish some success metrics for the project.
- Create a project team and generate some enthusiasm about what the team seeks to do. It's selling a Vision, not a list of tasks.
- Have ideas as to what some of the quick wins may be.
- Be able to raise awareness about the team's function, role and participating members.
- Plan to create a team which can work together well and grow to trust each other.
- Ensure the Pioneers can be released for sufficient time to work on this project. It is of no value if they come to one workshop and then cannot contribute further due to other priorities.
- There will likely have to be detailed conversations with Practice Area Heads. The Change Manager will need to have access to the staff members who are part of the pilot group for a limited period. The Pioneers' time needs to be freed up. This may result in having conversations about reviewing current fee and time recording targets.

This team cannot be an army of one.

TARGETS

The Pilot project will require some realistic and challenging targets. These could be:

1. Seeking to demonstrate an ability to increase prices charged on a range of services by, say, 20%.
2. Create Fixed-Price Agreements containing options for customers in, say, X work areas.
3. Collate and circulate feedback from clients regarding their support of choice.
4. Identifying, when given a choice, which clients chose Gold, Silver, or Bronze options.
5. Team profitability increases amongst Pilot team members.

NAYSAYER PENGUINS/RESISTORS

You want to avoid having Naysayer penguins or big negative egos in this Pioneer penguin team. It can slow down the process and make it harder.

Sometimes, a well-meaning leader may say, 'Let's include X in this project.' You may believe X is a Naysayer. Quite often, this suggestion will come from someone who has a Naysayer in their team and wants you or the Pioneer Group to confront and deal with their disruptive behaviours rather than them. Avoid this trap.

There will be lawyers in your business who will say, 'This VBP thing is all very well and good, but it doesn't apply to me or my Practice Area.' They will say it can't be done. They are wrong.

You will find – in the fullness of time – that those Naysayers will look back when the concept has been proved within other legal teams and come to ask how it was done and if you can do it for them.

Anticipate resistance from these areas:

1. **Management**: Will be apprehensive about leading the change. Is the business going to be exposed while the change happens? Will they be criticised if it is unsuccessful? Are they worried about their reputations? Are they able to lead?
2. **Partners/Owners/Shareholders/Directors:** They need to be reminded they are running a business, not necessarily just doing a lawyer's job. They must look at the bigger picture. It requires a change of focus. They must remain in the VBP tent and on message.
3. **Team Leaders/Heads of Departments:** May feel the whole of their teams and all processes will be impacted. They will be concerned about the current day job and finding time to implement the changes that may be proposed. They may give the project lip service and engage half-heartedly.
4. **Lawyers:** Will be concerned about the time they will need to spend in training and also becoming a salesperson. They may worry about the time it takes to learn new skills and get the work out the door at the same time. They will be worried about price increases as it may make it even harder to get legal work. They will have concerns that their clients will never accept price increases anyway. They will be concerned about having to have conversations with clients and presenting a number of price options.
5. **Finance:** May be used to a system which automatically generates invoices based on booked time. They will be concerned about any impact on the financial data they are used to dealing with. If there is no WIP, what can they measure? They will have to learn something new and will be concerned about doing battle with lawyers to get the financial information they need.
6. **Marketing: BD.** Will be concerned about how this impacts their teams. It will involve communicating new messages to clients. They will be concerned as to whether the lawyers will act and behave differently and embrace and communicate the message of VBP.

7. **IT Teams:** Will be concerned about any impact on the team and IT systems of delivering any coding/case management developments required. Pressure will be placed on them to get system reporting on whatever finance metrics are set.
8. **Human Resources:** Will be concerned about legal, emotional, and intellectual issues. Bonus schemes, if based on billable hours, will need amending. Lawyers may be upset about the changes. To deliver the project successfully, lots of training and HR support will be required.
9. **The Pioneers:** Will have to deal with resistance from Naysayer penguins some of whom will be senior to them in the organisation. Their colleagues may not be onboard. There may be elements of jealousy that they have been selected for the project. On occasion, Pioneers themselves may have Naysayer thoughts and questions. Keep close to the Pioneers and reaffirm how important the role is, and why the VBP project is essential.

FIRST PIONEER MEETING

Those that form part of the Pioneer Group should be held out and celebrated as champions.

The individuals who are selected to be part of the project should be able to open doors of communication into other Practice Area groups. Your Pioneers will be visiting and attending other team meetings to explain what is going on in the project and the successes that are being achieved.

You may decide that the team should meet regularly, at least once a week. Get these appointments in people's calendars as recurring appointments and stress to both participants and managers that these are important. Attendance is required. Remember, complacency will kill this project.

A more detailed explanation of what should occur at meetings is in the planning section of P#3 – Plan.

PSYCHOLOGICAL SAFETY AND PERMISSION TO MAKE MISTAKES

It is inevitable that many questions will be asked of the Pioneer Group. Very often, 'I am not sure' is the right answer for them to give. Ensure they know that.

Let's face it, you are embarking on a transformative process where you have to capture the hearts and minds of your lawyers. The learning is going to be continuous. You will need to create a framework and design processes, and then get people to understand and implement them.

You can tell people who are not part of the initial Pioneer Group (including the Naysayers) that they will be communicated with, they will be consulted, they will get involved, and they will be part of the process and brought in at the appropriate times. You may find some enthusiastic members of staff want to volunteer to be in the second wave of the Project Group.

It is crucial that those in your Pioneer Penguin Group know that volunteering to participate in this programme will not be career-limiting in any way. Lawyers are not very good at accepting mistakes – especially those made by others.

When I embark on a training project with law firms, I insist that the CEO and CFO attend the launch meetings and talk to the Pioneer Penguin Group about the firm's finances. Topics include the gross profitability of teams and how much work in progress got written off in the previous year (team by team). I then get the CEO/CFO to confirm that it is absolutely OK for the members of this group to get things wrong whilst on the project; whatever pricing mistakes they may make in the pilot, it won't be anything like a fraction of last year's write-offs.

As mentioned, (and underscored here), it's extremely important that there is a culture of psychological safety.

Typical things that may happen in the project include:

- Pitching for work and not getting it.
- Pitching for work and finding there was more to doing it than originally thought. So, there becomes a WIP write-off.
- Choosing not to pitch for work at all as the client or prospect was the wrong fit.
- Choosing not to accept work from some existing and prospective clients as it was the wrong type of work.

SHINGLES LOGIC

Turning away work from clients is hard for some lawyers to get their heads around. The Naysayers will be thinking:

- 'Surely any work is better than nothing.'
- 'How can we turn away X? We have done their work for 20 years… granted they are slow payers and don't respect what we do…. but they are old, established clients.'
- 'We must work for Y; they were referred to me by a member of my daughter's pony club.'
- 'You must work for X and do the work at a discount; they are an old personal friend/member of my family.'

POSSIBILITY THINKING

How can we possibly find out who – at our firm – knows about value-based pricing?

- Ask.
- One-to-ones.
- CVs.
- Appraisals.
- Interviews.
- Email.
- Leave books lying around.
- Ask who is interested.
- Team meetings.
- Family friends.
- Competition.
- Polls.
- Previous careers.
- Posters in toilets.
- Posters on walls.
- Questionnaires.
- WhatsApp.
- Social media.
- Comparing their billings to hours booked (recovery rate) if it's above they already doing it.

Usually, when I attend conferences or Partners meetings/away days and talk about value-based pricing, I will always get the classic Naysayer question from the floor where someone says, 'What do you do when you've given a client a value-based, fixed price of £15,000, and it later turns out that the work in progress – that has been recorded – is £20,000?' The answer is quite easy. You suck it up, you take the hit, and you learn from it. The Naysayer who asks the question never for one moment considers how much WIP was written off by their team the previous year.

> Being ashamed of our mistakes
> makes them a crime.
>
> **Confucius**

PRICING CONFIDENCE SURVEYS

As you are now aware, I am a great fan of undertaking Pricing Confidence Surveys with staff and guaranteeing anonymity to the participants.

I would strongly recommend that you survey all the members of your Pioneer penguin team. Ask them questions about the pricing policies that you currently adopt in your firm. You're likely to be surprised by the answers you receive.

Some example survey questions are set out below.

BIG SURVEY QUESTIONS

Pricing Confidence

Q1: I believe those who work in the firm understand the difference between the cashflow and the profitability of the business.

Q2: I believe those who work in the firm know how our revenue streams support the delivery of the firm's Strategy.

Q3: I believe all those working at my firm agree we should have a profitable business.

Q4: I believe that those who work in my firm understand how decisions impact profitability.

Q5: Our current pricing policy reflects my personal values (the way I like to do things).

Q6: I believe that my firm's pricing and charging model is a good reflection of our brand values.

Q7: We have pricing policies that are clearly defined, communicated, and adhered to in the firm.

Q8: I understand the relationship between running the business and pricing.

Q9: I am confident that our work helps and benefits our clients.

Q10: I believe my firm tends to reduce prices based on what our competitors may charge.

Q11: Those in my firm create accurate and well-scoped pricing proposals which they send to clients.

Q12: My colleagues and I know who the most profitable and strategically important clients are in our firm.

Q13: My colleagues and I know how to confidently deal with price objections from clients when we receive them.

Q14: We price clients differently based on a variety of factors, including current workload, time pressure, ability to delegate, and whether we feel we are going to enjoy working with them.

Q15: I would like to be taught how to price clients differently, based on a variety of factors, including current workload, time pressure, ability to delegate, and whether I feel we are going to enjoy working with them.

Q16: I believe that some of the clients my firm acts for should be dismissed as they are too painful and/or unprofitable to act for.

Q17: My team has a very clear idea of the clients we want to work for, and how they can be defined.

Q18: I believe that my firm has a mindset which requires lawyers to take on every piece of work that comes into the department.

Q19: I believe those in our firm understand that individual and group wellbeing directly impacts profitability.

Q20: My colleagues and I understand how to produce Fixed-Price Agreements which contain different service levels and price options for clients to consider.

Q21: When someone new joins your team, how is pricing training undertaken?

Q22: How are your pricing policies currently documented?

Q23: How is pricing reviewed at your firm?

Q24: How is pricing set at your firm?

Q25: I would be happy for someone else to price my work at the outset and leave me to get on and deliver the service to the client.

Q26: What is your view about your firm's time recording policy?

One question you may be surprised to see in the list above is Q3. 'I believe all those working at my firm agree we should have a profitable business.'

It may surprise you to learn that there will be some in your organisation who believe that you should not! I have asked this question on hundreds of occasions and have had ranges of percentages of yes from 60 to 100%. Anything less than 100% identifies a training need.

With the surveys you undertake, it's important that these questions are answered anonymously, so people do not feel that they are entering into a survey which may have career-limiting outcomes. This may mean you get someone to collect the data independently and report back. If you are prepared to ask the questions, you're likely to be very surprised by the answers that you receive.

The advantage of doing this kind of survey at the outset – either with the whole firm initially or with your Pioneer Penguin Group in particular – is that you can repeat the survey after three or four months and see how the dial has moved and attitudes have changed. Then, celebrate the successes!

HINDERING THOUGHTS

You will worry and question whether you have got the right people. Well, to be honest, you have who you have. You may need to think about bringing external people in to help, but the chances are you can do quite a lot of the initial preparatory work yourself.

POSITIVE THOUGHTS

You, hopefully, have some idea as to who the first wave of Pioneer penguins will be. They do not all have to be Partners or Team Leaders, far from it.

WORDS WITH THE WISE

Dr Jacqui Rigby, Rigby Pollitt Associates

Check that your Guiding Team includes those who really know the different areas of the business that will undergo change. It is critical to include team members who are customer-facing. Those that best understand customer needs, pain points and opportunities.

Ensure the Pioneers can be released for sufficient time to work on this change. It is of no value if they come to one workshop and then cannot contribute further due to other priorities.

Empowering the team will pay dividends. It brings greater motivation and instils trust in leadership. But empowerment does not remove responsibilities as a leader. Leaders must support the team delivering the change in managing issues and risks that are beyond their remit. Leaders play a key role in communications, managing senior stakeholders and ensuring recognition and celebration for those working on delivering the change.

Melissa Lyon, Hive Legal

The Pioneer mindset requires you to do things differently. Your courage to continue and be persistent and not revert to your old habits. You need to keep going and to make mistakes and learn from the mistakes. You may not want Naysayer penguins in the Pioneer Group, but you do need to learn from them and listen to them. Sometimes, a Naysayer penguin who comes in and stirs the pot a bit is really important because they are the ones who are going to tell you where the resistance is.

Robin Dicks, Thriving Consultancy

In one firm I'm working with now on a programme, there's a very clear belief that you've got the traditional long-in-the-tooth Partners, and then you've got the embryonic Partners and Partners-to-be. Those people will really be the decision-makers in five years' time and are those who are going to be very integrally involved in delivery and behaviour in a certain way. The drivers of that change are very clearly saying that the key people to make this change happen and to adopt it, espouse it, and live it, is that group of junior Partners.

David Gilroy, Conscious Solutions

Putting together a guiding team from a marketing perspective is all about process. Change vision and strategy, that's where it starts to get interesting. It's necessary to be aware of internal and external presentations; there's language that every business uses inside the business that they don't use outside the business.

Paul Roberts, My Customer Lens

When it comes to client experience, the most hated phrase is this, 'I know my customer, or I know my clients.' It's almost a shield. It gets used as I don't need to change because there's nothing you can tell me that I don't know. Anything you tell me that I don't know isn't relevant because my client hasn't told me, or at least I've chosen not to hear it when they did tell me. And so, therefore, I've got all the things that I need based on this relationship.

Simon Tupman, Simon Tupman Consulting

Who are the leaders? I think there is a fundamental belief (that still propels even the largest law firms in the world) that if you're a successful lawyer or Partner, and you've got a good book of business, then you're a leader. And we all know that is not always true. There are plenty of people in firms who may not be great lawyers, but they're exceptionally good legal professionals who have leadership qualities. They're good at leading their people; they have an understanding of how the business operates and they care about their communities.

The Pioneers might also comprise young people who are just coming into the business, who may be very tech savvy, who can speak for Generation Z, and who can feel free to say what they want in the company of people who are old enough to be their parents without fear of reprimand. If they're given free rein, they will be able to come up with something that is novel and fresh and encourage the Board to confidently introduce and implement change.

When creating Pioneers, I think a prerequisite is to clarify the governance in firms. This is sometimes a stumbling block as there are many Partners who struggle to relinquish control and feel it's their duty or right to make decisions about the smallest thing in the firm by virtue of the fact that they are the owners.

Matthew Burgess, View Legal

I think to implement value-based pricing, you need to create a Skunk Works project. Carve off a life raft. Give the pilot team complete autonomy to go off and have a go.

Sometimes, the billable hour recording 'rock stars' are the worst people that you can have in a value-pricing environment. Because they just don't get it. There's no velocity. There's no focus on what the value is to the customer.

Jon Whittle, Jon Whittle Consulting

The Pioneer team needs a facility to look out the window. You need someone who's looking out of the window. Because it's so easy in these change situations for things to become internally focused, it becomes about how do we reengineer? What do we do? What do we pull? What do we shut down? What do we switch on? And you need someone to remind the whole business in this pioneer team. That's the direction. We're going over there.

John Chisholm, John Chisholm Consulting

Sometimes, too, there is a disconnect between leadership and the 'rank and file' in a firm. I once did work for a global firm, and I genuinely believe the global leaders of that firm wanted to make some genuine change and be different from their competitors in a meaningful way – in this case to seriously pilot value-based pricing. But when it got to the rank and file – those Partners and professionals at the coalface – most of them were sceptical of real change primarily because the measurements and rewards didn't incentivise those embarking on the value pricing journey.

Quite the contrary, they believed they could be penalised if they perceived their journey to have 'failed' at any stage. There needed to be a safety net to back up the rhetoric, and in this case, there was not. If the guiding coalition want support, they too have to give support.

Kirsty Pappin, Aries Legal Practice Management

Let's just start with, and it's not a buzzword – there needs to be absolute *psychological safety* during the project. People must have zero fear that they can raise issues or thoughts without any repercussions on them and their careers. In fact, raising the most negative feedback can be the best feedback. And this safety must come from the top and be genuine, ensuring that those in that team provide honest feedback on the project. This approach is important to assisting the overall goal of just getting it right.

You need a cross-section of experience levels because some of the really good stuff can come from those just starting out in their legal careers – lawyer or business support. It can also come from seasoned professionals in the firm who are about to retire, all the way down to those who have just walked through the door. Some stereotypes can be true, but people can blow your mind away, so it's always best not to presume how someone may participate; just be prepared.

CRIB SHEET
READING & VIEWING

READ

10 Project Management Tips for Non-Project Managers

By Northeastern University Graduate Program

https://graduate.northeastern.edu/resources/project-management-tips/

TIPS/CHECKLISTS

1. Leadership is all about the softer stuff.

EXERCISES

EXERCISE 1 (COMPULSORY)

Pull Together a Pioneer Group: Find your Project Sponsor.

Identify who – in the leadership team – would be a suitable Sponsor.

EXERCISE 2 (COMPULSORY)

Identify the Change Manager who will lead the change.

Who – in your firm – has project and/or change management skills?

What supplementary skills or support might they need to take on the role successfully?

Finding a Change Manager: you may not have people who have a defined role as 'project manager' in your firm, but you may well have people who have the natural skills to take on the role for a VBP change. Ask your senior managers who might fit the bill based on the attributes below.

In a Change Manager, you are looking for someone with the following attributes:

- Good organisational skills.
- Delivery experience.
- Communicates well.
- Can lead a team.
- Works collaboratively with people at all levels.

EXERCISE 3 (COMPULSORY)

Find your Pioneers.

Identify your Pioneers who will be your guiding team and lead the change.

Your guiding team is a core group of people who really know the different areas of the business that will change. From IT to HR, from your Compliance Officer to Operations, from Finance to Marketing.

EXERCISE 4

How can the Pioneer penguin team build more trust with each other?

What authority is not represented in the team, but maybe should be?

POSSIBILITY THINKING QUESTIONS TO POSE

1. How can we possibly communicate the benefits of VBP within our firm?
2. How can we possibly find out who in the firm has knowledge of value-based pricing?
3. What challenges might we possibly face when managing change in the firm?
4. What might our SMART objectives possibly be?

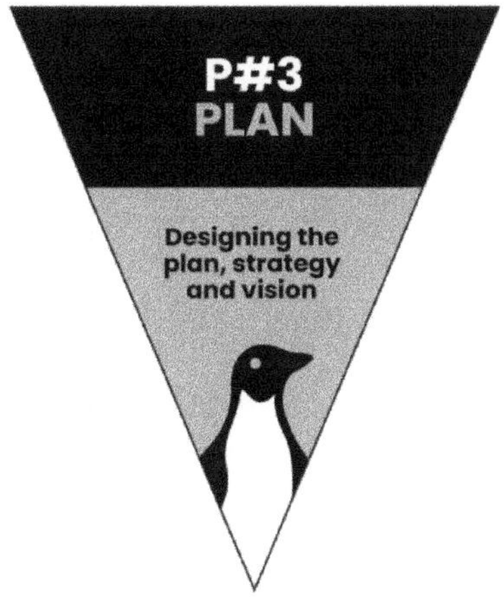

P#3 PLAN

DESIGNING THE PLAN, STRATEGY AND VISION

So welcome to P#3 Plan. This is where we create a Vision and a Plan for change. How will the future be different from the past, and how will the future become a reality?

You will recall, in the introduction, that I mentioned this was the section where the hard work starts. It's a long section, so buckle up!

> Our goals can only be reached through a vehicle of a plan, in which we must fervently believe, and upon which we must vigorously act. There is no other route to success.
>
> **Pablo Picasso**

This P#3 Plan is divided into four subsections.

1. **KNOWLEDGE:** A look at some VBP fundamentals. Here, you can learn more about what you need to know regarding the principles and mechanics of VBP and the logic behind it.
2. **TOOLS:** Details of the tools you will need to consider creating in your firm.

3. **VISION:** A glimpse into what your future might be like.
4. **PLAN:** Some guidance and tools to help you create the planning documents to deliver the VBP project.

PART 1: KNOWLEDGE

WHAT DO YOU DO AT YOUR BUSINESS?

To be honest, you may think this is an odd heading. 'What do you do?' Do you and your employees really know all the types of legal services that your law firm is able to deliver day-in day-out? Would you be able to list all the services you could offer clients?

Quite often, depending on the size of your firm, your own lawyers won't know what the full range of legal services available is. For most firms, it's not part of the induction process to educate new lawyers about what others in the business do.

Usually, when starting at a new firm, lawyers will be told where to sit and how to engage with accounts and the IT system, but precious little time will be spent explaining what the other people in the business actually do. Quite often, we just settle new starters into their silos and ask them to crack on. Don't believe me? Do a test at a team meeting.

How often have you spoken to a referrer or client, and they mentioned they had a need in one area of law but had instructed one of your competitors? You look aghast and ask, 'Why didn't you use us?' and they say, 'I didn't know you did that kind of work.' It happens all the time. Let's break down that sorry statement.

'I didn't know you did that kind of work.'

What you are being told in that conversation is:

- The lawyer who previously dealt with them had not had a conversation about the client's full needs, nor got to know them and their circumstances.
- Because they didn't take the time to understand the client's needs, they lost the opportunity to even mention we have lawyers who can help and support them when the time is right.
- The lawyer did not create a sufficiently strong relationship for the client to even think about picking up the phone and asking, 'Do you know anyone who can help with X….' It's sad!

8 PPP PENGUIN LOGIC

Do not expect your clients to educate themselves about your business

- We need to educate our lawyers about what we do.
- We need to ask our lawyers to educate our clients about the work we do.
- We then need to educate our referral sources about what a good client looks like.

If your lawyers don't know what an ideal client is, your referrers certainly don't.

WHAT DO CLIENTS BUY FROM LAWYERS?

When I ask at training sessions, 'What do clients buy from lawyers?', I usually get answers along the lines of:

- 'Our expertise.'
- 'Our time.'
- 'Our experience.'
- 'Our brain power.'
- 'Our brand.'

It's only after three or four people have had a go at the question, and I haven't written one of the earlier answers on the flip chart, that someone will tentatively suggest 'A result… an outcome', and they are 100% right.

I am sure you have heard the question, 'Why do people buy a drill?' and you know the answer is it's not because they want to own a drill; it's because they want to 'Make a hole'. Clients want outcomes and results. You will remember Jon Whittles' words of wisdom concerning outcomes in P#1. The outcomes our clients want are things like:

Property/Real Estate

- To own my dream house.
- To help my children get on the property ladder and leave home.
- A pension fund investment purchase for when I retire.

- To purchase a doer-upper, sell the property and buy another one.
- To extend the lease of my flat, which will increase its value.

Dispute Resolution/Litigation

- To stop my neighbour encroaching on my land and upsetting my family,
- To recover losses incurred following the purchase of a defective machine.
- To get a tenant out of my property who has not paid the rent.
- To recover cash due to my business from a debtor.
- To get compensation for an accident which has ruined my life.
- To challenge a will as I should have been left something. It's unfair.

Family/Matrimonial/Childcare Law

- To protect my child.
- To help me divorce a person I no longer love, and live a new life.
- To allow me to see my children/grandchildren.
- To help split up the matrimonial assets fairly.
- To help me get closure on an unhappy period of my life.

Wills & Probate/Private Client

- To sort out and distribute Mum's estate fairly between me and my siblings.
- To protect my family in the event of my death.
- To structure my assets so less tax is paid when I die.
- To help my family make the decisions I would like if I were ever incapacitated.

Employment

- To bring a claim against my employer for discrimination/unfair dismissal.
- To protect my business secrets from a competitor.
- To be legally compliant, so I don't get sued.

Company/commercial

- To allow me to fulfil the dream of opening my own business.
- To help me successfully run my business.
- To allow me to start my retirement and sell my business.
- To protect my business with robust contracts so we don't get sued.
- To create a shareholder agreement just in case we fall out and have a mechanism for parting company amicably.

BRACE YOURSELF…
incoming provocative statement

'To be a lawyer, you need to have a big ego. That is my perception as a client. They feel the service they are providing is above average. I wouldn't say so – I think they are pretty average.

'Nothing makes them stand out as good or client-centred. I don't find legal services very customised to the client, I see them as very standard, off-the-shelf services.

'That's why so many are in trouble. So many are going out of business, and in my view they should, because they are not providing the correct level of service.'

Now, don't shout at me; I am the messenger! This is an extract from the Lexis Nexis Bellwether Report, *The Age of The Client*. I suggest you read it.

So, let's accept clients want their outcomes to be delivered, and they are prepared to pay a price for their delivery.

We know the price we charge must be certain. No extras. No surprises. And be in their eyes represent value… but what is value?! Read on…

WHAT IS VALUE?

Getting to grips with value is not easy. I guarantee that you and I have different tastes in wine, watches, music, cars, houses, and holidays, to name but a few. A car might be very important to you, but it's not to me.

VALUE IS SUBJECTIVE

Because we are all different, it is important to understand that it's the customer's perception that matters. Because value is subjective, our own personal histories impact the way we look at value. Jewellery and watches may be important. Clothing and designer brands may be important. We are all different, and we all have different buying habits.

I spend a lot of money on a certain brand of American clothing that I like. I like the fact that I can buy it online, they usually have my size, they are easy to deal with, their returns policies are excellent, they are polite, and they have a loyalty scheme. Their clothing makes me feel good when I wear it.

> People buy good feelings and
> solutions to problems.
>
> **Michael LeBoeuf**

Buyers believe they get what they pay for. Higher fees convey higher quality. When you think of brands such as Rolls Royce, Rolex, Louis Vuitton and Prada, you tend to think of quality.

VALUE IS NOT RATIONAL

If you take the subject of cars. I only want a car to get from A to B. I don't care what I drive. It surprises me that some people will pay ten times the amount that I will pay for a car simply because they want to own a Bentley or a McLaren and can afford to do so. I think that it's not rational to do that. My friend Dave has a McLaren car, it's one of four cars he owns. He is a petrolhead. You would not believe the servicing costs of a McLaren! For me, it's not rational.

Why do people buy Apple products? When you speak to IT people, a large number will tell you that Android-based products are better, have more functionality and are cheaper. My IT guy, Kevin, told me this when I started Big Yellow Penguin. I ignored him and ordered an Apple iPhone. Why? Because I know how an iPhone works and couldn't be bothered to learn how another cheaper, better phone may operate. Not rational, according to Kevin.

When the new Apple iPhone is released, there are always some people who will queue up outside a store at midnight so that they can be one of the first people to get it. I am not one of those people, but I know some who would regard that as time well spent.

8 PPP PENGUIN LOGIC

£1,800 per hour, anyone?

At 4.30pm on a Friday afternoon, lawyer M – who had participated in value-based pricing training – received a call from a local businessman who was upset about a defamatory statement that had been posted on a Facebook page in his home town. He wanted a letter before action to be sent to the person who had posted the defamatory statement within the next 30 minutes.

Lawyer M knew a similar letter had been drafted earlier that week for another client. The know-how could be recycled. A conflict check was undertaken, which was clear. The prospect was told that a letter could be drafted and sent within the next 20 minutes. The price of doing so would, however, be £600 plus VAT, and payment would have to be made immediately. The prospect agreed. He was transferred to the accounts team, who took payment. An Engagement Letter was emailed, followed by a draft letter before action. The letter was approved and sent before 5pm. The prospect (now a client) was delighted. The offending post was taken down.

The client wanted immediate action and was prepared to pay the price, which if they had thought about it, equated to £1,800 per hour. The client wasn't interested in the inputs; they wanted an output – a letter being sent within 20 minutes. The client continues to recommend his friends and associates to lawyer M.

VALUE IS CONTEXTUAL

Value changes depending on where you are.

Let's take the most abundant product on the planet: water. The amount you pay for water varies with your location and circumstances. You will pay next to nothing for a glass of water at your home. You will pay more when you pick up a bottle of water from a service station. You will pay even more when you order a bottle of mineral water in a high-end restaurant. You would probably pay a huge sum if you were emerging from the desert – having been stranded without water – and were offered water by an unscrupulous vendor. Context and circumstances impact price.

What is particularly interesting, when you think about it, is that water – the most abundant product on the planet – is always the same. The chemical equation for water is H2O. It's never H30. It's never H2 O2. So, it's always exactly the same; it must be. But we pay vastly different prices for it.

If you are on a long car journey with a quarter tank of petrol, and you come across the last garage for 200 miles – and you need to fill up – you will buy the petrol and pay the price. You will probably pay much more than you would have had you stopped 20 miles earlier in the journey. It's just the way things are. Your situation, the context you were in, dictated the higher price.

8 PPP PENGUIN LOGIC

Water conundrum

Have you ever noticed that Evian is naïve spelt backwards… #Justsaying – are they messing with our heads?

VALUE IS A FEELING

> ‘Don’t tell me how good you make it; tell me how good it makes me when I use it.’
>
> **Leo Burnett**

When I’m training lawyers, I often talk about three wristwatches that I own. I bought one from Amazon 20 years ago for £100; it has a yellow face, stainless steel strap, luminous dial, stopwatch and shows the day and date.

When I received a bonus at work one year, I bought a Tag Heuer watch; it also has a steel strap, yellow face, stopwatch, luminous dial and day and date.

I also have another watch; it has a navy-blue face, steel strap, luminous dial; in fact, loads of dials all over it, so you can’t really see the date clearly. It’s made by a budget brand – Citizen. I don’t wear it.

The blue watch was given to me by my late father after he had a stroke, and he couldn’t see the time and date anymore. But he loved that watch, and he wanted me to have it. Of the three watches, which one do you think is most valued by me? Of course, you know… it’s my father’s watch, which is by far the least valuable in monetary terms. My father’s watch is not worth anything to anyone else. But – to me – it’s worth a great deal of money.

I have this continuing dilemma about how much I would pay for the blue watch if I ever lost it and it was held to ransom. In my head, I think I would go up to £9,500 or thereabouts. I can’t quite get over £10,000. However, even if I were to pay out £9,500 to get the watch back, I don’t think I would ever be brave enough to tell my wife. It’s not valued by her at all.

Do you watch the TV show The Repair Shop on BBC television? I watch it regularly, quite often with tears rolling down my cheek when I see what effect the repair of an old item has on somebody who really loves it. It might be a broken guitar, a shabby old teddy bear, an old leather case. We can physically feel and understand why it's valued by the owner.

I hope you agree that these examples demonstrate an important lesson. Value is a feeling.

We need to try to acknowledge that value is a feeling and factor this into account when we are selling legal services. Are we even aware of the emotions that our clients may be feeling whilst engaging with us as lawyers? Do we acknowledge them? Are we putting ourselves in their shoes? Do we see and understand why something might be so important to them? Do we know how they feel? Probably not. Do we care how they feel – I suspect yes, but we have to have a conversation and ask them questions to understand their feelings.

8 PPP PENGUIN LOGIC

Are we going bananas?!

One in three bananas sold in the UK is a Fairtrade banana, which costs far more than other bananas. Between 2000 and 2020, UK sales of Fairtrade bananas amounted to £144 million (fairtrade.org.uk). We pay the premium as we feel we are doing 'our bit' to help support farmers in faraway lands. It makes us feel good.

> Seek First to Understand,
> Then to Be Understood.
>
> **Stephen Covey, Habit 5, The Seven Habits of Highly Effective People**

8 PPP PENGUIN LOGIC

What is important to clients?

Educating lawyers to actively listen, show empathy and enquire about value is not taught at law school. It should be. Lawyers need to consider how clients define value.

We should ask clients. Record their answers and train our people.

Lawyers have historically believed that all our clients are interested in is an hourly rate.

They are not.

GIVE CUSTOMERS A CHOICE

If we accept that value is complicated and determined by the customer, then it should make it easier for you to agree that presenting clients with choices and price options is a logical step.

We all like choices in our daily lives. We choose our car wash menus. We choose what cars we drive. We choose what clothes we wear. We choose the wine we drink with dinner in a restaurant. Surely, the legal profession can move on from a choice of take-it-or-leave-it, which is often the only choice presented.

Let's aspire to get to a stage where we offer clients options with different price points and service levels, and let clients self-select and choose the package *they want* after we have explained the options to them.

CLIENT JOURNEY

> If you are not taking care of your customer, your competitor will.
>
> **Bob Hooey**

You will have gathered by now that it's very important to stand in the shoes of our clients and think about the experience they may have with us while we work for them.

How do we make them feel? Are we looking at what is important to them? The answer is to try to understand the customer journey they go on when dealing with your firm.

The chances are that customer journey mapping is something that you may have heard about, but very few firms ever implement. Most CEOs I meet know of its theoretical existence and mention how it's been on a to-do list for several years, but they have never quite gotten around to it.

With any customer journey mapping experience, it's necessary to look at the process from several different angles. Some of the more sophisticated customer journey mapping exercises will include creating different client personas and then mapping the journeys those customers receive as they engage with your firm. The idea behind the customer journey is that you collect the data and see how your lawyers engage with the customers, at what points, and how the customers feel about it. Then, once you know what happens, you make the whole experience better next time around.

If you want to see a customer journey map in all its glory, just Google 'Starbucks customer journey map' and then select from the plethora of maps you will be confronted with. It will give you some idea of the levels of sophistication that some organisations drill down to, as customer experience is so important.

Undertaking a customer journey mapping experience will probably be eye-opening for you.

If you take a service such as Wills, Trust and Probate, you can map the experience the customer has in the following ways:

1. Who says what to whom, and when.
2. What documents are created and sent relating to an initial enquiry.
3. How the enquiry is followed up (if at all).
4. What prices are quoted.
5. How work is delivered.
6. How payment was requested.
7. How the matter was closed.

You can then map the process again and look at how the client encountered your firm when they contacted you in different ways.

1. Was it a telephone enquiry?
2. Was it a web enquiry?
3. Did they walk in off the street?
4. Were they referred internally by another lawyer who took advantage and cross-sold a will service (rare, I know)?
5. Where they referred by a third party?
6. Were they a prospect responding to a marketing campaign?

If you have more than one office, then do the exercise at all of the offices you operate from.

When you undertake this exercise, you can even repeat it amongst the individual lawyers in the team. You will, I suspect, find that the enquiry is dealt with in completely different ways by the different lawyers in your firm. I guarantee that one lawyer will send documentation that is better than another. One lawyer will handle the initial web-based enquiry better than another. The challenge here is to look at what goes on in your organisation, select the best methodology, and then roll that out and ask all your lawyers to use the agreed best practice.

If you can then map the customer touchpoints – where customers engage with your lawyer/your firm – and see how and what kind of experience the client received, you can then look to increase the satisfaction rates by making appropriate adjustments.

YOU HAVE BEEN GOOGLED!

Customers will have formed a view about your firm before they've even got in touch with you and received any kind of service at all.

- Prospects will have asked for peer recommendations from friends.
- They will have visited your website.
- They may have looked at your Google and Trust Pilot Reviews.
- They may have even looked at the recruitment website Glass Door to ascertain what your own people think of your firm.

There is a valid reason that the most pages viewed on your website are case studies and lawyer profiles. Prospects want to know whether you can help them with their problem, whether you have done it before (case studies), and who is going to do it (profiles)?

Prospects – when they become clients – will form a view of you while the service is being delivered, and they will form a view after the transaction has been completed.

BRACE YOURSELF…
incoming provocative statement

If you can bear the painful read, obtain a copy of the Insight 6 Report – *Professional Client Journey 2021*.

It reports on the way new enquiries were dealt with by lawyers, IFAs, accountants and estate agents. It also looked at whether chatbots were more engaging than humans.

Spoiler alert… lawyers came out of this really, really badly! You have been warned.

I think Insight 6 found more than one firm with the Shingles mentality.

https://www.insight6.com/2021-professional-client-journey/

POSSIBILITY THINKING

What do we do that possibly hacks off our clients?

- Not responding to them.
- Inaccurate out-of-office messages.
- Voicemails.
- Going on holiday without telling the client.
- Awful coffee.
- No parking.
- Not delivering communications in the way that they were asked for.
- Legalese.
- Jargon.
- Not explaining the process clearly.
- Using Latin!
- Assuming that clients are also lawyers.
- Being aloof.
- Unexpected bills.
- Poor communication.
- Feeling you haven't got the client's back.
- Feeling the client's case is not a priority.
- Being impersonal.
- Swapping over fee-earners.
- Not giving updates.
- Not explaining why an action cannot be undertaken.
- Creating too many surprises.
- Not offering solutions.
- Not offering explanations.

- Not giving advice.
- Sending out bills without telling clients about the costs.
- Not allowing dogs into reception!
- Rushing clients to make decisions when they may not fully understand the process.
- Not checking in with clients.
- Not checking with the client that you have understood all the facts.
- Not creating options.
- Just not being quick enough.
- Sending huge, long emails with loads of jargon.
- Assuming the client knows what you are on about.
- Complying with timescales and not making it clear why this is the case.

CLIENT SELECTION AND DESELECTION

> Be sure you've done everything within your power to turn a low-value customer into a high-value customer. The fact of the matter is that your customers are not going to get better until you do.
>
> **Ron Baker**

Let me start this section with a few myths that need to be dispelled. They are:

- All clients are good clients.
- All clients are the same and should be treated the same.
- You cannot give a fixed price as you don't know what is going to happen.
- Clients are ringing around.
- Our competitors charge less so we should drop our prices.

- There is a 'going market rate' for the job.
- Clients won't pay more.
- Clients are not interested in VBP.

You must accept that if you are going to successfully implement VBP, your client base will change… for the better.

As you pursue your VBP project, you will find yourself quoting Baker's Law that 'Bad clients drive out good clients.'

One of the challenges of value-based pricing is adopting a policy to get rid of clients who make the lives of your staff a misery and who are not profitable. As I've already indicated in this book, the surveys that I take at law firms always indicate that there are clients that staff do not want to act for.

As part of your Vision, you may already be considering:

- Which clients to deselect.
- What types of clients to pursue.
- How you can work with clients more collaboratively.
- How to deliver on the promises you make about customer service.
- How to have more fun at work!

What is incumbent upon the Pioneer Penguin Group is identifying the D clients in your business. D stands for *ditch*… the clients who should be gently persuaded to leave the business. The characteristics of such clients are easy to identify.

Typical D clients:

- Someone who is unprofitable.
- Someone who doesn't pay their bills.
- Someone who doesn't accept or respect the advice that you give.
- Someone who doesn't respond to requests for information until the last minute.
- Someone who is disrespectful to your staff, is a bully, and makes them feel physically ill. (I am being serious. Ask them.)
- Someone who contributes to lawyer burnout and absences through sickness.
- Someone who negotiates lower rates on the basis of giving increased volumes of work that never materialise.

NO TWO CLIENTS ARE THE SAME

It is important to accept that no two clients are the same. You will often hear from the lips of your lawyers that 'All clients deserve a gold service.' They are wrong. All clients deserve a competent and compliant service.

- Customers are different.
- The facts of their cases are different.
- The customers behave and will interact with your lawyers differently.
- The expectations of customers are different.
- Your lawyers' workloads will be different at different times of the year.
- Timescales and priorities will be different and constantly changing (both yours and the customers).
- Lawyers on the other side will be different – let's face it, there are some lawyers that we know we dislike dealing with.
- The risks will be different.

You can make more money from certain types of clients and work. Identify them and make it a strategic objective to get more of that type of work.

You and your lawyers need to become more selfish, and by this, I mean seek to work with clients that you like and enjoy working with. You do not have to accept mediocre clients. You need to be prepared to walk away and refuse to be 'nickel and dimed'. You will earn more money as a result.

Remember, in VBP, client selection is key. When you start parting company with the 'D list' clients, you will find that your staff will come to you and say, 'We don't understand why you didn't do this sooner.' It is important to signal to your staff and customers that you have standards, and that you are willing to stand by them. The work your lawyers do competes for their time. Make sure their time is spent on the work that is worth doing, and for clients who appreciate what they do.

8 PPP PENGUIN LOGIC

Bad clients impact succession plans

As you now know, Baker's Law is 'Bad clients drive out good clients', and Ron is 100% right. But it can also be the case that 'Bad clients drive out good lawyers from your firm', and no one wants that.

In September 2023, I led a session at a national law conference looking at what Associates wanted from law firm management/owners to encourage them to join the partnership. Time and time again, the answers which came up included:

- Good quality clients.
- Nice clients.
- A client veto.
- Interesting work.

Going forward, you may find that your firm's succession plan is linked to a policy of sacking clients who are too painful to act for.

8 PPP PENGUIN LOGIC

Are The Clients in The Wrong Place?

(Courtesy of a Facebook post.)

A father said to his daughter, 'You graduated with honours; here is a car I acquired many years ago. It is several years old. But before I give it to you, take it to the used car lot downtown and tell them I want to sell it and see how much they offer you.

The daughter went to the used car lot, returned to her father, and said, 'They offered me $1,000 because it looks very worn out.'

The father said, 'Take it to the pawn shop.' The daughter went to the pawn shop, returned to her father, and said, 'The pawn shop offered $100 because it was a very old car.'

The father asked his daughter to go to a car club and show them the car. The daughter took the car to the club, returned, and told her father, 'Some people in the club offered $100,000 for it, since it's a Nissan Skyline R34, an iconic car and sought out by many.'

The father said to his daughter, 'The right place values you the right way.'

If you are not valued, do not be angry; it means you are in the wrong place. Those who know your value are those who appreciate you. Never stay in a place where no one sees your value.

8 PPP PENGUIN LOGIC

Talk about your D clients

In 2023, I facilitated a Partner away day for a large regional law firm. There were 26 Partners of the law firm present.

One of the exercises I led was asking them to write down three clients they would like to sack. When I asked the first person to list the three clients on his list, he gave the name of a large, well-known, international blue-chip company. There was a lot of laughing.

I asked how many other people have got the name of this blue-chip company on their list; five hands went up. The Partner responsible for this client didn't really know that this client was disliked by many of his Partners. When we drilled into the numbers, the client was not worth a significant amount of fees in any event and clearly was using other firms for more profitable work.

I do hope one of the outcomes of that meeting was that the client was politely told to go elsewhere.

CLIENT SEGMENTATION

Define the clients that you want to work for. This should be something considered in your Vision and Plan.

As we have established, every client is different. Segmenting customers into defined categories/work types can allow marketing strategies, communications and activities to become more targeted.

This is not intended to be a book which deals with marketing theory and brand positioning. I have already mentioned Tim Williams' book and recommend you read it.

If you ask any lawyer about their ideal client, they will usually tell you it is a 'High net worth individual or a blue-chip company'. When you ask them to define what high net worth or blue-chip means and how it gets measured, the conversation usually ends slightly abruptly. In a room full of 20 lawyers, you will get 20 different answers. So, give some thought to who you want to act for.

Work out who your ideal clients are. Some of the criteria behind category A clients could be:

- The profitable revenue they create for your business.
- They complement the categories of work you do, and are strategically important.
- They are in a niche sector you operate in and want to exploit.
- They have growth potential and cross-selling opportunities.
- The kudos of acting for them.
- The financial net worth of individuals.
- You enjoy working with them.
- They appreciate the work that you do for them.
- The work is simple for you to do.

BIG SURVEY QUESTIONS

I asked this question in a poll of 80 different law firms.

The answer is not unusual! Sad, but not unusual.

Q: I believe that some of the clients my firm acts for should be dismissed, as they are too painful and/or unprofitable to act for.

A: (Agree) 76%.

In a follow-up question:

Q: What prevents your firm from deselecting clients?

A: Included: 'worry about our reputation', 'inertia', and 'Partners'.

Your staff know which clients they would like to see the back of!

It is important to recalibrate the relationships with your clients and work out who your A, B, C and D clients are. Let's focus again on the D ones.

Before you decide to cease acting for your D clients – based on your chosen criteria – consider whether you can turn them into C clients. Can you increase their prices? Can you change their behaviour? Do they even know that their behaviour is considered bad?

You may wish to consider the following. Resolve to initially put your prices up with D clients and see what happens. I suggest the Ds because their low profitability may mean they are not crucial to the business. If the D clients can't become C clients, can they introduce you to new A clients?

Also, consider when the time is good to deselect the client. You don't want to leave clients in the lurch. If you can give them a lead in time and an introduction to someone else, then so much the better. I'm not for one moment suggesting that D-client relationships are terminated halfway through a transaction unless there is a very good reason to do so. You don't want any compliance issues. Just prepare the ground so that further instructions are not accepted. However, if a category D client is indicating that they are going to continue to send work, a conversation must be had to say that they are not the right fit for your business.

GOLDEN RULE #5

Bad clients drive out good clients AND good lawyers.

8 PPP PENGUIN LOGIC

'We like them.'

'They have supported us for years' (but never paid all their bills).

'They are friends of mine.'

'When they sell their business in a few years, we won't get the work.'

'I am not busy at the moment.'

'What if other clients don't instruct us? Surely, it's better than nothing?'

'It would look bad if the client went to our competitors.'

Prepare your responses to these comebacks.

I firmly believe that lawyers do not have to take on every piece of work that comes into their firm. What they must aspire to do, though, is to take on more than their fair share of the good quality work. Pricing cheap attracts cheap clients.

When clients are deselected, you will find that your organisation's morale improves. In fact, the health of your employees will improve. Acting for difficult clients is an emotionally taxing business. It is stressful! If you accept this as an employer, you have a responsibility to start looking after your people better, ending up with happier staff. You will also free up capacity to either take on better work and/or deliver better service to existing clients.

CRM SYSTEMS

Whilst on the subject of clients, it would probably be remiss of me not to mention the CRM system in passing. Chances are, your CRM system is that neglected, unloved, unused piece of software that hangs off your Practice Management System. I suspect many of your CRM data fields won't be populated, and many of your lawyers retain up-to-date client information on Outlook or their mobile phones rather than populate the records on the CRM system itself.

In most firms, the data held in CRM systems and the wills and deeds registers is, quite frankly, toxic and can't be relied on or utilised to their full potential. Don't believe me? Would you do an email shot to your client base now, pulling a mail merge list from your client database records of those you hold wills for, and advise them to contact you for an update? Thought not.

SHINGLES LOGIC

I have known firms that have tried to rely on databases that are not properly cleansed, updated, or maintained.

One firm did a mailshot to clients for whom they held wills to try to encourage them to be updated. The Senior Partner found herself taking calls from tearful widows who were saying, 'Why are you writing to me and Philip about updating our wills, when you know Philip died last year and you are dealing with the probate?'

It happens!

COMPETITORS

Whilst this is a book that deals with VBP, I will briefly mention your competitors for the simple reason I know that your Naysayer penguins certainly will.

Competitors come in all shapes and sizes and geographies. You may have High Street firms which you regard as your competitors, regional firms, or lawyer consultants – working from home for umbrella law firm practices, which have their head office hundreds of miles away.

Chances are, a detailed review of your competition has never been undertaken, and most of your competitor analysis is a mix of gossip, tinged with some bias and a small measure of jealousy. Let's try to do something a little more sophisticated.

In their book *Value Based Pricing*, Macdivitt and Wilkinson created a table for competitor analysis. It's set out below, although I have altered the key attribute columns to reflect a law firm.

Key attributes	Us	Competitor 1	Competitor 2
Quality Chambers/Legal 500 Industry awards Accreditations			
Work areas Any niches? Activity levels			
Innovator/Dinosaur Are you playing catch up, or are they ahead of you?			
Pricing Regime What methodology was used? Hourly? Fixed? VBP?			
Top lawyers Who are they? How senior? How long have they been there? Are they recruitment targets?			
PMS/Case Management What have they got? What are they developing?			
Marketing activity How good is it? Levels of activity?			
Reputation brand What do others say about them?			

(The table above has been reproduced with the kind permission of Macdivitt and Wilkinson.)

By populating the grid, you can identify.

1. How many competitors you have. These may be local; they may be sector-based.
2. What do they do? List their service capabilities.
3. Are they Shingles-type firms or innovators/iconoclasts?
4. How do they price? Can you ask your staff? Have any of your staff worked for your competitors in the past? Can you ask candidates who apply to work at your firm how they currently price? Can you ask your referrers? Can you mystery-shop them?
5. Who are the competition's star lawyers? You may wish to keep an eye on them and see what they produce on social media. Connect with them on LinkedIn. You may want to offer them a job.
6. What Case Management System do they operate? Have they any other innovative IT tools?
7. Do they carry out marketing activities that you would find difficult to replicate?

A competitor analysis is always a mixture of objective measurement and subjective analysis.

8 PPP PENGUIN LOGIC

Use Undergraduates… they will thank you for it

You may wish to consider employing undergraduate work experience students to undertake a competitor analysis during university holidays. This exercise is easy for them to understand and deliver, and it will provide you with some valuable data.

Undergraduates are always keen to get some experience of working in a law firm. I used to get students in every year to do this research. In fact, many MBA programmes at universities are desperately seeking projects for their students to do. Use them.

A BIG SURVEY QUESTION OF 80 LAW FIRMS

Q: I believe my firm reduces prices based on what our competitors may charge.

A: Not at all: 38.75%.

To some extent: 43.75%.

*

Comments received.

'We are the reverse! We intentionally charge more than our competitors!'

'We are mindful of competitor pricing when setting prices.'

'We are always checking what others charge but think we are probably a bit more expensive than others. We don't charge what we think the service is worth, as this would certainly take us out of the market.'

GOLDEN RULE #6

Be a price setter, not a price chaser.

Do not follow your competitors' pricing.

ONBOARDING SCRIPTS/DISCOVERY CALLS

So now, we get to the stage where – unbeknownst to us – the client/prospect has done some research, satisfied themselves they have a need, and have called us. Happy days!

It's important to remember that, when faced with a legal issue, a client has four options:

1. Do nothing at all.
2. Try and resolve it themselves.
3. Instruct a competitor.
4. Instruct your firm.

If you are receiving an enquiry from a prospect, they have effectively discounted options one and two. Let's face it, if they could have sorted the issue themselves or dealt with it in-house, they would have done so. They want to buy legal services. The choice now is who do they buy from – you or a competitor?

CREATING ONBOARDING SCRIPTS

I am a great fan of onboarding scripts.

Before you raise your quizzical eye and say this is nonsense, and that no one should have a script, bear with me. I'm not for one moment suggesting that the scripts are read out in a monotone voice and that you don't go on to question seven until you've extracted every piece of information required in question six. What I am suggesting is there should be some thought and structure given to the conversation and the information that needs to be obtained. In the real world, outside of law, they call them 'discovery calls'.

When you think about applying for a mortgage or sitting down with a financial advisor to discuss a pension, they will get huge amounts of information from you at the initial meeting. I take the view that – when engaging with clients of a law firm for the first time – most lawyers miss this opportunity to find out about the person in front of them.

> I bring my ignorance to the situation. Ignorance is the most important component for helping others to solve any problem in any industry.
>
> **Peter Drucker**

When I'm dealing with new clients, I will always try to get them on a Zoom call if they're making an enquiry about using my services. I want to see what they're like. I want to see how they engage with me. I want to see if they understand what engaging with me is likely to mean.

I am, of course, going to discuss the issue that has prompted them to get in touch. But I am also going to ask them lots of other questions.

I encourage firms to create a well-thought-out list of subject matter-related questions. During the conversation, the lawyer can elicit answers to questions as the conversation progresses rather than starting off with 'Right Question 1… what is your name?'

When you consider it, when a prospect is sitting in front of a lawyer for the first time, this is a golden opportunity to ask them absolutely anything. We can ask them about:

- Their families, children, elderly parents.
- Their work. The business they are in. Do they enjoy it? Why did they choose that area? Whether they own the business. Are they aspiring to own it? Who do they own it with? Have they an exit strategy?
- You can find out what prompted them to contact you, as opposed to other lawyers. Have they used lawyers before?
- How they would like to work with you?
- Preferences regarding communication by email, text, face-to-face, calls or letter.

8 PPP PENGUIN LOGIC

I often listen to a business development podcast for the accountancy profession called The Accounting Influencers. (I know, I know, I must get out more.) In one episode, the presenters likened the first client meeting to going out on a first date. I liked this idea and suggest lawyers should adopt the same mindset. They should:

- Take pride in the fact that they are going to see an attractive prospect.
- Appreciate the prospect will have researched them, too.
- Have carried out some research on the prospect. Look at websites and LinkedIn profiles as a minimum. What was their latest LinkedIn post? If they climbed Kilimanjaro the week before, for charity, start off by congratulating them.
- They should nurture and be excited about the opportunity available, and remember you only get one chance to make a first impression.
- They should dress to impress.
- They should show some humility and respect when meeting the prospect.
- They must not be late.

- If the prospect is bolshy and demanding at the outset, that is what they will be like as clients as the matter progresses.
- Is the prospect someone who will always want to be in control and won't listen to advice?
- The lawyer should understand that if they forget the prospect's name and don't show some genuine interest – and only talk about themselves throughout – they should not be surprised if they are not contacted for a second date.
- If the lawyer does not send a follow-up email or documents that they promised, the prospect will feel ghosted and will tell their friends how they were let down.
- Pick up the tab for the coffee. Don't be a cheapskate.

First impressions count! This could be a lifetime partner. You are investing in a relationship!

LAWYERS AND SOFT SKILLS TRAINING

Expect some pushback if any form of training is to be suggested. Don't get me wrong, your lawyers will need training. My surveys show they accept they need training. However, the pushback will usually relate to the fact that they don't have time to step away from their day jobs to do the training.

Many lawyers won't want to have anything to do with training if they think it relates to sales. Do not use the 'S' word! Expect to be told things like:

'I have been doing this for years. I don't need any help.'

'I have a great conversion rate.'

If these or similar reasons are given, ask the lawyers to produce the checklists they use when qualifying all these prospects. Explain you want to capture and document their knowledge so it can be recycled and help others. The chances are that lists won't be forthcoming… and that's the point here; we want to get this information written down and create a structure and process – so they and their colleagues can get better at 'dating', and others can benefit from their knowledge.

8 PPP PENGUIN LOGIC

What are the components of an initial onboarding conversation?

They are pretty much going to be along the following lines:

Preliminaries

- Where did the client come from?
- Was it a referral?
- Was it a cross-sell?
- Are they an existing client? You need to know this.

If it's a referral, then it might be quite nice to say thank you to the person who referred the client. If the client is an existing client, chances are they have not been ringing around getting free quotes from anybody else.

Have you had the chance to do any preliminary research?

On the call

- Relax. Remember, you've done this before.
- You need to introduce yourself (some lawyers forget to tell callers who they are, especially if the call has been transferred internally).
- Ask if it is okay to call them by their first name.
- Invite them to call you by your first name. Put them at ease.
- Take the client's full name and contact details, including postal address and email.
- Ask if this is their first experience of using a law firm. (It might be the first time they have engaged with a lawyer – they could be nervous. They might know what they need already. They may not have a clue.)

- Ask, 'Is it okay if I take 15 minutes to ask a few questions to establish how I can help you?' (The client might not know how long it's going to take.)
- Ask if it's okay to take some notes. (Again, it helps put clients at their ease.)
- Ask permission to ask a few questions, including what *they* may want, or what *they* are hoping to achieve.
- When you are delving into the specifics of the situation, ask 'why' the matter is important to them. (You may find that your initial thoughts are not at all what the client's priorities are. Remember the LexisNexis report.)
- Think about showing some empathy. There is nothing wrong in saying, 'I appreciate this must be a tough time for you right now, but don't worry, we can help you get to where you need to be or achieve your goal.'
- Ask questions to understand the situation fully. (We already know that the client's number one priority when instructing a lawyer is to ensure that the lawyer *understands* their situation. So, ask questions, checking to make sure that you do.)
- If you are being consulted as the second lawyer, what caused them to instruct you partway through the matter? What was the issue with the first lawyer? Was it response times? Was it cash flow and paying lawyers' fees? Was it a personality clash? Was it that they felt their lawyer was not being proactive?
- Seek to establish what the potential obstacles are.
- Delve into details. What are the issues involved? How long has it been going on?
- Once you have got confirmation that you understand the issues, ask more *why* questions.
- Why are they seeking legal advice now? Is this time-critical? What makes it time-critical? Why not in six months' time?

- What would be the impact of not doing anything? (This is always a useful question as it can help establish value.)
- Periodically, ask for confirmation that what you have said is correct; make sure that your understanding is correct!
- When you get on to the question of cost, you may want to ask, 'What is your budget?' – the budget that they have for you. (I stress the question is 'your budget'.) If they are, for example, enquiring about litigation and want to go all the way to the High Court, but have a budget of £5,000, you will have to manage their expectations somewhat radically.)
- You might want to ask how the client is going to fund the matter. Always beware if you are told 'money is no object'.
- The client might have legal expenses cover, which may help. It might well be the case that your firm is not on the panel of the legal expenses insurance company they have a policy with, and you will need to signpost them away.
- You will need to try to explore the gap from where they are now to where they want to be, and the outcome they want. Ask what a good outcome might look like, and why that particular outcome is important to them.
- Is this a case that can be fixed? Can you deliver the outcome they want?
- It is important to summarise as you go along, and reframe and rephrase what clients tell you. Doing this demonstrates to them you understand their issues. Use the words and phrases that the client has used when having the initial conversation.
- You can demonstrate that – based on what you have heard and the answers that they have given – you are confident that you can help, and they are in the right place.
- You may want to mention that you/your colleagues have dealt with similar cases in the past.

Buy some time

Once you have all the information, buy some time.

- At this stage, you can say that this looks like a great opportunity, and you are very confident that you can help.
- Explain that you would like to go away and think about all that you have been told, and would like to get the team together to prepare a Plan and establish exactly how you can assist the prospect. Explain that you will prepare some options and solutions for consideration. Ask if that is okay.
- Agree a certain time and date – it could be a few hours; it may be a few days.
- Point out that a future meeting will explain the Plan and options in detail, and deal with any questions they may have from the proposal.
- You may wish to ascertain whether anyone else needs to be at the future meeting if it is not immediately apparent the decision-maker is the person you have been dealing with.
- You can then take time to think and sketch out what you can achieve for this client.

Getting back in touch

- When you have thought about the matter, and crafted some options and solutions, you get back in touch with the client.
- Face-to-face is preferable, then Zoom/Teams, then phone, then an email. Once you send an email, you have lost control of the process.
- You outline your solutions.
- You need to demonstrate the prospect is at the right firm. That you have done this before. Your website may have case studies that you can refer them to. You may have industry expertise.
- You may need to refer to the fact that you are leaders in your field or in the region. That your firm

features in some of the legal directories and/or law society groups, demonstrating expertise in this area.

- Ask, 'Is that the solution that would work for you?' Bear in mind that your solution might not be the solution they want.

SPEED IS BAD

> The faster you price,
> the lower the price will be.
>
> **Ron Baker**

One essential skill that lawyers must learn when pricing their work is to slow down. As a rule, speed is bad when it comes to pricing. The pressure to give a quick quote and depart from your pricing process will rarely end well. If the client insists on a price being given, then the automatic response should be for the lawyer to go in very high.

You need to discuss value before you set a price, and you need to keep the customer focused on the objectives they want to achieve.

If pushed to give a price, give a wide range. I would often tell clients that the price at the top end of a piece of litigation could be as much as £100,000. You would see the colour drain from their cheeks. I would then say that these were the costs for going to a High Court contested trial. I would point out that all cases settle. It is only a small percentage that are settled by the judiciary. I would then seek to get back to discussing what the merits of their case were, and what they wanted to achieve.

If the client's only consideration is price, then they might well be a client you should not deal with at all.

You could say, 'I have no idea. We have only just met. In fact, I don't even know if I am the right lawyer for you.'

You could ask, 'What's my budget?' Sometimes, the client genuinely doesn't know as they don't know what is involved in pursuing the case. That is where options come in handy.

If pushed by clients via email or even face-to-face, some of your typical responses could be along the following lines:

'I need to discuss the case with you and understand all of the issues, to make sure I truly know all there is to know about your case. That will allow me to come up with a solution that meets your needs.'

'I have some more questions that I want to ask you before I can give you a price. I need to understand exactly what you want from me before I can give you a price and some options.'

'I need to understand your issues and then work out what services you will actually need from us.'

Let's face it, if you were having an extension built at your house and arranged for a builder to come over and look at the property at 4 pm, and the builder scratched his head, looked at the building and then – at 4:15pm – gave a price for a two-up two-down extension of £145,000 plus VAT (inclusive of labour), you wouldn't be terribly impressed. In fact, you might be petrified. You would ask how he arrived at that figure. He didn't even ask you about what kind of tiles you wanted in the bathroom. You didn't talk about door furniture, kitchen worktops, or window fittings.

Buying some time in the pricing process gives us time not only to think, but also to check and discuss the matter with colleagues, properly scope the work, and make correct assumptions. It can also give the impression to the client that we are thinking about their case in detail and crafting a personalised response, which is – of course – exactly what we are doing.

One of the other reasons to slow down the process is to make sure you understand *who* you are dealing with. Are you dealing with the economic buyer? Is it the person you are talking to? It might not be. You will never know until you have that conversation.

You may want to ask, 'Is anyone else involved in the decision to engage us?' If you are dealing with a gatekeeper, they can only ever say 'no', not 'yes'.

Who is paying for the work? If a company/opponent/third party is picking up the tab, then the person you may be dealing with may have zero price sensitivity. If, for example, the residential conveyancing costs are part of a corporate relocation package, the client you may be dealing with may have no issue at all with the costs you propose, as they are not paying them.

8 PPP PENGUIN LOGIC

The Fixed-Price Agreement can show you care!

Some years ago, I was invited to pitch for a piece of work, which was the formation of a company. It wasn't a terribly complicated piece of work. I knew that a competitor law firm had also been invited to quote for the work.

I created a fixed-price proposal which outlined the scope, and identified assumptions and exclusions – all that you've read about so far. My price was over 30% higher than that of the competitor firm.

The chairman of the organisation appointed my firm. He told me, 'We liked your detailed proposal as it showed you had really thought about our case.' As I say, it wasn't complicated, but the client liked the fact that the FPA showed we had thought about what they were doing, and that enabled us to secure the work at a premium price.

FREE WORK

> If you work for nothing,
> you will never be out of a job.
>
> **Shaun Jardine's neighbour, circa 1994!**

We have already discussed the four options that are available to clients when getting legal advice, which are:

- Do nothing.
- Do it themselves.
- Instruct a competitor.
- Instruct you.

We have already confirmed that if a client is ringing a law firm, they have excluded the first two options. So, what do you do when prospects or, indeed, existing clients don't want to pay for any legal advice?

Most law firms don't have a clearly defined pro bono policy. It is very much left to the individual lawyer not only to price their work, but also to decide how much free work they do.

Sometimes, management teams will dictate that their lawyers must do free legal advice clinics or participate in events like charity will-making weeks. This is all well and good, but lawyers will be concerned if their fee-earning targets are not adjusted accordingly. Free work also impacts realisation rates if you monitor this data.

SHINGLES LOGIC

One firm I have come across had a policy of offering free legal advice to all prospective matrimonial clients. They did so in the mistaken belief that this would eventually generate lots of work. It certainly led to lots of work, but it didn't lead to lots of instructions or cash. What happened was the firm gained a reputation for giving free legal advice. Competitors would send prospects wanting free advice to the Shingles-style firm.

The very big downside, here, was that in these matrimonial cases, the firm effectively excluded themselves from being able to act for the other party who might have been prepared to pay. They had conflicted themselves out for nothing!

Don't get me wrong, I know there is a huge unmet need for legal services and that an element of Corporate Social Responsibility is a good thing. However, it is important to understand what your pro bono policy is, and if there is not one, create one.

- What are the criteria?
- What type of clients?
- How much work do we commit to do?
- How is it communicated to your lawyers?
- How is it monitored?
- Is there a strategic link between doing work for free? Say for a charity/good cause that operates in a sector that is of interest to you.
- When do you say enough is enough?

If you contact your firm's compliance officer, you will probably find that the complaint registers are littered with issues where lawyers have given 'free advice' and then haven't undertaken proper compliance or conflict checks. Free advice is not free. It costs the business to deliver it, regardless of whether you get paid.

When you consider other professions, we don't expect our accountants to do work for nothing and deliver a tax return for us – just to see how they get on and then decide if we'll use them in the future. When we go to the dentist, we sign the paperwork at reception. We have unspeakable things shoved in our mouths and work undertaken.

We don't ask how much the X-rays are, or how much the filling material will cost. At the end of the appointment, we queue up back at the reception, get our credit cards out and pay.

I understand that lawyers entered the law because they want to help people. However, in order to continue to provide a service, we have to ensure that our businesses are profitable.

Finally, if you do free work, make it known you have done so.

- Ask the client for a Google, Trust Pilot review, or LinkedIn recommendation.
- Ask the client to introduce you to paying clients when they get an opportunity to do so.

WORDS WITH THE WISE

Melissa Lyon, Hive Legal

From a business development point of view, the timesheet hinders collaboration and creates competition within the firm. I worked in a BD team. I was often asked when preparing tenders, 'Mel, is there something that you and your team can give them as a free value-add?'

I always think that's a tautology, isn't it? If you're adding value, why is it free? I often thought, why aren't we charging for this? If we go in and help a client with their systems or their processes or provide them with a better way of doing their internal business development, or client relationship management, we are providing value, so why aren't they paying us for that as well? Why is it just something that you're throwing in for free?

8 PPP PENGUIN LOGIC

Be selfish

You don't have to do every bit of legal work. You should aspire to do more than your fair share of the good stuff.

Empowering your lawyers to turn work away is important. They will need to hear this from the management and from their Team Leaders.

CRIB SHEET

READING & VIEWING

WATCH (COMPULSORY)

Pals International Café: Generalist vs Specialist

Confused about how your firm should position itself? Watch this, and all will be revealed… (then again, maybe not)

By VeraSage Fellow Paul O'Byrne

https://www.youtube.com/watch?v=dZljwnvKlPs

WATCH

3 Things that Make a MEANINGFUL Vision

By Simon Sinek

https://www.youtube.com/watch?v=zpzZumZCdWA

READ (COMPULSORY)

The Riddle of Perception

By LexisNexis

The section dealing with what lawyers think clients want, and what clients actually want, is illuminating.

https://www.lexisnexis.co.uk/bellwether/assets/pdfs/Lexis-nexis-report-2016_interactive%20version03.pdf

READ

The Age of The Client

By LexisNexis

The balance of power in the client/lawyer relationship is shifting. This report explores how independent law firms and sole practitioners are responding to a new breed of client.

https://www.lexisnexis.co.uk/bellwether/assets/pdfs/bellwether-report-2015-age-of-the-client.pdf

READ

Restaurant Offers Budget Version of Salt Bae's Gold-Covered Steak

By The Guardian

https://www.theguardian.com/food/2021/nov/01/restaurant-offers-budget-version-of-salt-bae-gold-covered-steak

READ

Law Firms Could Learn a Trick or Two from Qantas

By Joel Barolsky

https://www.linkedin.com/pulse/law-firms-could-learn-trick-two-from-qantas-joel-barolsky/

READ

Time to Ditch your 'Batman' Clients

By Joel Barolsky

https://www.linkedin.com/pulse/time-ditch-batman-clients-joel-barolsky

LISTEN

How To Fire A Customer

By Ron Baker and Ed Kless, The Soul of Enterprise

https://www.thesoulofenterprise.com/tsoe/how-to-fire-a-customer

LISTEN

What Makes Something Valuable?

Chris Do interviews Ron Baker. Cost does not determine price.

https://thefutur.com/content/what-makes-something-valuable

TIPS/CHECKLISTS

1. Value is a feeling, and you don't know what your clients are feeling, so don't try and overthink it.
2. You are worth it!

EXERCISES

EXERCISE 1

Setting Prices?

In what ways have you given your power away when setting prices in your firm?

What needs to change?

Are there non-negotiable areas?

What must you unlearn?

What mindsets are at odds with your new Vision and pricing values?

What training must you forget?

EXERCISE 2

Comprehending Value

What changes do you need to make to upfront meetings with clients and potential clients to ensure that you comprehend value?

How does this differ from what you are currently doing?

What additional education and training do you require in order to implement this?

EXERCISE 3

Customer Journey

Select a work area:

- What would a typical customer journey into your firm be like?
- Who says what and when?
- What documents are created?
- Have you already got standard scripts and templates? Review them.

EXERCISE 4

Speed

1. If speed is bad (especially for new clients), how can you slow it down?
2. If prescribing without diagnosis is bad, how can you slow it down?
3. How can you not answer? How can you slow down?

EXERCISE 5

Client Selection Criteria

Ask your compliance team to give you details of a matter which ended up as a formal complaint. With the benefit of hindsight, what questions could/should you have asked about that matter? Retrospectively, score answers to five questions, with 1 being low and 5 being high.

For example,

1. How complicated was it?
2. Did you have capacity?
3. Was the client a good fit?
4. Etc.

Lots of 4/5s indicate that this is a matter which should not have been undertaken; alarm bells should have been ringing.

Once you have settled on some questions, think of what the scoring bands should be to assist with client selection.

POSSIBILITY THINKING QUESTIONS TO POSE

1. In what areas could we possibly offer pro bono legal advice to enhance our brand?
2. Where can we possibly get information to map customer journeys?
3. How can we possibly make our CRM system more popular?
4. How can we possibly get better at discovery/onboarding calls?
5. How can we possibly slow down the speed when we give prices?

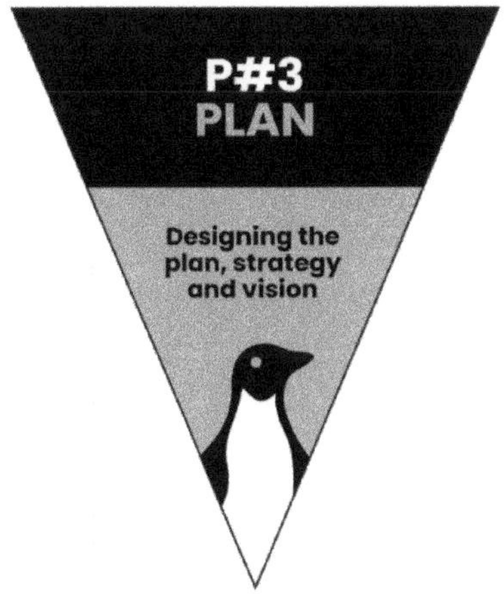

P#3 PART 2 TOOLS

LAWYER SCORING MATRIX

In his books on pricing, Ron Baker frequently talks about the human capital in knowledge businesses. The human capital leaves the office in the elevator at the end of the day. It cannot be owned; it can only be contracted. Baker makes the point that, ultimately, the staff are volunteers, and it is totally up to them whether they get back into the elevator the following morning.

We know, as lawyers, that our people – our human capital – are important assets of our business. However, you only have to look at some of the reports on social media detailing lawyer burnout to understand that we have some way to go as an industry in caring for our human assets.

One of the common misconceptions in many law firms is that when a piece of work arrives at a law firm, the lawyer must do it. In many of the surveys I've conducted over the years, I have asked, 'Does your firm require its lawyers to take on every piece of work regardless?' And, quite often, the answer is 'Yes'.

One of the important lessons to learn on the value-based pricing journey is law firms must create what I call a Lawyer Scoring Matrix. It's basically a series of questions they ask themselves before giving a client a price.

Listed below are some questions to consider.

ANALYSING THE OPPORTUNITY

Source of work

1. Existing client?
2. New prospect? Have they been referred to you by a referrer who is strategically important?

The work

1. Is the job on offer something that you have done before?
2. How complicated is it?
3. Do you have the skills within the team to deliver the work?
4. Who will be accountable for determining progress?
5. Can you delegate this work to other team members if required?
6. Do you like doing the work?
7. Do you have any existing financial information to indicate what previous fees have been charged for these matters?
8. Over what period will it be delivered?
9. Is it time-consuming?
10. Do you have the right resources, or are team members off sick or planning to go on holiday?
11. Is the lawyer on the other side easy to deal with?
12. Have you made a profit in similar cases?
13. Will you make a profit in this case?

Results

1. Are the client's required outcomes achievable?
2. How will you know if the objective has been achieved?
3. What is the best alternative to a successful outcome? Has the client considered this?
4. How will this project impact the client's reputation?
5. How will it impact your reputation?
6. Will you make a profit in this case?

The clients

1. How has the client been when dealing with you to date?
2. How polite have they been?
3. Will they value your advice?

4. How easy have they been to contact, and how quickly have they responded?
5. Have they kept their appointments?
6. How prepared were they for meetings?
7. Did they do what was asked of them?
8. What information do you need from the client? Are you confident they can supply it?
9. Are they the kind of client that has produced a beautifully crafted chronology and a paginated bundle of documents, or will they deliver documents to you in a plastic bag with instructions on the back of an envelope?
10. Have the clients the means to pay?
11. Have these clients instructed other lawyers already? If so, why was the relationship terminated?
12. Is the client strategically important? Will it lead to more work?
13. Is this a client that will generate more work in the future?
14. Will you and your team like working with this client?
15. Are they nice people to deal with?
16. Has the client used any phrases that have set alarm bells ringing? These could be things like:
    - 'My previous lawyers didn't understand my case.'
    - 'My previous lawyers were too expensive.'
    - 'This is not a complicated matter; I need you to just do XYZ.'
    - 'Money is no object.'
    - 'This is a point of principle.'
17. Will you make a profit in this case?

You/The Lawyer

1. How busy are you now?
2. Is this going to be time-consuming?
3. Does the client trust you?
4. Do you trust the client?
5. Can you fit it in with all the other work that you have?
6. Are you going find yourself apologising to other clients if you take this matter on because you haven't got round to dealing with their work?
7. Will you make a profit in this case?

Scoring the opportunity

I recommend a Lawyer Scoring Matrix is created where the lawyer asks themselves a select number of questions and scores them on an ascending scale of 1 to 5, with 5 indicating an increased price should be charged.

The scoring bands should drive you to take some form of action and have an open conversation with a colleague (depending on the score total) about increasing your price.

The questions I commonly recommend are:

1. How busy are you? (Not busy 1. Very busy 5.)
2. How complicated is this work? (Easy 1. Really hard 5.)
3. Can you delegate this matter to someone else? (Yes 1. No 5.)
4. What has communication been like with the client up until now? (Brilliant, really organised 1. Terrible 5.)
5. Will you enjoy working with them? (Lovely people 1. Difficult and argumentative 5.)

If you have lots of fours and fives to whatever questions are in your Matrix, you need to increase the price.

You may even want to create scoring thresholds with the following categories, directing action of some kind.

- Proceed.
- Consider uplift.
- Consider Substantial uplift.
- Refer to management.

8 PPP PENGUIN LOGIC

Warring siblings

A probate lawyer brought a matter to the firm's Value Officer (VO). The pricing spreadsheet used by the probate team, based on the size of the estate, indicated that the fee to be charged should be £6,000.

The Lawyer Scoring Matrix was applied, and the conversation that ensued was along the following lines.

VO: 'How busy are you?'

L: 'Manic.'

VO: 'Why not delegate this matter? You have junior lawyers in your team.'

L: 'The clients are too difficult for a junior lawyer to deal with.'

VO: 'Why are they difficult?'

L: 'They are arguing over their late mother's jewellery already, and she hasn't even been buried yet. The siblings don't get on with each other and – to progress the probate – each matter will involve speaking to each one separately.'

VO: 'Will you enjoy dealing with this matter?'

L: 'Not at all. It's going to be tough and demanding.'

VO. 'All the indicators suggest you should seek a very high price. What would you like to charge?'

L: (After a moment's thought) '£24,000.'

VO: Price approved. Good luck.

The next day, the lawyer confirmed the clients had accepted by return. She was delighted to have obtained the pump fist price and knew she would be happy dealing with the difficult matter as she was being paid a premium to do so.

PREPARING FOR THE VALUE CONVERSATIONS

> Prescription without diagnosis is malpractice.
>
> **Ron Baker**
>
> One of the most compelling things you can do after asking a question is to genuinely listen to the answer. Stay Curious, my friend.
>
> **Michael Bungay Stanier,**
> **The Coaching Habit**

Above, Ron Baker is essentially saying that professionals are quite often keen to start talking about the solution to the problem (the prescription) before they've actually checked all of the client's symptoms.

You see this all the time with some lawyers; they just can't control themselves. They almost can't wait for clients to stop talking when they meet, so they (the lawyer) can start telling them what they need.

Imagine if you went to the doctor, and you walked into the doctor's surgery – pale and a bit huffy – and before you have even sat down, the doctor says, 'Ah, great to see you; I see you have an atrial fibrillation of your heart.'

What? Eh?

The doctor hasn't taken any tests, carried out an ECG, taken your blood pressure or even listened to your heart. You received the diagnosis about what was wrong with you before you even sat down. The doctor might be 100% right, but you wouldn't feel you've been dealt with properly. You haven't told him how you feel, nor the impact the condition is having, and you would doubt whether the doctor was right.

The value conversation is important. It is a two-way conversation. It is vital it happens as we don't know *what a client values* until we speak to them, and we know what is important to clients is that we really understand their issues. How can we do this without a detailed conversation, or the response to an email, or (even worse) have our websites list prices without speaking to clients at all?

I believe that lawyers have almost created a rod for our backs with the language we use. When we meet a client, we talk about 'taking instructions'. When you think about the phrase 'taking instructions', it's nonsense. Clients don't know what they want to instruct us to do. If they knew what to instruct us to do, they would be out there doing it!

It's a shame to say that, for some lawyers, actively listening and showing empathy are not skills that come easily. We have all experienced doctors with poor bedside manners. Sadly, some lawyers are the same. I once came across a person working in a law firm who – when taking enquiries on probate matters – never even said, 'I'm sorry to hear about your loss.'

When I asked the person concerned why she didn't ever mention this, she told me, 'They know their mother has died; that's why they are calling us to deal with the probate.' Nothing wrong with her logic, just an appalling bedside manner on a human level.

Empathy can start with the fact that we recognise the client or their representative is feeling worried, stressed, and vulnerable. Instructing a lawyer is not an easy decision to make. Clients, in the main, are not used to instructing lawyers. They will have lots of preconceptions and unconscious biases about what we are like.

You have already heard from Jon Whittle regarding his take on law firm websites. Most law firms have the same navigation and wording on their websites.

- They talk about putting the client at the centre of everything they do.
- They talk about being the trusted advisor.
- They talk about their history.
- They talk about the qualifications that their lawyers have and how many people there are in the organisation.
- They talk about their rankings in directories that the clients have never heard of.
- They may even talk about the awards they have won, some of which you can buy online by paying a fee and responding to an email.

Clients don't care. All they're interested in is whether you have someone in your organisation who can deliver the outcome they want. Clients won't necessarily mind whether this person is newly qualified or someone who's been working in the business for 30 years. The fact that you employ competent people are givens. It only means something if other firms have website statements like, 'We employ decidedly average, well-meaning, mediocre lawyers', and we know they don't do that.

Clients want to be understood and heard. They want to make sure that your lawyers understand their needs and are the right people to help them.

You may be surprised to learn that clients have very low expectations of the way they are going to be dealt with when they meet a lawyer. Page 16 of the 2015 *LexisNexis Bellwether Report: The Age of the Client* does not pull its punches when outlining a client's expectations.

'Most clients aren't exactly excited about the prospect of having to find a good lawyer. Though they may respect lawyers' knowledge, clients are less flattering about their human qualities. Clients don't tend to expect a high degree of rapport when they enter into the relationship. As one client put it: 'Lawyers are not people people.

'Private clients don't always feel that their concerns are fully appreciated by lawyers. The legal situation itself prompts enormous anxiety in them – and then there's the worry about entering into an open-ended financial commitment. Uncertainty about what's included in the cost, the often-unpredictable timescales, and dependence on the knowledge of others can all lead to client anxiety. Add to this the stress of feeling in the dark about how the case is progressing – and constantly chasing to find out – and it's easy to see why clients have become so demanding. 'They talk more than they listen, which is a big turn-off. I judge them based on the questions they ask.'

8 PPP PENGUIN LOGIC

Listen Up

Remember the old saying: 'We have one mouth and two ears, and we should use them in those proportions'?

It is important to listen.

It is important not to subject the client to a cross-examination.

BRACE YOURSELF…

incoming provocative statement

Too often, lawyers are keen to tell the prospect all about themselves and their firm. I have some bad news for you; most prospects don't give a jot about:

- How many lawyers you have.
- How old your firm is, and how you can track its existence back to the eighteenth century.
- Your lawyer or firm accreditations with acronyms like ALEP, ACTAPS, LEXCEL, IIP or CQS.

It's not about you or your law firm at all. It's about them.

BODY LANGUAGE

In my view, the best way to engage with a client is face-to-face and then via Zoom or a Teams meeting, then phone, then email. We know that body language is important. If you can see a client, they will signal how they are feeling. You can see if a client doesn't understand something. You can see a client wince if they are given a price. You can see if they are confused at certain points in a conversation.

We know psychologists tell us that – within the first seven seconds – people are already judging the other person. In fact, there is evidence to suggest that people start to judge and can make accurate judgments of others within $1/10^{th}$ of a second!

8 PPP PENGUIN LOGIC

Remember to be WITY

We need to remember to be WITY when talking to clients.

What's

Important

To

You?

When you consider the nature of the work, private client, family, and conveyancing lawyers can become experts at having value conversations early on. They are nearly always dealing with the main decision-makers/economic buyers.

8 PPP PENGUIN LOGIC

Be a Farmer

As I have stated earlier, having a value-based pricing conversation is *not* selling.

Lawyers, in the main, absolutely run a mile if anybody ever mentions the 'S' word. If, however, you accept that what clients buy are outcomes, we know we have to have a conversation with them to determine what outcomes they want and whether or not we can satisfy the client. We are both working towards the same goal.

I suggest you never talk about lawyers being salespeople or even as hunters or rainmakers. They are not comfortable with these descriptions.

A Canadian legal market strategy and management consultant, Heather Suttie, in an article *When Sales Becomes*

Value invited lawyers to consider themselves as farmers when it came to client sales and BD. I like this idea.

We want farmers to nurture the clients they have (assuming we want to retain them). We know that the cost of gaining a new client is seven times the cost of trying to land a new one, so the lawyer will understand the logic of this. We want the lawyer to adopt the farmer mentality.

- Appreciate it might not be a quick win to cash in.
- There must be a long-term relationship.
- We need to look after the opportunity and nurture it.
- Keep a watchful eye on things.
- Protect the client from any storms on the horizon.
- Be observant and contemplative.
- Be quietly confident, as farmers know what they are doing.

And also, as farmers know, it's always necessary to work on the opportunity presented; doing nothing is not an option that will bear fruit.

Education and coaching are better words to use than sales training. I repeat, lawyers don't like the 'S' word.

WORDS WITH THE WISE

Chris Marston, Exemplar Companies Plc

We give all of our team an option to have business development plans with a private coach and share ideas, bounce off challenges, figure out how to get into clients in advance of meetings, and how to approach client circumstances. People can avail themselves of that training. It is not obligatory unless you're a leader. Leaders have to go through it.

Kirsty Pappin, Aries Legal Practice Management

As is the case with any conversation, lawyers need to listen closely and pay attention to the body language of their clients. Law firms should afford their lawyers the opportunity to experience coaching (and pay for it), as these lawyers will learn skills from these sessions that will benefit their conversations with clients. Learnt experience from experience.

CREATE VALUE-BASED PRICE QUESTIONS FOR EACH PRACTICE AREA

As we now know that value questions are important, it is worth spending some time working out which ones we should ask of our clients.

Customers and prospects will judge how competent we are, based on the questions we ask. If we ask questions that show we have done some preliminary investigation and research, the more confident they will be in our ability.

We need to have conversations about them and what they want to achieve and learn a new skill of asking good questions. The questions must be thought about and lovingly crafted. Chances are that you and many of your lawyers create good questions every day. However, I suspect they are not written down anywhere, nor shared, which would assist other team members.

As part of the value-based pricing process, I recommend your teams discuss which questions should be asked when meeting a client and discussing a new matter. What questions should be asked to find out about them and their issues? What keeps these clients awake at night when thinking about the issue?

Your lawyers should discuss them, write them down, hone them, work out the best ones and create a list that gets put into the departmental practice manual/BBU.

As this is such an important part of the process, I have listed a vast number of questions to consider. I am not – for one moment – suggesting every question is asked to every client/prospect. Your lawyers can and should select the ones they are comfortable asking and monitor the responses they receive.

Here are some examples to get you started:

1. What is your goal? What would you like to accomplish?
2. How would you like us to work with you if money were no object?

The important thing about this question is it can give you an idea of the service levels the client wants, and whether you can deliver them. It can identify boundaries and guidelines for working with clients who respect and value your services.

3. How would things improve as a result of this engagement?
4. Why are you instructing us now?
5. What is the current problem?
6. What is the solution you are hoping for?
7. What do you think the biggest threat to a successful outcome is?
8. Why do you think it's a threat?
9. What precise aspects are most troubling you about the case?
10. What is keeping you awake at night?
11. What is a good outcome for you?
12. What is a bad outcome?
13. What do you think are the important priorities in the matter?
14. Does this case impact you personally?
15. What does success look like for you in terms of this case?
16. How would you like us to communicate with you? Phone, email, face-to-face, text, WhatsApp, portals.
17. How often would you want to hear from us? Only when there is some development on the matter, weekly, daily?
18. How involved do you want to be in the case? What can you do? What are you prepared to do?
19. What did you not like about your former lawyers?
20. What did they do well? What did they do badly?
21. What is my budget? (The lawyer's budget.)
22. Is there a budget I need to keep within?
23. How did you arrive at that budget?
24. Why have you not set a budget? Have you given any thought to the costs?
25. How would you like to pay for our services?
26. Can you spread the payments?
27. How will you measure the quality of our service?

If it's a corporate client, you may want to add questions such as:

28. What's the benefit if this deal comes off? (In terms of increased revenue.)
29. What's the impact in terms of revenue if we lose the case or the deal fails?

30. How would your organisation flourish/be impacted by a win/loss/failure to achieve the outcome?
31. Any preference as to when an invoice should be raised?
32. Who are we reporting to?
33. Would the Board require progress updates at Board meetings?

Asking good questions – to find out what the problem is – will reassure the client that you can help them solve their problem. Good questions make clients feel at ease. It's important the lawyer is seeking to understand the problem and demonstrate that they understand their circumstances.

THE IMPORTANCE OF ASKING 'WHY' AND 'WHAT ELSE'?

Asking 'Why?' a client is taking a course of action is a very powerful question. Ask it often.

A solicitor friend of mine tells the story of a husband and wife who had a family-owned business in which their children were employed. The clients told him they wanted to sell their large and profitable business, which employed lots of staff. A great transaction – many lawyer mouths would be fed as it would involve corporate, employment and property teams.

My lawyer friend asked *why* they wanted to sell. The clients told him they were selling the business because one of their children was about to marry somebody who they – the parents – didn't think would be a long-term prospect. They were worried that the business might get tied up in all kinds of legal wrangling if a divorce happened later, and they thought the best thing was to sell the business and divide up the proceeds now, so all of the children benefited.

My friend was able to explain that they didn't need to sell the business. All they needed was a robust shareholders' agreement, which would protect the business. The clients were delighted. A shareholders' agreement was duly drafted.

I wonder how many other lawyers might have ended up selling the business because that is what the clients wanted or at least thought they wanted.

The question 'What else?' is also a very powerful question. Michael Bungay Stanier, in his book *The Coaching Habit,* describes it as a question with 'magical properties'. It may need to be asked a few times during the conversation.

- It shows that you are interested.
- It keeps you from proffering any advice until the situation is fully understood.
- It can buy you thinking time if needed.
- When you hear 'there is nothing else' from the client, you can move on and take it as a cue to start talking.

It is hard for some lawyers to take a step back, listen to what is being said, and then re-calibrate the conversation to see whether they can help. I have already mentioned 'assume' makes an ass out of you and me. As lawyers, we are quick to assume that we know what clients want when, in fact, we need to establish that we know what clients want, and that is very different.

QUESTIONS FOR THE LAWYER

Once the lawyer has asked the client value questions, it is then necessary to ask a series of questions aimed specifically at the lawyer and those who will work on the matter. It is important to give some thought to the opportunity they have been presented with. Remember, the client and their matter might not be the right fit.

QUESTIONS ABOUT THE CLIENT AND MATTER

1. Who is the client? What type of business? What do the lawyer and the team know about them? How long has the client been in business? Is there a track record of liquidations by the owners?
2. Have we worked with them in the past… what did they pay?
3. Is this really important to them… e.g., an injunction? Could the issue shut the business down? Does the part the lawyer can play make the business more valuable? It may keep it alive!
4. How urgent is it? Are there urgent deadlines? Can we adhere to the deadlines?
5. How hard is it to find the expertise to solve this problem? Do we have competitors likely to compete for this job? Are we better than the competition, technically?
6. What is the downside/cost of not solving the problem? If it's a litigation matter, has the lawyer factored in the requirement that the losing party may have to pay the other side's costs? Are there likely to be delays at court? What is the input and management time required from the client?
7. What is the client's benefit if the problem is solved?
8. Why are they acting now?
9. Is this risky? Is it a risk the firm can take on? Is it a conditional fee?
10. Has the client a contingency plan in case the identified risk becomes a reality?
11. Does this project need some serious analysis into potential risks?
12. Who is paying for the service?
13. Who are their accountants, bankers, and other professional advisers?
14. Who referred the client to us?
15. Is the referrer strategically important to us?
16. Why were they referred to us?

17. Were there former lawyers? If so, why have they changed? Do we rate those lawyers? Should alarm bells be ringing for us?
18. Has the client used lawyers like our firm before? Are they familiar with the process?
19. How solvent is the client? Can they afford us? Is the client losing money and in a perilous financial state?
20. Who are the decision-makers, and are we dealing with them? Do we know them?
21. How business savvy are the owners? How experienced are they when it comes to dealing with lawyers?
22. If we take on this piece of work, can we replicate the service delivered for other new clients? Does it open a new area of work that we can exploit, or is it a one-off?
23. Is it a strategically important area of work for us?
24. Should we take this on?
25. Is the best decision to pass on this opportunity?

QUESTIONS ABOUT THE INTERNAL RESOURCING CAPABILITIES

1. Who else in the firm needs to be involved with this to sell, deliver, and pitch for the business?
2. Who will do the work?
3. Have we got enough support staff?
4. Have we the expertise to deliver this, or will we rely on external counsel?
5. Do we need to recruit additional lawyers?
6. Can we upsell any other legal services?
7. Have we got the technology to support what they need us to do?
8. Is an urgent case going to impact the service delivery to other clients and their matters?
9. Are we prepared to fund any disbursements such as barristers' fees, court fees or expert fees? If so, why and to what extent?
10. Are we assuming any risk at all regarding the recoverability of costs? Are we going to have any skin in the game?
11. What if the matter goes abortive? Who pays what?
12. Will we make any money?
13. Is the best decision to pass on this opportunity?

As you will see from the above, none of the questions themselves are magic.

They are all similar. In fact, two of them are repeated: 'Is the best decision to pass on this opportunity?'

Your Practice Areas should select the questions relevant to their work area, write them down, use them, and review them frequently. Inevitably, new questions will make it onto the list and others will drop off. Add the questions to the BBU.

VALUE PROPOSITION WORKSHEET

In their book on *Value-Based Pricing,* Harry Macdivitt and Mike Wilkinson created an example of a Value Proposition Worksheet that they recommend is adopted. The template is copied below and can become part of your onboarding and value pricing process.

Key Issues Facing Customer	**How We Can Help**	**Benefits**	**Evidence to Support the Proposition**
These will be questions based around the key issues and seek to understand what is and what isn't important.	What solutions can we offer?	How does our solution improve their position?	How can we demonstrate the validity of our proposition?
Listen carefully	What can we offer?	What are they?	How can we prove it?

(The table above has been reproduced with the kind permission of Macdivitt and Wilkinson.)

What I like about this template is that it can also be looked at – again – as part of any After-Action review process. The information can also be used when it comes to the creation of a Fixed-Price Agreement.

WORDS WITH THE WISE

Steven and Jacqui Brown, Lynn & Brown

Steven and Jacqui ask the following questions at their firm:

1. What is your problem or opportunity?
2. Why do you want to attend or resolve this issue now?
3. What timeframe did you have in mind in reaching a resolution?
4. What aspects of this matter do you want dealt with urgently?
5. What aspects of this matter are causing you the most concern?
6. What outcome would you like to achieve?
7. What does success look like for you?
8. What is the cost of doing nothing?
9. Are you the decision-maker?
10. Have you used legal services previously? If so, why have you changed firms? We like to make sure your experience with us is positive.
11. What is the most important thing to you when dealing with your lawyer? i.e., urgency, communication, cost control.
12. How often would you like to hear from us? Would you like regular communication and weekly updates on your matter, or would you prefer to be contacted or updated as and when we believe it necessary?
13. How involved would you like us to be? Would you like us to completely guide you through the process, or would you like to do some parts yourself?
14. Why us? How did you hear about Lynn & Brown?

COMMERCIAL CLIENT AUDITS

When I was in practice, I really enjoyed carrying out client audits on new commercial clients that instructed my firm. I would ring the CEO/Managing Director, thank them for the instructions, and ask if I could visit them (if geographically suitable) so I could carry out what I called a 'self-preservation audit'.

I explained that my firm liked to get to know and understand our clients and their businesses early in our relationship. We did this as we felt it more appropriate to warn them about potential legal problems before they arose. I likened the audit exercise to my firm being diligent fence builders. We preferred to be fence builders at the tops of cliffs, rather than an ambulance driver at the bottom, waiting for someone to topple over. I explained that, in my view, the lawyer's job is to anticipate needs where we can, and then identify solutions to satisfy those needs. Clients were delighted to spare me their time. I would tell them that the best legal problem is the one they never have.

The audit questions themselves were very general.

1. Who owns the business? Shareholders? Partners?
2. Are you contemplating any new owners joining?
3. Do the directors have service contracts?
4. Do you have a shareholder agreement?
5. Are any shareholdings provided for in any of the owner's wills?
6. Has a lasting power of attorney been created, restricted to business issues?
7. Are there any disputes between shareholders or issues which may lead to disputes?
8. Are you planning any internal or external investment?
9. Are you planning to sell all or part of the business?
10. What is your growth strategy/exit strategy?
11. Do you have a succession plan?
12. Do you have a strategic plan? When was it last reviewed?
13. Are you planning to expand any part of the business?
14. How many clients do you have?
15. Would losing any client severely impact the business?
16. Are there any key suppliers who could cause issues if they ceased to supply you?
17. Who are your major competitors?
18. When were your terms and conditions last reviewed – both sale and purchase?
19. Do you have any patents/intellectual property?
20. Have you a written IP strategy?
21. Have you got confidential, commercially sensitive information? Who has access to it?
22. Do you have contracts of employment with restrictive covenants? When were they last reviewed?

23. What was last year's legal spend?
24. How do you like to work with your professional advisers? If money were no object, how would you like us to work with you?
25. Why did you choose our firm?
26. Are you planning on increasing or decreasing your workforce?
27. When were contracts and staff handbooks last reviewed?
28. Would you be interested in conducting an anonymous survey of any issues affecting your business with your staff?
29. Do you own or lease your premises? When do the leases end? What are the dilapidation provisions? Break clauses? Rent reviews?
30. Would a review of your leases be of interest?
31. Who do you bank with? How do you rate them?
32. Who are your accountants/auditors? Are they proactive?
33. What is the biggest risk to your business?

At the meeting, I would score the opportunity. For example, if the client said they did not have a shareholder's agreement, I would ask, 'How important is it that you get one?' They might say 'quite important', so I would score it as a 5 on a 1/5 scale.

I would then ask the client how long they would like to wait to get the shareholder agreement resolved, and ask them to give me a time frame of 1/3/6/9 months. They would answer. I would record the timescale.

At the end of the conversation, I explained that I would create a priority list for the client with the timescales that they had set. I had effectively created a ready-made list of work that needed doing in the future and permission to nudge the client to do it. I had the perfect excuse to keep in touch. Farming, not selling.

I always liked asking the questions about banks and accountants. If clients replied that they were not impressed with their banks or accountants, it would create a great opportunity to make a referral if required.

Before the meeting even took place, I would go online and look at the ICO Register (Information Commissioner's Office) and see if the client was registered. If they were not, it would allow me – at that meeting – to give them an early indication of the value of the audit and point out they were breaking the law… a sleepwalker at the edge of a cliff averted.

FIXED-PRICE AGREEMENTS (FPA)

Now that we've had a value-based price conversation with the client, and gained an understanding of what they want us to do, it now falls to us to create a Fixed-Price Agreement template that can be delivered to the client.

The FPA document is important. It helps lawyers to look at what they are proposing to scope the work, consider assumptions and exclusions, and then create options and prices. The aim here is to create a document which sets out clearly what will be delivered, identify options, and not have the lawyer fallback position of 'This is my hourly rate' – take it or leave it.

Detailed scoping is key. It never ceases to amaze me how some lawyers put very little effort into defining the scope. Very often, it's because they are so excited about getting stuck into the case. Time spent really thinking about the scope will be time well spent and will positively impact the price you seek to charge.

A detailed scope also allows clients to read and fully understand – and see – what's involved in their case, understand the process, stages, and time scales, and can help them understand the work and value you create.

It is always worth spending time on this document for a couple of reasons:

1. We want the client to understand the outcomes that we are offering.
2. A well-scoped document can be saved as a precedent, then later amended and recycled to use in the future. It will be added to your BBU.

FEATURES OF THE FPA

The FPA you create needs to feature the following:

1. The client's contact details.
2. List what you believe the client's pains/gains are. Use their language and mention the outcome they want. Give them what they asked for.
3. Identify what work you are going to do (in scope) and the work that you are not going to do (out of scope/exclusions). You will need to list the stages. Remember, the client may have forgotten what was discussed in the initial meeting.

   It is always worth spending time on identifying what work will and will not be undertaken. It's important that both the lawyer and the client understand their roles and what they're expected to do. If a client indicated that the matter is going to need three witnesses, that should be mentioned in the scope 'Taking witness statements from three witnesses.' If it later transpires that 23 witnesses are required, the matter is going to go out of scope, and you will need to have a conversation and create a revised price for the additional 20.

   If the client says they are going to prepare the first draft of a chronological bundle of documents and deliver them electronically in a paginated bundle, then put that into the agreement. If they ultimately deliver you a shoebox stuffed full of paper, then it is easier to have a conversation that the matter has gone out of scope.

It is wise to limit the number of revisions that may be made to a document/contract/heads of terms. Limit things to, say, two revisions. When you are asked to prepare the third draft, you can talk about the change in scope.

On commercial transactions, electronic deal rooms may need to be created. Set out whose responsibility it is to create them and who is paying. It's also worthwhile setting out and agreeing how documents will be filed and stored in these electronic environments.

Due diligence is always a thorny issue. Who is doing what? It may well be the case that the client's accountants are being involved. State who is carrying out what task.

It is necessary to state, in your agreement, that if circumstances change, any revisions to pricing will be the subject of a change order. You must get into the habit of stopping work when the matter goes out of scope, having that conversation with the client, and *not* continuing to do the work. It's the lawyer's responsibility to manage the work and the relationship and document revised scopes and prices.

It's always worth investing time in the scoping of the work and getting better at doing this. A well-drafted scope can be a good trade-off against a battle over fees later on, if a matter goes out of scope.

4. Who is going to be involved in the case?

   Who, at your law firm, is going to be acting on the matter? In this section, you can be quite creative, so why not list paralegals or legal assistants? Copy and paste photos of them from your website. People buy people! Insert their contact details.

   Who is getting involved in the work is important. At the outset, a lawyer may think it won't be necessary to instruct an external barrister. That may change.

   If an external barrister is going to be instructed, you may wish to specify the level of call (number of years of experience) you envisage to be required. If it is a run-of-the-mill case, it may be a junior barrister. If it is groundbreaking law, then King's Counsel may be required.

   Are expert witnesses going to be required, and – if so – how many, and what type?

5. You will outline what your plan of action is for achieving the outcome. You may even break the transaction down into a series of stages. This is particularly common when creating Fixed-Price Agreements for litigation matters. It is important that risks are considered.
6. Include a timeline indicating key dates. This should feature dates where clients may need to supply documentation/instructions to you. List other clients' actions. The timescales must be realistic. Delivery dates are important, so there is no point in having a deadline to file a defence and hoping that the client will

give instructions the day before. If you need the date three weeks before, then state that.

7. Create a list of assumptions. These are the things that you have assumed will happen. If an assumption later turns out not to be correct, then this gives you the opportunity to have a further conversation with the client about how the matter has gone out of scope and needs to be re-priced.

   Common assumptions can include:

   - That the only work to be undertaken is identified in the scope.
   - Where will meetings take place? Your offices, their offices or virtually?
   - It is assumed the lawyers on the other side will be competent and knowledgeable.
   - That the law does not change.
   - That all parties to the transaction are UK-based.
   - That work will be undertaken during office hours.
   - That the client and any other professional advisers will fully engage with the process.

   In litigation cases, it is common to make provision for matters to be resolved by mediation or other forms of alternative dispute resolution. It is common to exclude any mediation costs from the initial Fixed-Price Agreement. If mediation is going to happen, then another budget can be created.

8. Set up exclusions, such as things you're not going to do.

   - Tax advice is usually one that features in most lawyer FPAs.
   - Other areas you are not advising on. Cross-jurisdictional issues.
   - Limitations on due diligence.

9. Set out the payment terms. Your starting point should be payment in advance. Negotiate backwards from there.

10. Your Service Guarantee. Are you prepared to guarantee any aspects of your service? This could be indicating when calls will be returned, when deadlines will be met, what documentation and correspondence will be automatically provided to clients, and when members of the team working on the project will be contactable. What will happen on the matter if the lead lawyer is, for example, unavailable?

    I know one firm that regularly offers a Service Guarantee to clients. They invite clients to deduct up to 10% off an outstanding bill if they are not happy with the service. The only provision is that a conversation has to take place with a lawyer to enable them to explain why the client has chosen to make the deduction. The Guarantee was used hundreds of times and called in only three times.

For more detailed and complicated transactions, you may go as far as creating organisation charts and project plans.

When preparing these Fixed-Price Agreements, it's always worthwhile having conversations with other members of the department and sharing the proposal. Colleagues will have knowledge and experience that may identify risks and/or scope defects that you have not considered.

And then, finally, once the FPA is created, have a chat with your marketing team and see if they can create a template document for you to utilise that looks different, appealing, and on brand.

WORDS WITH THE WISE

Leanne Bentley, WonderWord Training

Microsoft Word is a wonderful piece of software which is used in most law firms worldwide. However, I have rarely come across a lawyer who can use it properly.

In my experience, new trainee lawyers arrive at their law firm for their first seat, having previously used Microsoft Word at school and university. They are largely unaware of how very different that experience is compared with amending a 100-page agreement with multilevel numbering and specific house style formatting. Word training is no longer undertaken in law firms because 'Everyone knows how to use Word.' They are wrong!

Year after year, lawyers continue through their careers unknowingly breaking and then trying to fix Word document formatting. Few will admit that they don't understand it. This results in huge amounts of wasted time and money, with the added stress of trying to force something to work until the early hours. When the apparently trivial task of amending a Word document takes six hours of lawyer time, all of which is written off, who is going to admit it?

Microsoft Word has a huge array of fantastic tools that can help manage complex documents. But if lawyers don't know what the tools do, or where they are, they will continue to spend too many hours on a task that could take a couple of clicks.

Putting lawyers on the right path from day one takes a bit of initial investment of money and time but will reap huge long-term rewards. The ramifications of not doing it are significant.

The creation of a Fixed-Price Agreement, as outlined in this book, can become dramatically easier for lawyers if they follow a few simple guidelines.

1. Create a good template at the outset. The template will set out the style and numbering format.
2. Choose or create your house/firm styles: the styles control function dictates how your numbering and formatting work. Applying styles is VERY simple when you have a good template.
3. Learn to paste correctly: if you use CTRL C and CTRL V, you're not pasting correctly.

DOING THE WORK

Once we have been awarded the work, we must ensure we do it efficiently. Project management is outside the scope of this book, however.

Nonetheless, your lawyers will have a project management system they use. In many cases, it's just not written down. Some work types may have very clear automated stages, such as conveyancing and debt recovery. You may use electronic onboarding tools, smart forms, and links that gather information and instructions from clients.

You will have seen from the journey mapping section that it is possible to look at who does what and when, and identify who does it best. All I am saying here is it's worth looking at processes that your lawyers operate carefully, and copy and replicate best practice.

You will have gathered by now that I like processes and writing things down! I like to be able to give lawyers checklists and precedents to follow. When I managed and led my litigation team, I created the Litigation Department's Big Book of Usefulness (BBU); it contained examples of:

- Specimen holiday notes that lawyers would create for colleagues.
- What to put on your Out of Office and when.
- Request For Assistance (RFA) forms (it's OK not to know everything).

- A Blind Spot form. Put the blind spot on a file on your desk so a colleague can see you have a problem. The idea behind this was that a colleague would see it and discuss it with you.
- Team Skills Matrix – areas of law undertaken by firm members, and who is good at what area.
- Examples of precedent letters.
- How you set up file structures. In a team of 14 lawyers, we needed people doing the same thing.
- Plus loads of other departmental/file hygiene practices.

> There is a tool to make behaviour more consistent and habitual.
>
> That tool is the humble checklist.
>
> Checklists help people avoid blind spots in a complex environment.
>
> People fear checklists because they see them as dehumanising. They think if something is simple enough to be put in a checklist, a monkey can do it.
>
> Well, if that's true, grab a pilot's checklist and try your luck with a 747.
>
> Checklists simply make big screwups less likely.
>
> **Chip and Dan Heath,**
> **Switch – When Change Is Hard**

Your challenge – when reading this book – is to decide how you are going to implement VBP at your firm. What are the nettles to be grasped? How will you structure pricing? What processes will you adopt? What will go into your Practice Area Big Book of Usefulness?

SCOPE CREEP – KEEPING MATTERS ON TRACK

> If you have to eat a frog,
> eat it when it is small.
>
> **Anon**
>
> Unlike wine, bad news does not
> get better with age.
>
> **Anon**

Quite often, people get confused between scope creep and scope seep. These matters can be easily defined. Scope creep is where the client effectively asks for more than is agreed. Scope seep, by comparison, is when the lawyer voluntarily decides to provide more than agreed (typically without the client knowing they have just had a free service upgrade!).

One essential skill that lawyers need to learn, develop, and practise regularly, is how to have a conversation with a client when the matter has gone out of scope. Frogs must be eaten.

As lawyers, we all like to get engrossed in the matter with which we are dealing; we want to create the best result for the client and show that we are really good at our job.

However, inevitably in some matters, what we thought was going to happen when we scoped the original proposal doesn't happen, and the matter goes out of scope. A typical example is a litigation matter where – at the outset – a client may have said only two witnesses will be required, and it later ends up being more than that number.

Getting a second pair of eyes on a proposal can help prevent scope creep from occurring if a colleague takes a look. The second pair of eyes can often spot a matter that hasn't been addressed. The better you get at scoping, the fewer problems you will have in the future. It is important to practise this skill.

What is important is that scope creep is identified and addressed *before* the additional work is undertaken. We've already established that clients don't like surprises. The conversation has got to take place either when the matter goes out of scope and the problem arises, or at the end when you try to deliver a bill which is higher than you originally told the client it would be. The best time for a lawyer to have this conversation is when you have leverage and a better negotiating stance, which is before you do the work, not at the end when the work has been delivered.

Quite often, scope creep happens because the initial conversation was not detailed enough. As I've already stressed, it is vital to have this value conversation and understand what the client wants and needs, and have an idea about how you are going to deliver the outcome. If expectations are mismatched, and the correct assumptions are not identified, then it is a recipe for disaster. What is still more disastrous is when scope creep happens and it's not addressed.

Sometimes, you might even decide not to charge the client for the extra work that has been undertaken. But at least you can let the client know how – on this occasion – they have 'got a good deal', and they should not expect the work to be the same price next time.

When scope creep occurs, it's necessary to document the change of scope and the additional cost that has been agreed upon. Lots of books on pricing talk about creating 'change orders'. The change order for a piece of legal work can be evidenced by either sending an amended version of the FPA or a letter or an email. It's an important document; make sure it is sent!

GOLDEN RULE #7

The response to scope creep is
'I will speak to the client and agree a revised price.'

One of the advantages of creating a formal documented process is that these changes in scope can be saved with your Fixed-Price Agreement templates in your BBU, and then – the next time a similar matter arises – the original template plus the change order can be looked at and incorporated into a better document. It's all about learning.

Situations when cases go out of scope should be discussed within team meetings. For all you know, a colleague may be undertaking a similar matter, and the same issue may arise. Knowledge is power.

> One Senior Partner reports,
>
> 'We have people who recognise that the scope of a project has changed, but you would think that they were 15 years old again and asking a girl to dance.
>
> They never get round to making the phone call.'
>
> **Jim Hassett, Client Value and Law Firm Profitability**

VERSIONS AND OPTIONS

As we have already established, people value things differently, so we need to price differently.

If everyone valued everything the same, we would only need one price.

The problem with only giving one price is that we leave value on the table for those who would pay more, and we exclude those who cannot afford the price we have offered, so you lose a sale.

Options solve this problem. If we can differentiate a service, we can let the customer justify the price they are willing to pay.

WHY OPTIONS ARE ESSENTIAL

It is inevitable that, at some point, we will have to have a conversation with the client about how much they will get charged for the services provided. What could be better for clients than to receive a choice, and we let them decide the price they would like to pay from the options? We all love choice. We are used to exercising choice every day: what we buy in the shops, the size of coffee we buy, the car wash program, mobile phone data contract limits, and menus and wine lists at restaurants.

Our clients would be delighted to have a choice regarding legal services. If you don't believe me, have a word with a client and ask them whether they would like to be given price options by your lawyers. I have *never* had a client tell me 'No'.

8 PPP PENGUIN LOGIC

It makes mathematical sense!

If you are still not convinced, let's do some maths.

A choice of one price is a 50/50 choice. It's a take the price (one choice) or leave it (a second choice).

If you create three actionable choices (and one leave it choice), it increases your chances of making a sale to 75% and reduces the leave it option to 25%.

This is a great example to use with Naysayer penguins when they tell you they can't create options. There is one school of thought that it is the height of laziness if you only create one option. You know the percentages are against you.

Creating options gives clients clarity about what you are proposing to do, what you are offering, and how you will define and deliver the work. Options also help frame the conversation – you can discuss the work identified within the context of the options.

Some clients may be quite happy for the lawyer to do absolutely everything and be prepared to pay for the privilege. Others will happily get involved in the transaction and do lots of the legwork. A client may want one feature from a Gold option included in a Silver price bracket. That allows you to see what is important to that client and enables you to navigate the conversation; rescope and requote if required.

Prepare options with prices for a number of eventualities. Don't forget, not all clients fully understand what lawyers even do. Clients are only interested in outcomes.

In our personal lives, we have all encountered situations where we thought something was too expensive and didn't select it. We will also have come across things that we thought were too cheap and didn't buy them either. If we can create options, our clients decide what they want to buy, and it becomes less likely that they will not want to work with us at all.

When creating options, there are a number of elements to consider. These can include:

- Access to talent. Partner/Associate/newly qualified lawyer.
- A Guarantee that an initial case will be conducted by a named senior lawyer.
- Advice and access to the lawyer (It's not abused, but Naysayers say it will be).
- Access to other teams/departments.
- Response times. A Gold option may offer a mobile number with 24/7 access.
- Technology may play a part. You may decide that if you have a client portal, your Bronze option will be communication via a portal rather than daily emails.
- Different payment terms.
- Ability to visit sites/locations.
- Involve meetings with key personnel.
- Transfer of skills. You may be teaching/training clients how to do something – so they don't have to pay in the future.
- Commercial clients may be offered a free legal audit.
- Free admission or discounted rates to attend webinars and seminars.
- Provision of in-house seminars for the client's employees.
- Introductions and referrals via your network of clients.
- A Service Guarantee.
- Abortive costs are capped or even insured.

Carry out a Possibility Thinking brainstorming exercise and seek to create a Gold service for work types within your Practice Areas. Once you start brainstorming with your team, the Gold service options will soon be uncovered. Silver and Bronze service levels can then easily be created by taking away some of the features offered in the Gold option.

I have set out, below, just a few of the ideas created by lawyers I have worked with. This list is not intended to be in any way exhaustive. Believe it or not, with one firm, we created over 50 features for a Gold Residential Conveyancing service.

RESIDENTIAL CONVEYANCING

- Access to talent. Partner/Head of Department.
- Extended business hours, including weekends.
- Lawyers with lower-than-average caseloads, so they can respond quickly and efficiently and are available to suit the client's requirements.
- Completion monies priority service. On completion day, the client's funds will be sent at the earliest opportunity by the finance team.
- Site/new property visits, if required.
- Holiday Assurance. If the lawyer dealing with your matter goes on holiday, the firm will facilitate an introduction.
- Meetings in person. Zoom. Your office. Your home.
- Rapid Response. Chain buster – a commitment to ring up and down the chain to ascertain issues.
- Unlimited progress updates.
- Service guarantees a 24-hour response.
- Specialist funding introductions if required.
- Meeting your surveyor. Visiting the property. Negotiating price reductions.
- Transferring guarantees into your name.
- Speedy/same day completion.
- Digital property logbooks/electronic bundle of reports/deeds as PDF/house manual.
- Free meeting with a private client lawyer for Will, lasting power of attorney advice.
- Registration of property with Land Registry alert service.
- Legal and surveyors' fees insured if the matter goes abortive.
- Service guarantees.

WILLS LAWYERS

- Unlimited meetings.
- Next-day delivery if required in urgent cases.
- Will drafting plus an annual review (where you contact the client) for, say, the following three years to see if circumstances have changed.
- Home visits.
- Meetings with Independent Financial Advisors to understand all the assets available and planning undertaken.
- Advice regarding setting up a Family Investment Company (FIC) and alternative to a trust.
- Meetings with proposed executors to explain the obligations of being appointed.
- Meetings with proposed guardians of children.
- Calculation of inheritance tax liabilities.
- Advice on life interest trusts.
- Trust asset protection.
- Specific tax relief on agricultural and business properties.
- Review of shareholding structures of business.
- Holding Wills in The Workplace drafting sessions for employees of commercial clients.

LITIGATORS

I have heard litigators talk about their Gold options, including:

- Access to talent. This could include meeting all available team members and selecting which ones the client is most comfortable working with.
- Turnaround time.
- Daily/weekly updates.
- Visits at client's premises to interview witnesses.
- Meetings with Board/family members to explain litigation risks and likely outcomes.
- Creating Board reports or attendance at Board meetings to discuss the outcome of cases.
- Including drafting any necessary brief to counsel.
- Reviews to see if work is eligible for Conditional Fee Agreement.

- Updates should case law impact litigation.
- Creation of personalised, secure email/WhatsApp groups.

COMMERCIAL LAWYERS

Gold options include:

- Visit the client's commercial premises.
- Unlimited revisions of documentation.
- Visits to a client's office to explain – to the sales team – the intricacies of a SAAS agreement the lawyer had drafted.
- Same-day turnaround.
- Annual review of the contract to see if it requires updating.
- Setting up meetings with accountants early on tax planning review before completion.
- Abort fees.
- Free Legal Audits.

COMMERCIAL PROPERTY LAWYERS

Gold options include:

- Time/talent/visits etc., as above.
- Unlimited revisions.
- Lease summary review pack detailing break clauses, rent reviews and dilapidation obligations.

EMPLOYMENT LAW SERVICE

Gold options include:

- Employment contract drafting with the speed of delivery as a variable.
- Provision of employment law bulletins, on-site seminars, and free telephone advice of up to two hours a month about employment law issues.
- Conducting settlement agreement advice meetings in the employer's workplace, if required.
- Offering your firm's HR expertise to clients to assist with disciplinary proceedings and the recruitment of their staff.

NAMING OPTIONS

You will need to decide what you call your options. In this book, I refer to Gold, Silver, and Bronze options. In my proposals to clients, I badge my options Mega, Midi and Mini. In one proposal, I even named them after types of penguins. I went off that idea after someone asked me for the 'Emperor Penguin Service'… it just sounded very odd!

American Express offer Green, Gold, and Black cards. Other credit card providers offer Platinum cards. You could offer good/better/best. I have even seen proposals which talk about 'All-In', 'Virtual Lawyer' and 'Back-Office Lawyer'; a 3-star, 4-star, 5-star service; Essentials, Plus, Power. You will know that Tesco has Tesco, Finest, and Value. You can create whatever naming conventions work for you. Be creative.

POSSIBILITY THINKING

I recently worked with an ex-magic circle lawyer who had gone out on her own. We carried out a Possibility Thinking exercise on a SAAS contract offering.

Q: What could you possibly include in a Gold option for your Practice Areas?

- Review of Intellectual Property Ownership.
- Unlimited rounds of drafting to create the final version of the template agreement.
- Guidance regarding the tone of language to be used in the contract.
- Option to turn the agreement into a template.
- Offers to amend wording for
- Fast delivery.
- Assistance with explaining terms to the client's salesforce.
- Agreement to amend terms of the agreement if required in different sectors.
- Creation of the Order Form and Terms and Conditions to accompany the document.

different jurisdictions.

- Creation of set-up service documentation (what will be delivered) when software is on the customer's site.
- Post-agreement (pre-signature) checking service (making sure it's correct).
- Annual update/review of the template.
- Pre-sale negotiating support by the client's side.
- Review of customer journey and sign-up procedures.
- SAAS alert service. A 'saw this and thought of you' update if the law changes.
- Digital Signature advice. Electronic Signature and Clickwrap vs Wet Signature.

> Kate Fox once wrote about a 'truly English protest march' – 'What do we want? Gradual change. When do we want it? In due course.'
>
> This sentiment could apply to many people in law firms. But large-scale change is happening now; no protest will change that. So, we need to win over hearts and minds. AI will transform what we do and how we do it.
>
> **Paul Caddy, Shoosmiths**

SHINGLES LOGIC

You will inevitably receive a comment from a Shingles-affected lawyer who tells you, '*Every* client should have a gold service.' They are wrong. Every client should get a competent and compliant service. How and who delivers the service is another question altogether.

I've met Shingles-type lawyers who tell me they would point-blank refuse to answer the phone or respond to any form of email at the weekend, and also refuse to agree that other members of staff should do so either.

When I asked if this would still apply if it was their best client – in the middle of a multi-million-pound deal – they replied, 'Yes'.

My response to lawyers like this is not to be surprised if clients, at some point in the future, decide to instruct someone else.

We are in a service industry. Sadly, many lawyers are still unaware of this.

PRICING PSYCHOLOGY

Pricing is a complex dance of numbers and psychology. It's not just about setting a number; it's about conveying value, quality, and a compelling message to potential customers.

I do seem to be telling you – quite often – what this book is not. Here is another exclusion! This book is not an authority on the psychology of pricing, even though it is a fascinating subject.

If you would like to learn more about pricing psychology and value-based pricing, I recommend you read *Pricing Value* by Rhondalynn Korolak, which explores the impact of psychology and neuroscience on value-based pricing. The book was written for accountants, but the contents are equally relevant to lawyers.

Marketing professionals know that when it comes to pricing, it's all about understanding human behaviour. Remember the Ogilvy quote at the beginning of the book and Mark Ritson's great quote, 'Pricing is the worst managed of all marketing areas. How prices are decided is often a mixture of voodoo and bingo.' The problem with the legal profession is we have not been taught this. We don't know any voodoo! We were not even told customers don't care about time; they care about outcomes!

Quite often, lawyers will automatically believe that their clients are price-sensitive. Naysayer penguins will raise this with you.

Think about price-sensitive people; what are they really like?

- They cut out coupons and trawl the internet for discount coupons and codes.
- They will never fly long-haul direct as they will get cheaper flights with layovers in other countries.
- They have time to shop around.
- They will buy the cheapest watch... in fact, they might not have a watch at all as they can look at the time on their phones.
- They will have the cheapest mobile phone.
- They won't buy coffee in Starbucks as it is cheaper to make coffee at home and take it to work in a thermos.
- They will have packed lunches at work.
- They will only sit in the cheapest seats in the theatre.
- They will drive the cheapest car.
- They will shop at the cheapest clothes stores.
- They only make a will with a lawyer as part of charity's legacy campaign, and then not leave a legacy to the charity who has paid for the will to be drafted. (This happens!)

Do you know anyone who fits every one of these criteria? I suspect not, and that is because people are, in the main, not price-conscious at all; they are *value-conscious.* We know we have to have a value conversation with them to find out what is important to them.

BRACE YOURSELF…
incoming provocative statement

Price Sensitivity

It will always be a myth that price is the only factor.

If the lowest price was always the only factor, the lowest price would always win every contract.

Let's take a passing look at price discrimination and price tag psychology.

Price Discrimination is essentially pricing identical or largely similar goods or services at different prices by the same provider in different market segments.

- Rail companies do it all of the time. Peak fares are higher than off-peak fares.
- A Marks and Spencer sandwich meal deal is more expensive at a garage service station than at a town centre store.
- Cruise lines offer discounts if passengers book early.
- OAPs and students get different prices.
- Pubs offering happy hours sell drinks cheaper earlier in the evening than later.
- Male and female haircutting prices are dramatically different.
- Airlines charge more for a last-minute flight than one booked six months earlier.
- In fact, Southwest Air (southwest.com) charges 'customers of size' double if they can't get the armrests down when they sit in a seat.
- Online retailers of Viagra charge more than pharmacists as it is less embarrassing to buy the drug for erectile dysfunction online. (NB. This is not the voice of experience here; I read this in Tony Cram's book *Smarter Pricing*, page 55 to be precise.)

Price discrimination is rife. Why is this relevant to lawyers? Well, I think we should be prepared to embrace the concept. I am not suggesting we charge 'people of size more', but we should be prepared to alter our prices when things change and impact our businesses. This could be when there are staff shortages or spikes in the amount of work. If you are a UK property lawyer, I am sure you remember the aforementioned stamp duty holiday spike in conveyancing instructions in 2020/21. Prices can go up and down. Your pricing policies can and should be kept under review, not just set at the beginning of the year and forgotten about.

PRICE TAG PSYCHOLOGY

This is a fascinating subject as context is important when it comes to pricing. Take a look at the RH website here: https://rh.com/gb/en/england

RH is based out of a large 400-year-old stately home. According to the website, the property is 'Reimagined and open to the public for the first time… the 73-acre, 60-room property seamlessly integrates RH Interiors, Contemporary, Modern and Outdoor collections with rare art, antiques and artifacts from across the globe.' It is the UK outlet of a US global interior design brand RH.

At the property they have valet parking, they have two fantastic restaurants, a juice bar and tea salon. In the rooms of the Grade I star-listed mansion, they have fantastic furniture. There is not a price tag on anything… if you have to ask, you can't afford it!

In turn, higher fees create higher value in the buyer's eyes. How did the celebrity chef Salt Bae manage to charge £850 for a gold-plated steak? He did, and people bought them.

A small price looks smaller than a big price. That, you may think, is self-evident.

Car leasing companies usually mention a price of £259 a month, rather than £259 plus VAT x 36 months with a £3,000 deposit. The headline figure is usually a low number. You may have noticed that some menus in restaurants now omit the £ sign on the price. Why? Because taking off the £ sign makes the number for the price of the dish look smaller.

Give some thought as to how your prices can be presented. If a fee for a piece of work is £7,500 plus VAT, you could present the total (we need to be compliant at all times) and then break the fee down into, say, three instalments of £2,500 plus VAT. Three instalments make it appear more reasonable. The *Clio Legal Trends Report 2023* (which surveyed 1,446 US law firms) reported that firms which offered payment plans to clients collected 49% more monthly revenue per lawyer than firms that did not. Smaller affordable payments may help.

Pricing psychology and left-digit management (where people place greater prominence on the leftmost digit of a product's price) play a crucial role in how consumers perceive the cost of products and services. The human brain tends to process information in a way that makes it more responsive to the leftmost digits of a number. In the context of pricing, this means that the leftmost digit has a disproportionate influence on our perception of the value of a product. When we see a product or service priced at £5,999, our initial impression is that the cost is in the £5,000 range rather than the £6,000 range. This perception makes the product seem significantly cheaper, even though the actual difference is just one pound. It's a psychological trick that businesses employ to make their products appear more affordable.

Prices ending in a zero are even more interesting. Whether it's £10, £100, or £1,000, prices ending in zero have a unique psychological impact. Zeroes convey simplicity, transparency, and a sense of completeness. When we see a price like £100, we perceive it as a whole number, and our brains tend to process it as a fair, rounded value. This is why many luxury brands price their products with a zero at the end – it communicates sophistication and quality. When you set a price ending in zero, you are subconsciously communicating quality. The zero at the end makes the price look more substantial and conveys that the service is worth it.

Believe it or not, even weather plays a part in pricing. On sunny days, people are prepared to pay a premium for products and services. I'm not sure whether that works in legal services though… maybe in book 2, I will explore this!

Price tag psychology is interesting stuff and something you may wish to consider and play around with.

ESTABLISHING A PRICE

Once you have worked out who you are acting for, scoped the work, and thought about options, you need to create a price.

In many cases, your lawyers will still be linking the price they want to charge to the time they think it will take. Be alive to that.

BRACE YOURSELF…
incoming provocative statement

The process of getting to a value-based price is uncertain and ambiguous. You know this. Read the Ogilvy and Ritson quotes again.

8 PPP PENGUIN LOGIC
Are lawyers experts?

The most important question on a client's mind, and one they will ask a lawyer is, 'How much is it going to cost?' If you are holding your lawyers out as experts and they can't give an answer to that question, what kind of experts are they? They must have an answer or a way of calculating one.

LAW IS NOT A COMMODITY

To be honest, it drives me mad when I hear people talk about legal services as a commodity product/service. What you may find is that most people who attach the label 'commodity' to legal services are lawyers usually repeating what they have been told by their clients! The commodity label is particularly common in residential conveyancing and wills drafting. Let me repeat… quite often, it is our 'clients' telling us law is a commodity! What do they know? If law was simple, they would be doing it themselves and buying a will drafting kit from their local supermarket.

A commodity is a process where the service delivered is uniform in value and quality and, therefore, indistinguishable; the only distinguishable feature is price.

How can legal services EVER be a commodity? Clients are not the same. Their problems are not the same. The lawyers exercising their judgment will not be the same. The facts of their cases are different. If water – the most abundant product on the planet – can be differentiated, and we know it's the same (it's H2O), then legal services most certainly can be differentiated.

If all lawyers do is give a client a price without a value conversation taking place, then all a client has to decide on is price. So, create differentiation and communicate why it's different and the value created.

If you think that you have a 'price problem', the problem could be your proposal and the way it is communicated.

8 PPP PENGUIN LOGIC

Ditch website calculators

When you go online to certain law firm websites with a conveyancing fee calculator, you enter the value of the property, you identify if it is freehold or leasehold, then indicate if you are buying with another person and if you need a mortgage. That's pretty much it.

Behind the scenes, the website sends you a standard proposal with a fee for the basic legal work and a long list of terms and conditions and exclusions that tell you if any extra work is required you will be billed for it.

At this stage, the client has no idea if they will need a Deed of Easement, a Declaration of Trust, a licence to occupy, has a defective legal title or whether titles need to be merged… how could they know if these are required? Clients are not lawyers.

So, from automated websites, clients get a headline fee plus the uncertainty of other charges coming down the line at some point. In many cases, the websites will be from law firms who profess to 'put the client at the centre of everything we do', other than wanting to speak with them.

> Now, you will think that the problem can't get worse. It can! In 2023, I did some research into the 'add-on charges' that residential conveyancers can potentially impose on their clients. I identified over 120 separate charges. Now, I am not for one moment saying that you can cover every eventuality in an initial conversation with a client, but you can make the process easier and give choices by versioning a service offering with some of the add-on costs identified and added to the options. At present, a low entry price with up to 120 add-on charges is – in my mind – bordering on confusion marketing.

Our lawyers are in the knowledge business, selling their knowledge and judgment backed by processes and procedures. It is the knowledge and the outcomes that are being created and which are being priced.

Legal knowledge comes in many forms.

- The law, statutes, case law, rules of procedure. These are all available online. Everyone can access them.
- There is procedural knowledge. How the business of law works. What you have to do and when. Where you have to do it. Who can help you do it.
- Then there is the lawyer's judgment. The experience. The personality. The impact they can make. The training that has been received. The legal cases they have been involved in. It is back to the engineer and the hammer… it's the knowing where to tap. And that legal judgment and knowhow are key to the value and benefits that get created and delivered to clients every day.

Law is not a commodity.

At this stage, your lawyers will:

- Know the customer has decided to buy legal services. This is why they consulted a lawyer in the first place.
- Have ascertained the customer has a pain or gain need.
- Have had a value conversation with a customer who has explained their issues, and knows they have been understood.
- Understand the customer's issues.
- Will have planned out and scoped the matter.
- Have created some options.
- Be confident that they can deliver the outcome the customer wants.

Your lawyers will now need to use their judgment, but in a different way. The judgment is used to create a price which reflects the value they will create. The more experienced your lawyers get at pricing, and the more they discuss this process with colleagues, the better they will become at this. They will back themselves more often as their confidence grows. They will feel they are worth it!

Remember, at this stage, it's the lawyer judgment call… not a calculator call. Time does not feature. VBP is an art, not a science. Value is subjective; it's not rational, it's a feeling.

The proposed price(s) your lawyers come up with will not be the final signed-off price, that will be reviewed by a colleague or maybe a Value Council you set up.

At this point, encourage your lawyers to be brave and trust the system you are designing.

GOLDEN RULE #8

No one prices their own work in isolation.

You will always get two pairs of eyes on every price.

BASE PRICE

It is important that we know what our bottom line 'walk away' prices are for delivering any service. Hopefully, your Practice Management Systems will enable you to extract meaningful base cost information.

As you will have read, time recording must always come with a health warning, in my view. Depending on the culture and policies operating in your firm, and the way that your people have engaged with time recording, you may find that the data you have is inaccurate.

If, for example, your commercial lawyers are told that if any lawyer wants to write off any time, they have to have a serious conversation with their Head of Department, then don't be surprised that your lawyer's default is not to record all of their time. They will only book the time that is going to be billed, and their utilisation figures will look awful.

Your lawyers should, in their Practice Areas, create a menu of base costs for certain services. These will only be starting figures, which they are not allowed to go below.

WHEN TO DISCUSS PRICE AND VALUE

Having a conversation with the client about the value of the work you are being asked to do is fundamental to embracing and succeeding in a value-based pricing project.

Let's face it, we're always going to have to have a conversation with the customer about price and value at some time. It's better to have the conversation before the work is done rather than afterwards. It's far better to find out that the customer cannot afford the price for doing the work before the work has been delivered.

I would encourage you again (yes, again) to look at the 14 attributes of the LexisNexis report *The Riddle of Perception,* to see what is important to customers. Lawyers don't know what clients want, and lawyer assumptions are usually wrong. You won't find out what clients want until you speak with them. The LexisNexis report shows that price is not the most important factor for clients.

Common mistakes and hindering thoughts that lawyers have about pricing include:

- A belief that the lawyer is not worth their hourly rate.
- Being uncomfortable about justifying a price.
- Being unwilling/afraid to deal with price objections.
- A dislike for talking about money.
- Feeling uncomfortable about negotiating with a client.
- A mistaken belief that the client won't pay the price put to them.

BIG SURVEY QUESTIONS
LEGAL ICONOCLASTS

In 2022, I commissioned a thought leadership and Pricing Confidence Survey for an event I co-organised. I was delighted to receive responses from 63 firms located all over the world.

One of our questions was:

Q: Does your firm have a clearly defined Pricing Strategy, or do you leave it to individual lawyers to price matters on a best-efforts basis?

As I previously indicated, this is a question first asked during a webinar I did for the Law Society of England and Wales. The response came out at 53/47 with 53% of individual matters being priced by individuals on a best-efforts basis, and 47% of firms saying they have a Pricing Strategy and policy which is consistently applied.

One of the other questions that we asked was:

Q: If you made no changes, what would you expect to happen to the firm's profitability in the next three years?

Read the question again. It was if you make **no change** … what will happen to profitability?

- 18% of respondents said profitability would decline.
- 24% said the profitability would be static.
- 10% said an increase of less than 5% per annum.
- 22% said an increase of 5 to 10% per annum.
- 19% said an increase of 10 to 30% per annum.
- 7% said an increase of over 30% per annum

What was interesting about this question, was the number of firms who were going to grow by 10% or more and *not change anything.*

We looked at those firms that were expecting a 10% plus increase in profits, and the following characteristics became evident.

- 21% were charging by billable hour.
- 48% gave a fixed fee.
- 7% were a hybrid of the billable hour and a fixed fee.
- 24% priced based on the known value to the client.

Crucially, other differences included:

- 81% asked clients what success looks like on their cases.
- 85% had a clear business development and positioning strategy.
- 77% had a clear Pricing Strategy and Vision.
- 62% asked the client about service expectations.
- 75% asked what business or personal outcome they wanted to achieve.

- 69% agreed clear service standards with the client.
- 62% empowered their people to decide not to work with a client if they believed that the client's value was low.
- 75% had strong management and capable champions who could implement change.

Remember this survey. You may need to refer some of your Naysayer penguins to it.

If any reader would like a full copy of the Legal Iconoclasts survey, drop me a line at: shaun@bigyellowpenguin.co.uk

SHINGLES LOGIC

In the Legal Iconoclasts survey, we also asked:

Q: What proportion of your client relationships are profitable?

This was either based on what respondents definitely knew, or at least had strong evidence about.

Worryingly, 40% of firms did not know what proportion of their clients were profitable.

PRICING HIGHER OR LOWER

There will inevitably be times when a lawyer – after they have had the second pair of eyes on the price – will make an impassioned case to propose a higher or lower price.

Some of the factors which may impact the price change are listed below.

You may decide to price lower:

- To get into a niche market if you have to effectively 'buy' some work to gain experience.
- You are reusing established knowhow. You may have the precedents and documentation already.
- You can delegate the work to junior personnel.
- There is the opportunity for customers to do more of the work.

- You are pitching against known competition, and winning the client from them could cause them some difficulty.
- There are cross-selling/upselling opportunities for other departments.

You may price higher:

- If the customer is going to be difficult to manage and serve.
- To try to make the work go away.
- If there is a risk of not being paid.
- There is a degree of urgency.
- The fact that you are a renowned expert in your field.
- You may be a brand that is known for charging high, and brand protection is important.
- There may be no competition.

PRICING LITIGATION – PEBBLES IN A POND

If I am talking about VBP in a room full of lawyers, I will inevitably get a question about pricing litigation. It's usually, 'How can you price litigation when you don't know what is going to happen?' My answer is always the same. It is 'you can'… at least the initial steps of a matter.

In 2017, I met an American lawyer called Chris Marston at a conference I attended in Texas. Chris produced a drawing showing a number of concentric circles, which he and his team use internally to decide what to include in his firm's scoping documents.

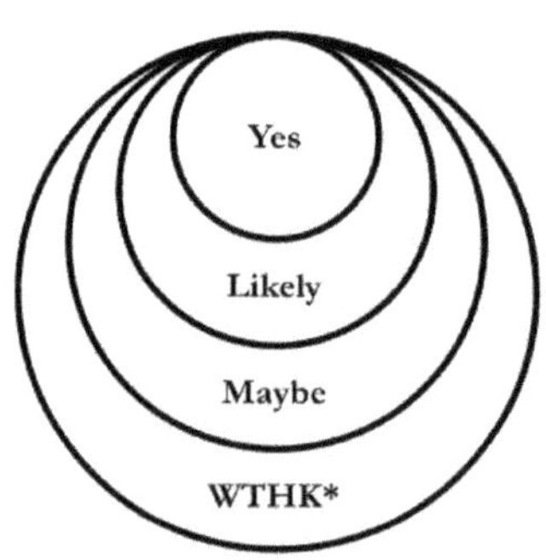

* Who The Hell Knows

- The inner circle is 'Yes' work. Work you know you have to do; say, file a defence to a claim or draft a letter before action.
- The next circle is 'likely'. What is likely to happen.
- Then you get into 'Maybe'. What theoretically may happen.

- Last circle – WTHK – Who The Hell Knows.

In England and Wales, the Courts have required litigation cost budgets to be filed for some years. Most law firms in England and Wales that practice litigation will have created many costs budgets. There are many cost lawyers who do nothing else. There is a wealth of knowledge about the stages and cost 'estimates' of what you should put into a scoped litigation case. To be honest, I don't understand why litigators get so anxious about this.

Let's look at a worked example.

8 PPP PENGUIN LOGIC

I use Chris's circles slightly differently. I explain the circle concepts to clients and mention that what I would like to show is what happens when you drop a pebble in a pond.

The innermost circle is the first event. I believe that lawyers should initially just price the 'yes' and 'likely' work to start off with. If you take a boundary dispute, for example, can your lawyer draft a letter before action on a neighbour/boundary dispute (the innermost circle)? The answer is 'Yes'. Can they give a fixed price for that? 'Yes'.

What is likely to happen after the letter before action is sent? The answer is one of three things. Firstly, nothing; the letter is ignored. Secondly, you receive a vitriolic letter from the neighbour themselves. Thirdly, you receive a vitriolic letter from the neighbour's lawyers. Can you price for those three eventualities? The answer is yes.

The third circle is 'maybe'. You're not quite sure what's going to happen.

The 4th circle is 'Who The Hell Knows' (WTHK).

Price what you know and explain to clients that you will price the outer rings of the concentric circle – the 'maybe' and 'WTHK' work – when you get there. It's very rare a client would be unhappy about that. They know we are not mind readers.

Clients are not usually expecting a price for the whole matter to completion. They know that not all cases go to trial anyway.

However, if they are adamant that they want a cost for every eventuality, look at cost budgets or engage a good costs lawyer/cost draughtsman and scope out the matter to conclusion. As happens when doing these budgets, if a client does want a fully costed, guaranteed price, some brainstorming will be required. The price will be high.

VALUE COUNCIL/TWO PAIRS OF EYES

> Lawyers must learn to accept no one has a silver bullet perfect solution that many committees seem to be waiting for.
>
> Many firms that wait for the proven perfect solution could go out of business before it arrives.
>
> **Jim Hassett, Client Value and Law Firm Profitability**

One of the golden rules of value-based pricing is that no one prices their work in isolation. If you think about it, in the legal profession, we come across 'two pairs of eyes' on many occasions. Why do barristers have clerks? You agree the fee with the clerk not with the barrister. Often, you receive an eye-watering quote for what the clerk wants to charge, and you may try to haggle and get it down, although usually these attempts are unsuccessful. The clerks know the value of the tenants in their chambers, and know that they are in demand and that others will pay more. The clerk's job is to extract every pound they can from the solicitors that are instructing them, and they are usually very good at it.

Why do footballers have agents? Why do actors have agents? It's the same reason.

Within whatever structure you create, you will need to have a mechanism for checking the proposed prices that are created by your lawyers.

CREATING A VALUE COUNCIL

The Value Council will be the guardians of the VBP process you create. It is important that the members of the Value Council are evangelical about the strategic project and enthusiastic about overseeing its success.

The Value Council will see cases week-in, week-out – possibly even daily – and will ensure that there is parity in pricing.

When lawyers come to present cases to the Value Council, they have to give confidence boosts to the proposers. They must be alive to the fact that lawyers who present to them might be suffering from low Pricing Confidence. They have to be enthusiastic about the work that is being undertaken and become a critical friend of the options that have been created.

The Value Council must undertake a profit protection role. They must be prepared to identify if a customer is not a good fit and turn the work away.

They should ensure that teams are creating their own BBUs and processes. If teams are not bringing cases to the Value Council, then they should enquire why this is the case. Teams should not be allowed to opt out of the process.

The Value Council should be champions of the training systems you create and be the custodians of the knowledge management processes where the learning is stored.

When setting up a formal Value Council, expect the group to meet more often at the beginning of the project. The reason for this is that all participants will be on a learning curve and will need to get into a rhythm of working together. There are likely to be more questions from participants in the beginning, and more questions will be asked of lawyers bringing cases to the Council. Eventually, you will develop business rules and set parameters in relation to new business and business-as-usual projects.

Authority limits may need to be set between teams with Heads of Practice Areas being involved. There may be mission-critical projects which have to come to the Value Council as they may impact a whole firm.

The role of the Value Council is as follows:

Oversight

1. To oversee the pricing, opportunity management, and onboarding of work coming into the firm.
2. To carry out reviews of work coming into the business. If they don't know the client, it works even better as they will be more objective and have no emotional baggage that impacts the lawyer-client relationship.
3. The chair of the Value Council must be a passionate champion of the process. Leadership is essential and it may demand that some unpopular decisions are made. Sometimes, individual opinions have to be sacrificed for the good of the firm.

Financial

1. Ensuring the firm are price setters, not price chasers.
2. They need to ensure the work undertaken is profitable.
3. To increase prices if required.
4. They need to ensure the firm does not embark on a race to the bottom in certain areas. Some lawyers will start talking about the mythical market rate.

5. They must crucially set up a framework for dealing with base cost pricing. Any lawyers ignoring the base price figures will have to be challenged.

Act as ambassadors and champions of change

1. Adopt a heads-up looking role, and continually think about how prices can be packaged and improved.
2. The Value Council need to act as ambassadors of change and be enthusiastic about the work that they undertake.
3. They need to create an atmosphere where lawyers feel confident about pricing – where success is celebrated. Recognition and congratulating people on a job 'well done' will become commonplace.
4. Create a list of probing questions that they make sure are asked. The lawyers will get used to the fact that the questions are coming and will anticipate them and prepare answers. As a result, the process gets better.
5. The Value Council will need to attend team meetings, evangelise about pricing, and ensure it is kept on the radar of all teams.

Quality Control

1. They need to ensure that clients instructing the firm are the right clients.
2. Ideal customers should be identified. Teams should be prepared to explain why the subject of the proposal meets those criteria.
3. They need to be sense checkers. Are the assumptions and exclusions valid? Is this work in accordance with the firm's strategic aims?
4. They may amend options.

Guardians of the process

1. They need to ensure that the necessary tools and materials for the implementation of VBP are created and developed.
2. They need to ensure that bad pricing practices are called out.
3. They need to set the frameworks upon which pricing will operate, and ensure the frameworks are amended when needs be.
4. They need to agree the processes for how the pricing documentation will be created, stored, and reviewed. And how learnings will be disseminated.
5. They must keep the pricing momentum going in the firm. It may well be the case that there are some lawyers in your organisation who should not price at all.
6. They need to be passionate advocates of training.
7. They need to ensure that HR teams change their recruitment policies and that prospective lawyers joining the firm are asked how they currently price at their existing firms. This information needs to be reviewed, collated, and stored.

8. They will need to make sure AARs happen.

Questions that lawyers should anticipate from the Value Council include:

1. What happens if the client doesn't use us?
2. Have we got the experience and knowhow to solve this problem?
3. Have we identified all of the areas that require our attention?
4. Are there other work areas where we can get work from this customer?
5. Is the customer's outcome realistic? Is it something we can deliver?
6. What are the risks associated with this work?
7. Who referred this customer to us? Are they likely to be upset if we decide we do not want to act?
8. Is the timeline for undertaking the work likely to cause problems?
9. Have they consulted other lawyers? If so, who? If so, why have they come to us?
10. How profitable is the organisation? Can it afford to pay us?
11. Are they a sophisticated buyer of legal services?
12. Do we know and/or rate their other professional advisers, such as banks and accountants?
13. Does taking on this matter open a new market for the firm?
14. Do you like this client? Are they likely to be easy to deal with?
15. What have they been like dealing with to date?
16. What is your (the lawyer's) gut feeling?

A Value Council is not just the preserve of a larger firm. Perth-based lawyers Lynn & Brown have 13 lawyers but have a formal Value Council made up of lawyers and operations staff to review their cases.

Obviously, how and where your Value Council meet is a matter for you.

The size of the Council will vary by firm. As a rule, smaller is better. Have a mix of members across the firm. Invite operations, finance and marketing professionals to be members, in addition to lawyers. Consider a fixed term for members. Spread the knowledge and increase the experience across the business.

In many cases, once the Value Council has become established and developed its own rhythm, the meetings can – in some cases – be a series of emails.

One large regional law firm I know has Value Council rules of engagement, which are essentially:

- The Head of Department would approve to one level.
- Significant jobs were subject to 'Colleague Challenge'.

- Hold a pricing forum monthly and highlight exemplars of innovation. This creates conversations.
- Premium price for urgency. Price for Value. Price the customer. Price the risk.
- Versioned products.

A BIG SURVEY QUESTION

Q: Would you (the lawyer) like pricing to be carried out by another person so you can be left to get on with the job?

A: Usually, when I ask this question, I find that 20% of lawyers in a firm would rather not price at all. They would prefer to be given the work once the price has been agreed.

Depending on the makeup of your firm, it might be something that you have to consider.

8 PPP PENGUIN LOGIC

Own the prices you set

Quite often, particularly with residential conveyancing, lawyers maintain that they should lower their prices because their competitors have. They will suggest this even though they might be dealing with returning, existing customers; customers who haven't even rung around asking what the competitors' prices are.

Lawyers also often complain that the amount of work they have to do on a real estate transaction is so much more than the estate agents have to do, and bemoan the fact the estate agents are charging much more.

My response is always the same. It is the residential conveyancing lawyers who set the prices for their services, *not* the estate agents. They may be envious of the fact that estate agents are able to charge more, but they conveniently forget each legal team is responsible for their Pricing Strategy.

PRESENTING OPTIONS

> Take pricing away from people who don't feel confident in doing it.
>
> Better to let someone else take it on, and not leave value on the table.
>
> **Ron Baker**

So, we've got to the stage where we know that price has to be discussed. The question is *when* and *who* should discuss it.

You won't be surprised to read, again(!), that I believe the price should be discussed when you have maximum leverage, and that is before you've undertaken the work. It is very difficult to have a pricing conversation after the work has been undertaken and the work has been delivered.

There are a number of tips when it comes to presenting options.

1. Present your most expensive option first. It's the one that will be read first. It is the one that you should be most proud of. Once the client reads the second and third options, they will realise they're not as good as the first one that they have read. We want the client to experience FOMO (fear of missing out).
2. When talking through the options, there is no need to negotiate against yourself. Do not use language which talks about 'our normal rate'. You may wish to consider amending your language here by talking about 'price' and not 'fee'. You can talk about an 'agreed price'.
3. Put a time limit for acceptance of the proposal. No proposal should last forever. If a client comes back in three months' time, you may be far busier then.
4. You should also copyright all of your proposals to ensure that you retain ownership. Make it difficult for your client to show the proposal to others.
5. If you genuinely have lawyers who dislike discussing prices, get someone else to do it. Chris Marston (of concentric circles fame) incentivises his staff to make sales and allows those who are good at pricing to have those conversations. I

appreciate that for some firms, this might not be an option. But where you can, I would suggest you play to your strengths.

GOLDEN RULE #9

Present your most expensive option first
and be proud of it.

MEETING THE CLIENT

Again, this will come as a shock to many lawyers, a face-to-face meeting is usually the best option. However, it is probably the one that is least utilised. A face-to-face meeting allows clients to deal with any questions and objections quickly. Think about it, when you want a new kitchen at home, the builder/kitchen designer will want to take you through what they are proposing on-site and explain how the project works. They will want to find out – sooner rather than later – if there are areas where you may change your mind. When sending a proposal by email, you completely lose control of the process.

Where you meet, and in what circumstances, will also impact the proposal.

If you want to charge a premium price, then it is important that you/your firm look and feel premium.

We all know that we can buy a bottle of branded beer from the local corner shop, and it will cost us less than in a luxury hotel. We pay the hotel price for the same beer because of the context in which we are drinking and experiencing the serving of the beer. If you have looked at the website of the palatial furniture shop near my house (mentioned earlier), I can tell you a bottle of mineral water there costs £9. I am still not quite over that!

If you want to charge higher prices, you must look and act like you are worth it.

You may need to take a good look at your business and how it operates.

- Is your website up-to-date?
- Is your marketing collateral high-end?
- Are your office meeting rooms clean and tidy?
- Do you offer decent coffee? Do you offer coffee at all?
- Do you have clean bathrooms?

- Do you and your lawyers look quality?

These are all things that will influence a client's perception about your operation.

DEMONSTRATE YOU UNDERSTAND THE CLIENT'S PROBLEM

The important thing when discussing the proposal with the client is to convey that you really do understand the issue with which they are faced with. Remember the LexisNexis report that highlighted the number one feature between parties: clients want their lawyers to *understand* their circumstances. You can explain to the client with authority how the matter is going to progress.

You can explain what you will be doing and what the client will be doing. If it is a litigation case, where you need to adopt the pebble in the pond principle, you will talk about the stages.

You will explain the options that you have created. You can reassure the client that all of the options will get the outcome that they desire. It's just the mechanics of getting there that will be different.

You will want to talk about the team that will be representing the client. You will supply contact details.

If you have testimonials or recent articles that are relevant, you will mention them.

If any trade legal directories rate your firm or individual lawyers in the area of interest to the client, you may wish to mention them.

If your lawyers are real experts in their field, point it out. In, say, a complicated trust matter, you may want to point out that the lawyer is STEP qualified, but do not make the mistake of assuming that the client will understand what STEP means (Society of Trust and Estate Practitioners). You may have to explain that the lawyer has just had to take extra legal exams over a period of years to gain this extra qualification in a complicated area of law.

You may want to talk about relevant industry awards that you have won in certain areas to demonstrate your sector knowledge. Meeting with a client is the opportunity to blow your own trumpet. However, you may want to anticipate any hindering thoughts that the clients may hold, and which they have not asked you.

- They may want to know if you had successes in this area of law.
- They may be interested in your client feedback.
- They certainly want to know that you understand their needs.
- They want to know that you are efficient.
- They want to know that you will keep to the timetable and keep them informed.
- They want to know how you will communicate with them.

This is your opportunity to reassure them.

WHY YOU?

Always be prepared to answer the question, 'Please sum up why we should choose your company.' It's a question that will be in the purchaser's mind; sometimes, they even ask it. You may even want to raise it for them.

If it is asked, you need to link your answer back to your FPA and the value proposition.

- Demonstrate you understand the issues and have understood the client's pain/gain.
- You have created a choice of solutions for them, which demonstrates your superior capabilities.
- You have given the client a choice. This shows your confidence in being able to deliver the outcome the client wants.

And then deliver the final and most compelling reason that differentiates you from the competition. 'We will always agree a price with you for the work we carry out.'

8 PPP PENGUIN LOGIC

Clients like choice and don't always choose the cheapest option

I worked with an employment lawyer for a large Midlands firm that had a commercial client who wanted some employment contracts. The options which the employment lawyer gave the client were:

1. I can send you some template documents with some explanatory notes. You can create the documents yourself, and I will check them. Price £2,000.
2. I will do the work for you in three weeks' time. Price £5,000.
3. I will do the work for you tomorrow. Price £8,000.

The client chose the £8,000 option. For them, delivery in a timely manner was very important. They knew they could get the work done cheaper by the same lawyer, but they chose not to take this option. Was the client happy? Yes! Was the lawyer happy? Yes! Was the firm happy? Yes!

GUARANTEE

If you are offering a Service Guarantee, this is the opportunity to talk about it. In reality, we guarantee our services every time we open a file. However, in most cases, we never *talk* about guaranteeing our service. It is important to remember that you are offering a guarantee of the service, **not** the outcome. Remember, even if you are offering a fixed discount off the price on a Service Guarantee, very few clients will ever call on it, as long as you deliver what you told them you'd deliver.

ASK FOR THE BUSINESS

It is absolutely vital that your lawyers get used to asking for the business. So often, I will hear and see lawyers 'if' the work away. By this, I mean that they will either say on the telephone, 'If you want to go ahead, please ring us back' or 'If you need anything further from me, please let me know and I will await to hear from you.'

Our conversations with clients should conclude with phrases such as:

- 'Shall we go ahead and get started?
- 'How does this sound to you? Shall we proceed?'
- 'Can I ask you to sign the agreement now, so we can start with the compliance paperwork and then start work?'
- 'Would you like me to get the team together so we can start on Monday?'
- 'Which of the three service options are you looking at choosing?'

Remember, the client is a buyer of legal services. They are going to buy from someone. Ask for the business before your competition does.

8 PPP PENGUIN LOGIC

You are worth it!

A conveyancing lawyer developed a premium/urgent price offering for removing the matrimonial restriction from a title to a property. Often, when the finances on a divorce are settled, the parties want any restrictions removed immediately. The base fee for the work increased from £195 to £495.

An employment lawyer – faced with a pressing restrictive covenant matter requiring an urgent cease and desist letter

– asked the client to agree to a price of £3,500. The client did so as they were keen for action to be taken straightaway since the commercial consequences of not taking any action were severe. The lawyer applied his version of the lawyer scoring matrix and the answers to the questions prompted a higher price. Ordinarily, the lawyer would have only asked for £1,500.

Two litigation lawyers become very bullish implementing the golden rule of 'two pairs of eyes' on every price on their respective cases. The more they practised, the more confident they became. Between them, on one matter, they increased the initial proposed base price from £3,500 to £7,500. Their confidence became infectious, and they realised they were worth it!

Two lawyer partners became slightly competitive in seeking to increase prices on what they regarded as standard matrimonial documents, such as separation agreements. Initially, the partners started for an additional £100 or so when enquiries were made. As they became more confident, and saw that the price increases were not being objected to, they continued to charge more. By the end of my project with the firm, the starting base costs for some standard documents had increased by over £850.

A lawyer sought to gain their first 'pump fist' price of £950 on a matter they would have ordinarily charged out for an hour of their time at £250. It was an important first step towards value-based pricing as the lawyer sought to move away from linking the price to time and towards the value created.

AFTER-ACTION REVIEWS (AARS)

An After-Action Review is a methodology used by the military to review combat missions. They are an essential debriefing exercise. The review involves asking four simple questions:

1. What did we think was going to happen?
2. What actually happened?
3. What went well and why, and what can be improved?
4. What lessons have we learnt from the exercise?

The nearest thing lawyers get to an AAR is when a formal complaint is made, and a Compliance Partner will ask a lawyer to dig out the old file and explain how they should respond to the client's complaint. The Compliance Partner will ask:

1. What was expected to happen?
2. What actually happened?
3. What went wrong?

The fourth AAR question is rarely asked or considered, and rarely – if ever – is the information communicated to the rest of the team.

Lawyers have a tendency to be ashamed of complaints that are made against them. In fact, many lawyers regard complaints from clients as a personal attack on their integrity. They will often come up with a dozen reasons why the client is wrong. They may even go on the offensive with the client.

GOLDEN RULE #10

Create an AAR Process.

Let's learn from our mistakes… lawyers are human!

When you are considering how the AAR process could work in your organisation, it is necessary to set some ground rules. The following will assist:

1. A genuine, no-blame culture. Discussing a mistake should not be regarded as a career-limiting exercise.
2. The review should not be used as a forum to play the blame game. The idea is to learn from mistakes so they do not happen again.
3. AARs are not a lecture. Your Compliance Partner, in particular, will need to understand this. They are an opportunity to learn, and they should not be an opportunity to berate.
4. The review should involve all of those who worked on the project. Everybody should be encouraged to participate in the review.
5. You should work through the four questions.
    - What was expected to happen?
    - What happened?
    - What went well and why, and what can be improved?
    - What lessons have we learned?

Some firms even go as far as involving the clients in the review. The important thing is to record the results, share the results, and learn from them.

In his book, *Implementing Value Pricing*, Ron Baker listed several AAR questions to consider. I've selected some here.

1. Did we add value for this client?
2. Could we have added more value?
3. Did the fee represent a fair portion of the value we created? Could we have captured more?
4. Did we leave money on the table?
5. If we were to do this engagement again, how would we do it? Have we created any new intellectual capital that we can use with other clients? Have we communicated the lessons learned to our colleagues? What were the needs of the client? Did we address them?
6. Did this engagement enhance our relationship with the client?
7. Did we have the right team on this engagement?
8. What could we do better next time?
9. How can we thank the client for their business?

I have added a few more.

1. What do we think the client would say about our performance?
2. Should we have taken this case on at all? Did we have the skills?
3. Were there any red flags we missed?
4. Was this enjoyable to do? Was it fun? Would we like more of this work?
5. Should we avoid this kind of work in the future?
6. Was it profitable, financially?

One of the reasons why I'm so keen that After-Action Reviews take place is to capture learning, experience, and intelligence. It also serves to make public that cases do go wrong and that lessons can be learned. The learnings will enable you and your troops to develop and continue to develop your pricing tools and scope, craft conversations, and ultimately create better proposals. Confidence and skill levels improve as a result.

The Big Books of Usefulness – that I encourage you to create in your teams – can become part of your knowledge-capturing process.

WORDS WITH THE WISE

Kirsty Pappin, Aries Legal Practice Management

With any project, especially one that has not been ventured before – there needs to be a main person overseeing the entire project, and this person must take responsibility for ensuring the roadmap is followed. But, as should be the case with any project, there needs to be complete transparency, so if anything were to happen to the lead, someone else can step in and continue the good work.

David Gilroy, Conscious Solutions

Are people price-sensitive? If you're lucky enough to see inside somebody's world, whether that's physically or virtually, you can absolutely get a sense of their appetite for money based on what you see on the wall behind them.

A Managing Partner once asked me, 'Would you mind sitting with our conveyancing team?' I went and sat with them, and just did my own work whilst listening in. We changed one thing, which was when they were talking about the property price, particularly on the buying side, when you'd say, 'Where are you buying?'

'I'm buying in Banbury.'

'How much are you spending?'

'I'm spending £550,000.'

Then I told the employee to say, 'Wow! That's a lot of money. We had better make sure we get this right for you.' Their conversion rate went up something like 40% as they had reiterated the value in the client's mind.

Katherine Thomas, Free Range Lawyers

A fundamental issue to consider is lawyers' own perceptions of the value that they deliver. That is both as a firm, but also personally and psychologically; what is my value in this profession? I produce a lot and I work a lot. I bill a lot of time, which enables me to make a lot of money, and so – therefore – I am worthwhile. I mean, that's pretty existential.

When we're talking about using AI and flipping the way that you price, there's so much more. There is such an education piece around how to have those value-based pricing conversations with clients and then how to come up with a price. Value-based pricing is far more complex and requires much more interaction and collaboration, and I think that's a real challenge.

Chris Marston, Exemplar Companies Pbc

What is key for the lawyers at Exemplar is to have the relationship level right. And that is done by the people best suited to do it, which is often sometimes not the person who's going to do the work. Sometimes, not even the person who brought in the work.

We have a team approach. The person to close and secure the work has to be a subject matter expert and understand how to frame a value proposition, and not miss any major gaps. They'll almost always accompany the relationship holder to the client meeting,

They just don't have to lead the meeting.

We have reserved pricing spreadsheets. We developed a reserve pricing tool which helps people estimate resource utilization as a means of establishing a reserve price. A reserve price is not the price. It is the minimum price which we should be willing to work for. And then we have a value-based price, which is the price that it is worth to the customer. And the difference between the two is the alpha. The alpha value is what we seek to create in client situations, the gap between the reserve price and the value price.

Jon Whittle, Jon Whittle Consulting

Clients don't understand law firms, and they don't understand the law. That's why they're briefing a law firm. So, the mechanics of what law firms do under a hood for most clients, even quite big clients, is irrelevant. The reason you buy a professional is you don't know how to do it yourself. You don't care how they work. By and large, you don't care what the mechanics are of fixing something.

With the gold, silver, and bronze approach, it must be carefully managed in the communication. If you have a leaking tap and call a plumber, and he says, 'I could use the big wrench, or if you want me to, I could use the power wrench, or if you want me to, I could take out the plumbing and put in some new plumbing', you're thinking, I've just got a dripping tap. I don't care. And you're telling me I could spend £50 or £1,000 getting the tap fixed. Unless there is a compelling reason for me, as a consumer, to spend more money, why would I? Unless the value is explicit to me, not to you.

If you are to band your service in different levels of quality or different levels of value, however you describe the banding, it has to be communicated in a way that makes sense to the consumer. What I see, when I talk to law firms about improving services, is they are like plumbers. It always comes back to the mechanics of what they do.

CRIB SHEET
READING & VIEWING

WATCH

Choice, Happiness, and Spaghetti Sauce

Don't believe options are a good thing? Watch this 17-minute Ted Talk. Ask yourself what options we can offer our clients.

Tipping Point author Malcolm Gladwell gets inside the food industry's pursuit of the perfect spaghetti sauce – and makes a larger argument about the nature of choice and happiness.

https://www.ted.com/talks/malcolm_gladwell_choice_happiness_and_spaghetti_sauce?language=en

WATCH

Legally Yours

Karen Finch from Legally Yours interviews David Wells from Moores Law in Melbourne. They discuss VBP, including MAP Moores Agreed Pricing.

https://vimeo.com/515534945

READ

When Sales Become Value

By Heather Suttie

https://heathersuttie.ca/insights/when-sales-becomes-value/

READ

Solicitor Lambasted by Judge over 'Primark service' for £100m Will

Read this article (and weep). What do you think would have been the correct price for the will in question?

https://www.lawgazette.co.uk/news/solicitor-lambasted-by-judge-over-primark-service-for-100m-will/5111349.article

READ

A-Z Retail Tricks to Make You Shop

https://www.spacehijackers.org/html/ideas/archipsy/tricks.html

TIPS/CHECKLISTS

1. Preserve your pricing integrity.
2. If you like playing with tech or know someone who does – have a play with the Smapley Journey Maps tool. You can use them for two weeks for free:
    - https://www.smaply.com/tools/journey-maps

EXERCISES

EXERCISE 1

1. Create a draft FPA for a typical matter that your team deals with.
2. What Service/Price Guarantee are you prepared to offer?

3. Create your own pricing vocabulary list.
    a. Look to strip out references to hours/time in your proposals.
    b. Talk about the agreed price. Not a fixed-fee.
    c. Will your price options have names? E.g., Gold, Silver, Bronze/Mega, Midi, Mini?

EXERCISE 2

Lawyer Scoring Matrix

Select questions you can pose to your lawyers to get them to think about price uplifts. Choose questions which resonate with your team.

Some questions you may want to consider as part of this process are:

1. Have you done this work before? Is it urgent? Is it complicated? Is it very time-consuming? Is it risky?
2. Are they likely to pay well, and on time?
3. Are the lawyers (if any) on the other side going to ease or hinder a successful outcome?
4. Was the client referred? Does the referrer send lots of work? Is this a special case matter?
5. Are the clients a good strategic fit for the business?
6. Is the client likely to create a highly profitable relationship?
7. Is this client a good, desirable commercial proposition?
8. How needy are they likely to be?
9. How has client communication with you been to date?
10. How busy are you?
11. Do you like them? Will they be fun to work with?

Create a scoring mechanism 1-5, with 5 being high (e.g., really busy is a 5).

Once you have settled on some questions, think of the scoring bands to prompt you and a colleague to discuss the uplift bracket the matter falls into.

The scoring bands should drive you to take some action and have an open conversation with your colleague/pricing buddy/Value Council (depending on the score total).

What would be the scoring thresholds/brackets for a table which had the following categories:

- Proceed.
- Consider uplift.

- Substantial uplift.
- Refer to management.

What else can you ask yourself and your team? Be creative.

Below is a Scoring Matrix created by Lynn & Brown.

Create your own template. What should go in?

Overview	LOW 1	2	3	4	HIGH 5	N/A- known
Complexity	☐	☐	☐	☐	☐	☐
Urgency	☐	☐	☐	☐	☐	☐
Desirability of client	☐	☐	☐	☐	☐	☐
Sophistication	☐	☐	☐	☐	☐	☐
Overview						
Likelihood of early agreement	☐	☐	☐	☐	☐	☐
Level of negotiations required	☐	☐	☐	☐	☐	☐
Level of disclosure required	☐	☐	☐	☐	☐	☐

Notable Client Qualities	Difficult	Poor	Fair	Excellent	N/A- known
Communication with us	☐	☐	☐	☐	☐
Organisation	☐	☐	☐	☐	☐
Expectations	☐	☐	☐	☐	☐
Dependence / neediness	☐	☐	☐	☐	☐
Communication between parties	☐	☐	☐	☐	☐
Expectations of other party	☐	☐	☐	☐	☐
Level of negotiations required	☐	☐	☐	☐	☐

EXERCISE 3

You present a price.

Your client objects.

What could you say to the client to explain your price without discounting it?

EXERCISE 4

Does your firm look and feel as though it offers a premium service?

How does it physically look?

What is 'premium' about it?

Are there examples of your firm being a budget operation in the eyes of a customer?

EXERCISE 5

Focus on the value you offer. Write down what makes you different – why you charge what you do – then say it out loud, over, and over until it becomes natural; then be confident saying it to the client or prospect.

POSSIBILITY THINKING QUESTIONS TO POSE

1. Ask each Practice Area to create a list of the possible assumptions and exclusions they could incorporate into their FPA. Complete a list of the most likely ones and save them in the BBU.
2. How can you possibly get two pairs of eyes on every price in each Practice Area?

EXPOSURE DRAFTS
BY GREG KYTE
IT'S NOT THAT I CAN'T SLEEP. IT'S THAT I CAN'T BILL MY TIME WHEN I DO SLEEP.

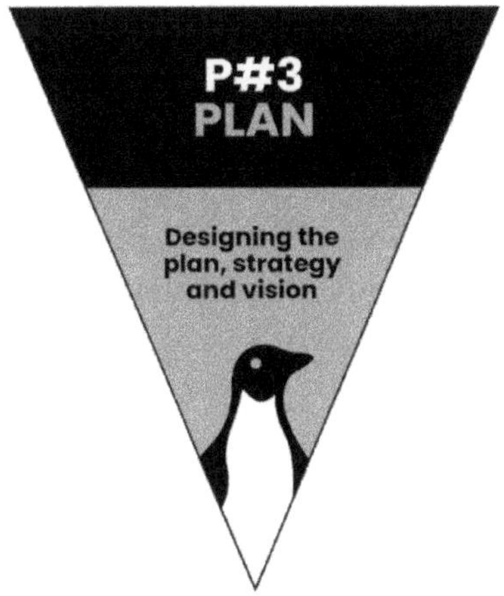

P#3 PART 3
VISION

> A good Vision Statement explains in specific terms what the world would look like if everything we did was wildly successful.
>
> **Simon Sinek**

YOUR VISION

So, at this stage, you now know the basics of value-based pricing and, hopefully, your head is swirling with thoughts about how – in the future – VBP might be developed in your firm. Your thoughts may include:

- What do you want to achieve?
- Where do you want to be in the future?
- How will you build psychological safety into your process?
- Is it going to be built on shared beliefs?
- Is it a commitment to shape the future?
- Does it involve trust and accountability?
- Whether the Vision has a commitment from the leadership to develop and support the strategy and make it a reality.

It's absolutely crucial – if you're going to embark on a value-based pricing project – that you have a Vision of what you would like the outcome to be and a Strategy to achieve it.

As you know, my strong recommendation is to write down your Vision thoughts and develop a Pricing Strategy and process. A process that can be followed, stress-tested, amended, and developed again.

The quotation below should be motivation enough to create a Pricing Vision.

> Pricing for value is, to my mind, one of the most critical challenges for providers of legal services at the moment. The need to understand value – from a client's perspective – and the ability to construct an appropriate pricing offer are now key attributes of a modern practitioner.
>
> **Professor Stephen Mayson**

LEGAL WORK IS HARD

Let us start with a few home truths about legal work:

- It's a risky activity. Let's face it, that is why Professional Indemnity Insurance premiums are so high.
- If a case is handled negligently and a claim arises, it can result in a professional indemnity insurance claim of tens/hundreds of thousands of pounds.
- The work is complicated.
- The work is high-pressure.
- We work in a regulated environment.
- High attention to detail is required.
- There are loads of litigation firms that will pursue negligent lawyers on a no-win, no-fee basis.
- All transactions and clients are different. No two are the same.
- Some clients will be a joy to work with. Others are difficult… we know this.

In their book, *How To Lead Smart People,* lawyers Arun Singh and Mike Mister created a Vision 'do list', which they have kindly permitted me to reproduce here. They identified that creating a Vision makes two demands on leaders. The first is to orchestrate and manage the human dynamics in the team to enable a Vision to be created. The second is to cope with the uncertainty that comes from relinquishing control to allow others to make a significant contribution to the destination and the journey. The aim is to enable the team.

To be inspiring and uplifting, your Vision needs to be 'big picture' and go beyond the technical, numeric, and issues of day-to-day management. It needs to engage, energise and enable local decision-making to drive productive action in the business. The Vision has to be realistic and not so far 'out there' as to be unattainable. Above all, it needs to have been built with the initiative, creativity and the involvement of the team – it is their efforts and commitment that will determine how well it is executed!

BRIDGE THE CURRENT REALITY TO THE NEW VISION

Prepare the way, ensuring that others can follow by defining goals and showing how they are attainable. Smart people will make links between where they see themselves and where you – their leader – are proposing to take them. They will not be convinced to sign up if they think it is completely unattainable.

CREATE A SHARED VISION

Start with some initial and incomplete ideas and start to share them. Make it crystal clear this is initial thinking and a collaborative effort to build something bigger and better than any individual can do on their own. The leader's responsibility is to get the best ideas and input from a lot of smart people and collectively craft them into something you can all rally behind to build a better future place.

MAKE THE VISION LIVE

Take every opportunity to share the Vision, initiate action, and take steps towards making it a reality. The Vision needs to become more than just words – it needs to become alive and visible to the people. The leader's role is to energetically remind and rally people behind the Vision and the steps being taken to make it come alive.

PAINT A VIVID, ASPIRATIONAL PICTURE OF THE FUTURE FOR YOUR ORGANISATION

A Vision states where an organisation is going. Make it long-term (18 to 24 months) and agree on appropriate, stretching metrics with the team. Make it something that connects with people at an emotional level.

To be understood, be crystal-clear about what the destination will look, feel, and sound like. Getting the right blend of aspiration and challenge will be key.

SET OUT THE STRATEGY FOR THE ROUTE TO ACHIEVE YOUR VISION

Creating a Vision means articulating a place of advantage for your business in your sector; it is about anticipating and planning for market changes.

All these factors contribute to strategic thinking. Strategy cannot be formulated without knowing the destination. Vision provides this overarching goal; Strategy is the means to achieve it.

BUILD IN SHORT- AND LONG-TERM GOALS

The strategic journey to the Vision should have milestones against which the entire team can monitor progress. You need to be able to build in and celebrate short-term wins that will help achieve long-term goals.

CREATE A VISION STATEMENT

A Vision Statement should be a clear, brief statement of intent.

Write it in the present tense, make it emotive – and instil passion.

Summarise the Vision Statement into a short, pithy, powerful phrase that is distinctive and impactful, and which people can easily grasp and identify with. And ask your team to critique it before going public.

CLARITY IS KEY

Forget buzzwords and corporate-speak and ignore the temptation to use slogans or simplistic alliteration. Use language that is easily understood, unambiguous, and as simple as possible. If you are going to use an acronym or a slogan, make sure that some witty individual cannot have fun with it by twisting the meaning or rephrasing it.

ENSURE EVERY PERSON UNDERSTANDS

Communicate and discuss the Vision with everyone who will be charged with making it a reality. Remember, a Vision Statement drives not just what they will do, but also how they will go about doing it.

KEEP IT UNDER REVIEW

Regularly review the statement and metrics. Are they still relevant? Have things changed?

Is everyone still on course and doing what is needed? What does the team think? If things are changing, then a team conversation is needed about changes and revisions.

> People generally prefer problem-avoidance and problem-containment to problem-solving.
>
> **Richard Susskind, The Future of the Professions**

WHAT CAN YOUR FUTURE LOOK LIKE?

Could your Vision feature any of the following?

MANAGEMENT

1. A committed management team that will review the firm's charging structure for all work types.
2. All Team Leaders, Partners, and Heads of Departments will look at how and why they price what they do. On a department-by-department basis, there will be an analysis of how the current pricing structure came to be. Was there any method in the madness, or was it just keeping with the processes that the company has always had and leaving it to 'best endeavours'?
3. Hidden files on the PMS system and Excel spreadsheets containing departmental pricing data will be outed and discussed.
4. A commitment to looking at the service lines that your firm offers. Are there any that should be made redundant?
5. Agreement to regularly mystery shop your own practice, and review what pricing information you get when you act as a customer.
6. A policy of looking at the customer journey that your clients experience.
7. A policy decision to be a price setter, not a price chaser. You will not undercut your competition.
8. You and your lawyers accept that you are not selling a commodity service.
9. You do not need every bit of work that comes into your organisation.
10. You will have looked hard at any referral fees that are paid and will forensically analyse the referral fees you are paying. This might mean that you even consider stopping work in a particular Practice Area.
11. You will have accurate figures of base charges that you are not prepared to go below for various services.
12. You may have come to the conclusion that some of your lawyers should not be involved in the pricing process at all. They just aren't comfortable dealing with it. They are comfortable pointing out some of the errors and complications, which is perfectly valid, but they are not comfortable asking for the price.
13. Your Vision is to play to the strengths of other team members.
14. You won't hide behind websites and Excel calculators. If you really do believe in offering excellent client service and putting the client at the centre of everything you do, then you will put your money where your mouth is and prove it.
15. Any time recording is only so that you can use it to help establish base costs, not prices for clients.

16. You will have made a decision that someone in the organisation – at Board level – will be responsible for the pricing. Your firm will know who is responsible for owning the pricing function.
17. You will have identified how clients prefer to be communicated with as part of that journey.
18. You will have created a clear and simple message about the future and what it looks like in your organisation and ensure that it is understood by all.
19. Your Vision will incentivise the people who are going to be involved in this process.
20. You are considering setting team targets rather than individual targets.
21. You are considering how you can incentivise teams to overperform.
22. Your Vision will show that you are confident, and that you have enough quality clients and opportunities.
23. Your Vision will be simple, aspirational, feasible, flexible, and capable of being easily understood and communicated.

CLIENTS

1. Accept that you will not act for some of your current clients in the future.
2. Accept that you will be providing clients with options when it comes to price.
3. You will help your clients understand the value you provide.
4. You will not capitulate when clients say they won't pay a given price.
5. Your lawyers will accept that all clients are not the same and should not be treated the same.

PRICING

1. When someone says (and they will), 'This is the market rate', you will ask how this rate has been calculated and where this market is. It is usually the case that this is the price that they are comfortable charging. Interrogate those who say this, and ask them where their research is that has led them to this pricing. Usually, it will be, 'We have found out our competitors charge less, so we should seek to charge a little bit less.'
2. Your lawyers will take time to have conversations with clients and seek to determine the value of the matter.
3. Your lawyers will take time to create Fixed-Price Agreements which are properly scoped to show that they understand what the task entails. The FPAS will include details of assumptions made in the scoping document and exclude work that is not included.
4. You will follow up on proposals that are sent to clients.

5. You will have – somewhere in each team/on the PMS – a departmental Big Book of Usefulness, which contains all of this information. A BBU that is freely available to team members. You will have frequently detailed value questions and details of common price objections and how to handle them in the BBU.
6. You may have gone as far as banishing the term 'non-chargeable time' and regard time spent with clients as 'investment time'. Investment time changes your people's thinking.
7. Your lawyers will know that sending a bill after the work has been completed is not pricing. Pricing occurs before any work is undertaken.
8. You will have onboarding scripts for Practice Areas which will be warm, engaging, and empathetic. These scripts and the questions you ask will allow you to get the information that you need to determine a price.
9. You will commit to creating a staff training and induction program.
10. You will help overcome resistance to change by educating your people about how law firm finances operate, how profit is made, and even why profit is important.
11. You will regularly repeat the phrase from L'Oreal and be able to convince your lawyers that 'They are worth it.'
12. You will create a new breed of VBP lawyers.

> Once we realise that there is almost no chance we'll get it right the first time, we can embrace the opportunity to sign up for better instead of perfect.
>
> Get it wrong the first time.
>
> Then make it better.
>
> **Seth Godin, Getting It Right The First Time**

Set out below is an extract from the website of View Legal, a firm owned by Matthew Burgess from Brisbane in Australia. I met Matthew in Dallas. His website mentions how he wants his firm to be regarded as a 'firm of the future' and lists five things that have been abandoned and five features that have been embraced. You may think that some aspects of it are too radical, and that's fine. This is Matthew's Vision for his business.

WORDS WITH THE WISE

Matthew Burgess, View Legal

At View, we believe that there are a number of attributes shared by professional services providers that are acknowledged as innovators – or, to coin a phrase, businesses that are 'firms of the future – now'.

Ten examples from View's journey to date are listed below – five that are abandoned and five that are embraced.

Five things abandoned:

1. Timesheets – with timesheets, all that is focused on is what is 'chargeable' – without timesheets, the focus is on what is valuable.
2. No leave policies – leave policies are a hangover from the industrial age – it is time to move on.
3. No individual budgets – while there will certainly be team goals, these are never broken down into individual monetary targets. Targets are aligned around performance in the eyes of customers. If a firm gets those right, everything else flows (including money).
4. No performance reviews – again, a very poor hangover from the industrial age.
5. No diversity goals – seeking to mandate minimum percentages of certain genders, cultures, religious beliefs, or sexuality disguise much bigger problems with the underlying business model. While 'leaning in' is critical, it is diversity of thinking which is the key to success.

Five features embraced:

1. Guaranteed, fixed pricing – the definition of a competent service provider is someone who can devise a scope of work and provide an upfront fixed price that they are willing to refund in full if the customer is not satisfied with the performance.
2. ROWE (that is, a Results Only Work Environment). To learn more, see: https://en.wikipedia.org/wiki/ROWE

3. Solution choreographed teams – analogous to the movie industry, disruptive firms are structured to allow them to work with whomever and on whatever terms are best to achieve the client's objectives.
4. AAR – a concept developed by the US military. After-Action Reviews are arguably the single most important learning tool for professional firms. To learn more, see: https://en.wikipedia.org/wiki/After-action_review
5. Diversity of thought – when two people in business are constantly of the same opinion, one or more is irrelevant. Embracing diversity in every sense of the word ensures arbitrary, politically correct, percentages become irrelevant.

As you work on your Vision, you will be confronted with lots of hindering thoughts and problems. Embrace Possibility Thinking and turn the problem into a possibility question and answer it.

POSSIBILITY THINKING

How can we possibly track and record our value-based pricing efforts?

- Look at what our IT people can suggest.
- Implement a sign-off on our Case Management/Practice Management system.
- Sign-off on file processes.
- Allocate a new file number code to those we VBP.
- Whiteboard.
- Paper.
- PowerPoint.
- Voice memos.
- Folder.
- Active campaign on CRM system.
- Monitor bills delivered and utilisation to identify candidates

- Sign off by Head of Department.
- Monitor files open on a spreadsheet.
- Asking at team meetings.
- Create a competition.
- Circulate thinking to colleagues.
- Create a bonus incentive scheme and competition.

embracing value-based pricing already.

- Team goals.
- 360° feedback.
- Diarise.
- Surgeries.
- Questions and answers.

During a conference organised in July 2023, I interviewed Jacqui Brown about working life at Lynn & Brown, a firm that operated without timesheets. I have had the interview transcribed. It's worth reading as this could be your future.

WORDS WITH THE WISE

Jacqui Brown, Lynn & Brown

Q: Can you just give us five minutes about what it's like to be a lawyer at Lynn & Brown? It must be better.

A: It's so much better. Filling out timesheets used to be one of the pains of my existence. I filled out a timesheet every day for 20 years. And not having done that for six years has just been life-changing for me.

Not filling out a timesheet is awesome. It frees up the way you practise law when you're not constantly thinking about, who do I charge this to? It means that you can collaborate so much better within your firm. It's not like you've got someone thinking, but I need to get some more time on the clock so I can't have that conversation, or I don't know which one of us is going to bill that. You sit down and you have a conversation. You don't even think twice about it, about the file. So, collaborating on files works really well.

We involve non-lawyers in our Value Council, and I think that it really helps to have non-lawyers as part of the process. It's because lawyers think in a particular way. Once you've been doing it for so long, you don't even realise that other people don't think that way. It's good to have other people's perspectives on some of the things that you do.

I love feeling like my client and I are on the same page. I like not having to write down the time that I start a conversation with a client and the time that I end the conversation with a client. And I love that a client knows that if they need to talk to me, they can ring me and speak to me and not have to worry about, 'Oh, is that two units? Or is it, oh, wait, it's pushing into the three units.' I remember one client that I used to have; he would say, 'It's five and a half minutes now. You're only charging me for one unit, aren't you?' before the end of a phone call. And you don't have to worry about that.

We used to have debtors in our office of about 500,000 before we went to value-based pricing. Now our debtors are below 100,000. We would regularly spend the week after we'd issued our monthly invoices, explaining to clients the bill rendered, going line by line through the time. I would dread that week at work.

I find that my relationship with my clients is much better. I think the feeling in the office is much better. People enjoy coming to work more. Not having to fill in a timesheet is better. You don't have that fear of sending out a bill at the end of every month and thinking, 'I know this client is going to hate this.'

It's such a cleaner, better, happier way of practising. I don't know if I'd still be practising law if I hadn't changed. I feel like the way I practise now is vastly better.

I think that my mental health has improved because I don't have that horrible pressure of filling in a timesheet and the expectations of that. And if we can make work better and easier for people, a mentally healthier place for people to be working in as well, I think that's really important in this day and age.

Matthew Burgess, View Legal

We've basically only got three KPIs:

1. Zero inboxes at the end of each day.

2. Conduct After-Action Reviews. By undertaking AARs, you can sometimes get performance feedback within an hour of the project being completed.
3. Have fun.

If you're turning up and having a good time, it means that your customers will pick up on that.

We've got no holiday policy. There's no annual review. There's no budget.

When it comes to looking at performance, it's not a long discussion. We operate a Results Only Work Environment (ROWE). Our lawyers have three KPIs. We're not going to just look at you once a year. It's an adult discussion. What do you think you're worth? What can the business afford? Let's see what we can do here.

John Chisholm, John Chisholm Consulting

Someone once said, 'If you don't make your Vision and your values and your strategy public, it's just a wish list.' I haven't come across too many law firms in my 15 years plus of consulting that have a Vision and a strategy that they genuinely believed in. Many have a 'wishy washy' Vision, an annual 'strategy' which is really a financial budget under the guise of a business plan, and a culture by default.

In one of the firms I worked with, the Managing Partner and their guiding coalition really 'got it' and understood that moving to a value pricing model was not simply a billing or even a pricing model change. They realised it was a whole business model change.

They would be the first to admit that it was hard for a while. They had some Partners leave. They lost some clients who still wanted to pay them by time, but they had made a 'blood pact' at leadership level that they were going to give this a red-hot go. If it didn't work, deep down they realised the firm might implode, but if it did work, they understood the world's their oyster and it would be a much better way to practise their craft.

Now, did it work? Yes, because there was a genuine guiding coalition, and the leadership was so strong to make it work. They didn't shy away from making some tough decisions. That's a huge commitment and most firms wouldn't be prepared to do that.

They didn't have all the answers, but they had a Vision and a strategy to achieve that Vision.

CRIB SHEET
READING & VIEWING

READ (COMPULSORY)

Should You Have a Value Manifesto?

By Tim Williams

https://www.linkedin.com/pulse/value-manifesto-professional-firms-tim-williams/

READ (COMPULSORY)

When Two Worlds Collide in a Good Way – What do Value Pricing and Design Thinking Have in Common?

By Melissa Lyon

https://www.linkedin.com/pulse/when-two-worlds-collide-good-way-what-do-value-pricing-melissa-lyon/

READ

Avoiding Extinction: Reimagining Legal Services for The 21st Century

By Mitchell Kowalski

An innovative legal practice management book. It could be a blueprint for your whole business.

READ

The Law Firm of The Future

By Ronan Hynes Sellors, LLP

https://www.irishlegal.com/articles/ronan-hynes-the-law-firm-of-the-future

READ

Defining Our Company Values: How We Screwed Up (And Fixed It!)

By Luke Kyte

https://www.corporate-rebels.com/blog/finding-value-in-your-company-values

WATCH

The Key Differences Between Leading and Managing

By John Kotter

https://www.youtube.com/watch?v=SEfgCqnMl5E

WATCH (COMPULSORY)

Creating A Change Vision

By John Kotter

https://www.youtube.com/watch?v=yA1a0khcuKo

TIPS/CHECKLISTS

1. Practise your 'Vision speech' often. Say it out loud, and over and over until it becomes natural; then be confident saying it to the client or prospect.
2. Ensure that your Pioneer penguins can describe the Vision in five minutes or less.
3. A clear Vision can help everyone understand why you're asking them to do something. When people see what you're trying to achieve for themselves, then the directives they're given tend to make more sense.

EXERCISES

EXERCISE 1

What does your Vision of the future look like in relation to your pricing?

Do you have a visible example of the case for change?

Is there a clear and simple message about the future – and what it may look like – that is understood by all?

EXERCISE 2

When you first start thinking about change, there will probably be many great ideas and solutions floating around. Link these concepts to an overall Vision that people can grasp easily and remember.

Focus on the value you offer; write down what makes you different and why you charge what you do.

EXERCISE 3 (COMPULSORY)

Let me introduce you once again to Steven and Jacqui Brown from Lynn & Brown in Perth, Western Australia.

View this short video on their website. It's what we are aiming for.

https://www.lynnandbrown.com.au/pricing/

POSSIBILITY THINKING QUESTIONS TO POSE

1. What might our Vision possibly include?
2. How might we possibly communicate the Vision?
3. What factors might possibly have an adverse effect on our Vision?

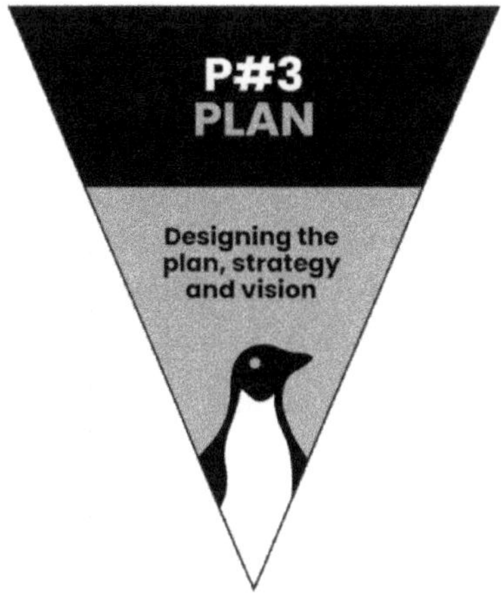

P#3 PART 4
PLAN

We have now arrived at the planning stage of P#3 Plan – designing the Plan, Strategy and Vision.

At this stage of the book, you have knowledge about the principles of VBP. You understand some of the tools that must be created to make VBP a reality. You will have thought about what your Vision may look like.

This book is not a blueprint for a one-size-fits-all VBP Implementation Plan. Every law firm is different, and the attitudes of those in the business regarding their willingness to embrace change will vary widely.

In this – the final section of P#3 Plan – I have incorporated some best practice and simple project principles into the real world of a legal firm. My hope is that by following the steps below, you can create your Plan and successfully deliver change *without* burdening yourself with unnecessary paperwork and Gannt charts. As mentioned in the acknowledgements, Dr Jacqui Rigby, an experienced COO, has assisted me in documenting the planning process and templates in this section.

> Vision without action is merely a dream.
> Action without vision is just passing the time.
> Vision with action can change the world.
>
> **Joel Barker**

DESIGN A PLAN AND PROCESS

When you consider it, a legal business is quite simple. We have to implement a number of processes which enable us to get work. Do the work and then get paid. I accept that legal work in England and Wales is highly regulated, and that brings its own challenges, but I also think that lawyers – particularly owners of law firms – sometimes seek to overcomplicate processes because they want to practise law and do things their way. Even if it means rewriting part of a Case Management System.

As you know, I believe that you need to create a process to implement VBP, and the process needs to be documented. The problem with legal services is that the processes about how to do *what* and *when* are quite often in the heads of the lawyers. They're not written down. They are not shared and discussed with colleagues. So, different lawyers work in different ways. We must not let perfection become the enemy of good.

In the next few pages, we will set out how to create the Plan you need. We are creating a Plan within the Plan, if you follow my drift.

> The secret of getting ahead is getting started.
> The secret of getting started is breaking
> your complex, overwhelming tasks into small,
> manageable tasks and starting
> on the first one.
>
> **Mark Twain**

STEP 1 PARADIGM: DEFINE YOUR CHANGE GOAL

DEFINE THE GOAL

Where are you now, and where do you want to get to?

If you are setting off on a journey in your car, you need to know where you are starting from and where you are going. Basic stuff, right?

If you are going somewhere new and longer distance, you may decide to check the weather forecast, the traffic, where you might stop for a coffee, how much fuel you have in the car, and how much charge is in your battery.

You might also check the oil, water, and tyres. You might set up the satellite to alert you to any delays and offer alternative routes. All to smooth the journey and reduce the risk of issues and delays.

Planning a change is like driving to a new destination. You need to know where you are going and where you are starting from. And just like a long car journey, if you plan a change and are prepared in advance to manage the unknowns, you will get there sooner and with less fuss and bother.

> Create a strong emotional bond
> with your vision.
>
> **Simon Alexander Ong,**
> **The Power of Vision**

WRITING OUTCOMES

An outcome is a statement that makes a goal more concrete. Outcomes describe the specific changes you aim to achieve when reaching your goal. So, to take the analogy of the car journey, the goal might be 'To get to Manchester for a 2 pm meeting'; the outcome you seek might be, 'Impress the client and win the new business.' To achieve this outcome, it might mean leaving home 45 minutes early so you can freshen up, get a drink and snack, and then reading through your notes again.

In delivering change for Value-Based Pricing, examples of outcomes might include:

- Higher conversion rates.
- Reduced complaint levels.
- Increases in customer satisfaction scores.
- Increases in staff morale.
- Reduced costs to serve (reduced administration costs).
- Increased cashflow.
- Increased profits.
- Decreased debtors.

We have discussed what may be the reasons for your paradigm shift in some detail in P#1. Now is the time to think seriously about *the Goal* and write it down.

Some tips for writing your Goal:

- Make it a Vision that is exciting for the firm, as this will help get buy-in to deliver the change.
- Ensure the Goal articulates the 'Why'.
- Goals are most powerful if you incorporate how the firm will look, how it feels to work there, and what the customer will experience (i.e., rational and emotional outcomes).

- Goals are not measurable objectives, so make them tangible, but don't worry about figures.
- Engage a couple of people to help build and/or review the Goal. Ask people who are big picture/visionary thinkers, who won't get tied up in 'how' the change will happen.
- Don't worry about how you will achieve the Goal or when you will get there at this point.

> Spectacular achievement is always preceded by unspectacular preparation.
>
> **Robert Schuller**

CONDUCT GAP ANALYSIS

Just like preparing for that car journey, organisational change is multi-dimensional. Change is not about IT. Change is not about people. Change is not about process. It is all of these and more. The organisational dimensions are also interrelated, which makes it critical that Plans and delivery are managed holistically right through to the end state.

OPERATING MODEL DIMENSIONS

The following dimensions or components will be impacted by the change – to a greater or lesser degree – to implement VBP successfully:

- People and organisation.
- Processes.
- Systems.
- Customer service.
- Regulatory.
- Measures and motivators.
- Marketing promotion.

To start your change journey, the text below and the exercises in the Crib Sheet will guide you in defining the 'change gap' in your firm against each of these dimensions. The framework can be applied in any change situation. Each starting point is unique. Each journey is unique. Make it real for you.

DEFINE YOUR FUTURE STATE AGAINST OPERATING DIMENSIONS

For each of the dimensions below, write a few bullets to describe what the FUTURE state will *look* and *feel* like.

- People and organisation.
- Processes.
- Systems.
- Customer service.
- Regulatory.
- Measures and motivators.
- Marketing promotion.

CHANGE GAP ANALYSIS

big yellow penguin

DIMENSION	NOW	FUTURE STATE
PEOPLE & ORG		
PROCESSES		
SYSTEMS		
CUSTOMER SERVICE		
REGULATORY		
MEASURES, MOTIVATORS		
MARKETING PROMOTION		

GAP ANALYSIS EXAMPLES

Some examples against the operating model dimensions are shown below to help you with your thinking. These are only guides to help understand the process and may not all apply to your firm. It is key that you conduct a Gap Analysis that applies to your own firm.

FUTURE STATE EXAMPLES

People and organisation

- Our people understand the benefits of VBP.
- Our people can explain pricing more clearly and more effectively with potential clients.
- Morale has increased due to an easier sales process and a reduction in the difficulty of conversations with clients over pricing.
- Our training has been updated to inform people of the benefits of VBP, the conversations to have with clients, and the processes they should follow on and off system.

Processes

- We have mapped the end-to-end customer journey for VBP.
- A series of VBP agreements are available for services in each of our Practice Areas.
- Value-Based Pricing processes run alongside billable hour processes.
- Our processes for updating and billing clients support VBP.

Systems

- Our systems accommodate pricing options alongside billable hour pricing.
- The system's logic has been updated to accommodate billing for VBP.
- The system's logic has been updated to accommodate when a client is managed via VBP.
- Our letter templates have been updated to accommodate VBP.

Customer service

- Our customer conversation and onboarding guides have been updated to accommodate VBP.
- Our complaints handling service has been updated to accommodate VBP.
- Changes to the customer journey have been implemented across the firm.

Regulatory

- We have understood and applied any relevant regulations to our products and services in using VBP.

Measures & motivators

- Our reward mechanisms incorporate metrics based on VBP targets and behaviours.

Marketing promotion

- Our website and marketing collateral have been updated to promote the benefits to clients of VBP.

HURDLES AND BARRIERS

Looking at the gaps between the current state and the future state:

- Taking each operating dimension at a time, what are the hurdles and blockers that may impact success?
- What are the top three blockers or hurdles to the success of the overall change? Identify them.

> **8 PPP PENGUIN LOGIC**
>
> **Education, Education, Education**
>
> This Gap Analysis is really important, and time spent working on it will pay dividends.
>
> One of the crucial areas to think about, here, is the training element. How do you train people now in the current state? How will that look different in the future state?

STEP 2 PIONEERS: INITIATE THE CHANGE

So, you have your firm's Goal for Value-Based Pricing, and you have defined your current and future states against the operational dimensions. How do you now get from the current state to the future state?

SIMPLE PROJECT PRINCIPLES

Some core principles in planning change are very useful to know about. You don't need to be a professional project or Change Manager to use them. Here are some common tools that will help greatly in planning and delivery.

Sponsor: every change management project should have a Sponsor. The Sponsor has a vested interest in the outcome, is fully supportive of the Goal, can take the bigger decisions, will assist the team in overcoming key issues and mitigating risks, and supports stakeholder management and internal communications. The Sponsor is part of the change team and is equally invested in success.

Scope is a key area to define in any change. Scope definition allows you to ensure the following:

- All stakeholders have a common understanding of the boundaries of the change.
- Helps to gain stakeholder buy-in and manage expectations throughout.
- Reduces the risk of the change.
- Aligns change activity to the Goal and objectives.
- Drives your Plan.
- Drives your budget.

Make scope items tangible, for example:

- Update pricing tables on the Case Management System.
- Update all customer letters that refer to pricing (pre-, during, and post-the case).
- Train your Practice Area team on conversing with customers on VBP, including objection handling.

Documenting out of scope is just as important as documenting in scope. Out of scope says what you will not do and usually provides the most conversation with stakeholders when discussing boundaries.

Be as clear as you possibly can on scope items to avoid misunderstandings. It is not uncommon for someone to say mid-project – 'But I thought this change would deliver X' which causes debate and bad feeling at best, and delay/unexpected cost at worst.

Limit scope to what is absolutely needed to deliver the change. Keep it simple to drive success. Avoid the temptation to add in 'nice to haves' or associated activity.

Assumptions: an assumption is pretty much what it says on the tin. An assumption is something you assume to be true in relation to the change. The funny thing about assumptions, though, is that one person's assumption may be different to that of another. By discussing and documenting, you use the power of the team to highlight additional actions, issues, risks, or dependencies.

Dependencies: some tasks require other tasks to be started before another task can be started, one task may need to be finished before a particular task can start, or two tasks have to be completed together. Understanding and managing dependencies is critical in any Plan and successful delivery of change.

Issues: an issue is something that is happening now/has happened that causes a problem. Issues need to be managed with actions and owners. Issues are classified on a scoring system to focus on the most important issues at any one time. Note that the severity of an issue can change over time. A Project Issue template can be found below.

Risks: a risk is something that *might* happen and, if it were to do so, would create an issue. Risks need to be mitigated with owners and often actions. It is perfectly fine to 'accept' a risk and take no action if that is a conscious decision concerning an appropriate course of action at a particular point in time.

Risk management is an important part of project and change management to reduce surprises and to plan contingencies. Risks are classified using a simple scoring system to allow the team to focus on the most important matters for the change. Note that the probability of a risk happening and even its impact can change over time. A Project Risk template can be found below.

Milestones*:* these are the points in the Plan that are key 'end points', decisions, or deliverables. They include 'Sign off User Acceptance Testing (UAT) and 'Lawyer Scoring Matrix agreed'.

Milestones are usually the key points on the Plan that have dependencies on other deliverables and/or are critical to the overall timeline. Milestones are the key points to track on your Plan. Milestones often drive dependencies. You can then drop down into the tasks driving each milestone to manage a particular delivery.

Project Triangle*:* A simple, useful tool to keep in mind is the project triangle. As you pull on one side of the triangle, you impact the other sides as well as on quality, which runs through the whole triangle. For example, if you fix time (i.e., you set a date, don't move it), then should there be a request to add more scope to the change, something has to give – cost or quality. Note that you should not look to use quality as a variable that you can adjust – otherwise, you will likely fail to deliver on the change completely.

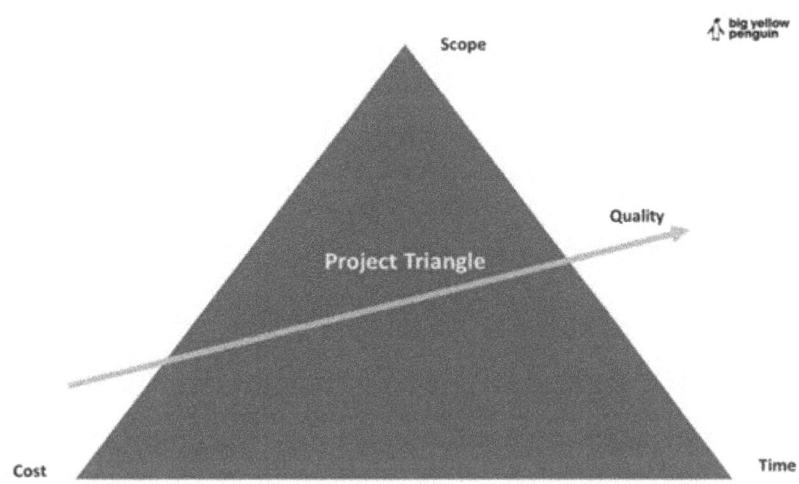

INITIATION DOCUMENT

Create a simple document that is the blueprint for the change. The Initiation Document will be developed over a period of time.

An Initiation Document usually contains:

- The Goal (from the Change Gap Analysis sheet).
- Change Objectives (make these SMART and business-focused).
- In Scope.
- Out of Scope.
- Summary Business Case (see Step 3, Build a Business Case).
- Sponsor and Pioneers (see Step 2, Initiate the Change).
- Governance details.
- Plan.
- Key risks, issues, assumptions, and dependencies.

To get started on the Initiation Document, think about the following three questions:

- What might your SMART change objectives be? (Include them in your Initiation Document.)
- What might be in scope of the change? (Include them in your Initiation Document.)
- What might be out of scope of the change? (Include them in your Initiation Document.)

Once you have completed all sections, ask key senior stakeholders impacted by the change – as well as the Sponsor – to review the document and sign it off. Ensure time is given for debate and dialogue; failing to do so invariably causes issues later that take up more time.

Don't skip this step! This is your anchor document to manage change and align key stakeholders. The time invested avoids more issues later when you discover different people have different views on what is changing, how much it costs, who is needed, and when the change will be delivered.

STEP 3 PLAN: CREATE A PLAN AND BUILD A BUSINESS CASE

> ' It does not do to leave a live dragon out of your calculations, if you live near him. '
>
> **J.R.R. Tolkien, The Hobbit**

EXPOSURE DRAFTS
BY GREG KYTE
I CAN'T BILL THIS TIME, SO WE'RE DONE.
OH, I GET IT.
#MENTORING
GREG

CREATE A PLAN

KICK-OFF MEETING WITH YOUR PIONEERS

The role of the Change Manager is to *facilitate* the session to engage the team and to gather information to build a High-Level Plan using the High-Level Plan below.

In organising your kick-off workshop, prepare the agenda (see example below), the flipcharts and the 'ground rules' in advance.

Set up flip charts around the room – one for each of the topics below – to capture the following dynamically throughout the discussion. Flip Chart headings:

- Plan activity (milestones/tasks).
- Risks and Issues.
- Assumptions.
- Dependencies.
- Decisions.
- Questions.
- Actions.

OUTLINE KICK-OFF MEETING AGENDA

1. Introduction from the Sponsor.
    - Communicate the Goal for VBP and the Vision for the future state.
    - Underscore the psychological safety of the Pioneer Group.
    - Finance and historical WIP write-offs.
2. Ground Rules. Typical ground rules include:
    - Everyone's views are equal.
    - Listen to other people's ideas and seek to build on them.
    - There is no such thing as a silly question or a silly idea.
    - Leave your baggage at the door.
    - No war stories.
3. Session Objectives & Roles.
    - What the session is aiming to achieve.
    - What the outputs will be used for.
    - The role of the Pioneers.
4. Planning.
    - Share the work on the Gap Analysis – current and future state – and work through the operating dimensions, stimulating discussion.

- Stimulate conversations about HOW you will get from the current state to the future state.
- Capture key tasks and milestones.
- Capture risks, issues, assumptions, dependencies, decisions, questions, and actions as they arise on the flip charts.
- Identify the key resources needed to deliver.
- Identify third-parties that need to be involved in delivery, e.g., an IT supplier.
- Check for Dragons!

5. Key Actions.
   - Ensure you have key actions from the meeting with timelines and owners.
   - Anyone with an action needs to agree to own and deliver to the timeline.
   - Do not give an action to someone not in the room.
6. Wrap Up (ideally with the Sponsor back in the room).
   - Summarise the achievements of the session and check them against the objectives of the session.
   - Outline the next steps for the Pioneers; reassure them that they will continue to be involved.
   - Ask everyone in the room to share (briefly) how they found the session with the group.
   - Agree a common key message to other members of the firm on what you did in the session and the next steps.

HIGH-LEVEL PLAN TEMPLATE

You can use the simple High-Level Plan template which you can create in PowerPoint. This is the sort of view suitable to communicate to all levels internally. You can adapt the template to meet your needs. The rows can be amended/added to as appropriate. You can move the arrows around, add more, or delete them.

High-Level Plan template

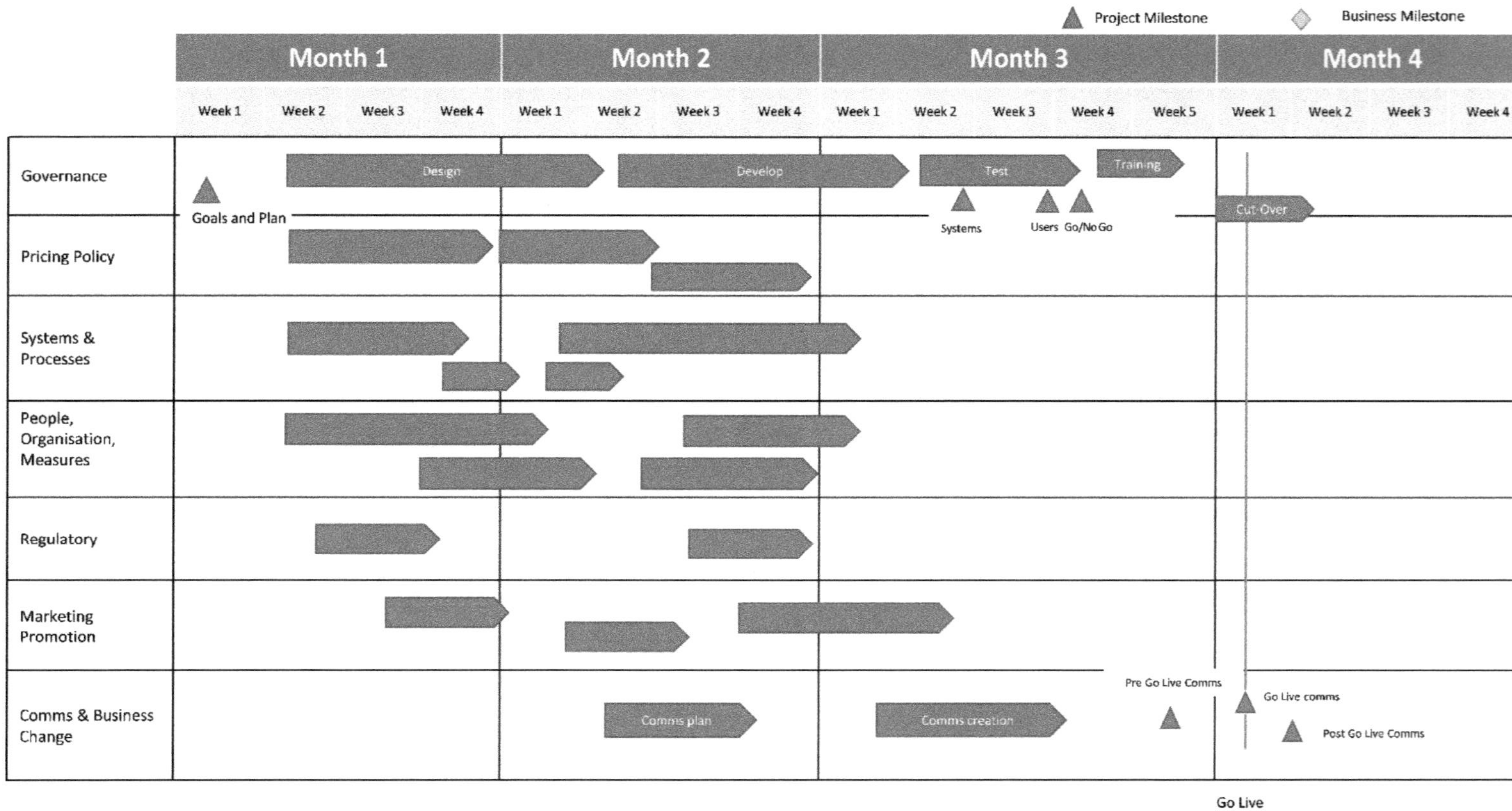

Using the High-Level Plan template and the information from the kick-off planning workshop, develop your Plan. Put real months and week dates in the timeline at the top. Update the rows, if appropriate, to best group activities together. We would recommend using the top row of Governance and the bottom row of Comms & Change Management in all instances.

Review dependencies between activities and check that the flow is logical and possible – both within and across the lanes. Make changes to the Plan as appropriate. Document dependencies.

Write up the flip charts from the session and ensure you have actions in place, filling any gaps missed in agreement with the appropriate owner. Share the session output and VBP High-Level Plan with the core team and the Sponsor, inviting comments and questions.

RISKS AND ISSUES

After the Kick-Off Meeting, add the issues and risks to the Issues and Risk templates, respectively.

Project Issue Template

big yellow penguin

Number	Issue Description	Impact of issue	Priority (H/M/L)	Action	Action Owner	Target resolution date

Project Risk Template

big yellow penguin

Number	Risk Description (including impact)	Probability score 1-5	Impact score 1-5	Risk score (P x I)	Risk (L/M/H)	Mitigation	Owner

Risk scores	
1 - 8	Low
9 - 15	Medium
16 - 25	High

BUILD A BUSINESS CASE

Now you have an outline of what is needed (having developed your Plan), you can build a Business Case with a budget.

The first step is to talk to your Finance team, who will guide you on what is required for a Business Case in your firm and any templates they use. However, there are some common principles for building a Business Case:

- Build a simple table of the different cost lines, and bring in expertise from each area to advise on costs.
- Work with your Finance team so they can advise on what components can be capitalised and what will be put against revenue.
- From the work you have done on the benefits of value-based pricing, develop a simple table of the benefits with financial metrics, with support from your Finance team.
- Work with your Finance team to combine the costs and benefits information to see the overall impact on the business P&L (profit and loss).
- Identify the budget needed to deliver the Value-Based Pricing Change.
- Agree what Finance need from you in tracking spend versus budget and sign-off approval levels.

DESIGN AND DOCUMENT THE BBU PRICING PROCESS

- Having looked at knowledge, tools, Vision, and an outline Plan for the project, what will your firm's actual pricing process, governance, and documentation eventually look like? I appreciate – at this stage of the book – you may well be thinking, 'I have no idea! I am only halfway through the book!' And your point is well made.
- You have heard me refer to the BBU already. I don't mind what you call it or what you create as long as the knowledge is captured, stored, documented and made available. These processes should now be mentioned in your Plan.
- Can I suggest that each of your Practice Area BBUs should cover some of the following topics:

1. Introduction from Team Leader/Head of Department.
    - Why you price the way you do.
    - That this is a psychologically safe process.
    - Who participated in the VBP Pilot Project.
    - Categories of work which are subject to VBP.
    - A commitment to creating options/versions and giving clients options and choices.
    - How pricing works in the team.
    - Pricing training available. How existing team members and new starters will be trained.
    - How prices are set and reviewed.
2. Outline the price approval process.
    - Where documents, templates, precedent questions and knowledge are stored.
    - How base price calculations are made and where the data is stored.
    - How the process operates.
    - How the Lawyer Scoring Matrix works.
    - How the 'two pairs of eyes on any price' decision operates.
    - Agreed payment terms with monies on account.
    - How AARs are conducted.
3. The Value Council's terms of reference and how they guide people in the firm.
4. A draft agenda for regular pricing meetings within the team/Practice Area. It could be such items as:
    - Number of VBP quotations sent in the previous 30 days.

    - Percentages of work won and prices obtained.
    - Gold features added to options lists.
    - Feedback from clients/referrers.
    - Feedback from lawyers.
    - Clients won.
    - Proposals lost and why.
    - Clients deselected.
    - Update on templates created and added to the knowledge bank.
    - Training updates.
5. The mechanism of reporting VBP progress to the Pricing Group.
6. The questions that candidates seeking to join your firm should be asked about their current pricing practices.
7. How you will gather and collate information about competitor pricing.

THE IMPACT ON HR

> Tell me and I forget, teach me and I may remember, involve me and I learn.
>
> **Benjamin Franklin**

As you will appreciate by this stage, one of the areas of the business that the VBP project will impact significantly is the HR function.

We already know we are dealing with human capital. We know our people are one of our biggest assets, and we must make sure they are looked after.

COMMON HR ISSUES ARISING IN CHANGE MANAGEMENT PROJECTS

Implementing a change management project within an organisation can bring about various human resource department issues, including:

Resistance to Change: Employees may resist the changes due to fear of the unknown, job insecurity, or a reluctance to abandon familiar processes.

Communication Challenges: Insufficient or unclear communication about the changes can lead to misinformation, rumours, and confusion among employees.

Employee Morale and Engagement: A poorly managed change project can lower morale and engagement levels, potentially leading to decreased productivity and increased turnover.

Skill Gaps: Employees may need new skills or training to adapt to changes, and HR must address these skill gaps through training and development programmes.

Leadership Alignment: Ensuring that all levels of leadership are on the same page regarding the change's objectives and implementation can be a challenge.

Employee Wellbeing: The stress of change can impact employee wellbeing, and HR may need to provide support, such as counselling or wellness programmes.

Retention Issues: Some employees may choose to leave the organisation if they disagree with, or cannot adapt to the changes, creating retention challenges.

Legal and Compliance Concerns: HR must ensure that the change process complies with employment law and contractual obligations.

Resource Allocation: Managing the allocation of HR resources, such as time, budget, and staff, for the change initiative can be demanding.

Measuring Success: Defining and measuring the success of the change project can be challenging, and HR may need to establish relevant KPIs and metrics.

Cultural Shift: Changes often involve a shift in organisational culture, which may require HR to facilitate cultural alignment and adjustment.

Feedback Collection: Gathering and analysing employee feedback during and after the change is crucial to making necessary adjustments and improvements.

Employee Burnout: Overloading employees with too many changes or unrealistic expectations can lead to burnout, which HR must monitor and address.

Addressing these issues proactively and with a strategic HR approach is essential for the successful implementation of a change management project.

TRAINING IS ESSENTIAL

It is absolutely crucial that a comprehensive training programme is designed and implemented if the VBP project is to be successful. We all know that people learn in different ways. Some of us are audible learners, some visual, and others learn by doing. We have to practise and develop the skills to implement VBP.

What procedures will be put in place to train new and existing staff in your new pricing methodology? How will induction alter? What does the Strategic Training Plan say? Is there a Strategic Training Plan?

Your troops need to know:

- That pricing mistakes are expected. They will not be career-limiting. They are psychologically safe.
- The knowledge base and processes have to be built.

- Confidence and competence need to be expanded, and that will be done by doing.
- Pricing is a skill to be learned. It is an art, not a science.
- There will be some mechanism in place, be it a Value Council or pricing buddy.
- Lawyers are not allowed to price their own work in isolation.
- As the project proceeds, there will need to be policies and procedures created.
- Training will be available.
- Lawyers will be trained on how to have value conversations. The questions will be documented in the team manuals/BBUs.
- Knowledge management systems will gather together, as will departmental pricing tools.
- Training will be given in the firm's Case Management System and Financial Management System.
- FPA templates will be created, stored, and made available for amending/recycling.
- Lawyers will be trained to create and present the FPAs they create.
- Lawyers will be taught how to deal with price objections.
- Lawyers will understand that the firm is committed to identifying and ceasing to act for customers who are not profitable or too difficult to deal with.
- Lawyers will learn your firm are price setters, not price chasers.
- After-Action Reviews will become commonplace and be regarded as opportunities to learn.
- HR will create a new series of competency questions that can be used when interviewing prospective employees to ascertain what level of pricing experience candidates have.

> With AI, quality increases with workload, not decreases as it does with junior lawyers. But AI can't do the soft human bit.
>
> **James Hutt, Paradigm Junction**

WORDS WITH THE WISE

Dr Jacqui Rigby, Rigby Pollitt Associates

Plan

A plan needs to be owned by the team responsible for delivering, and endorsed by the leadership team, so make sure you run a session or sessions to talk through the plan face-to-face. Simply sending a plan by email doesn't cut it!

Ignore dependencies at your peril. Dependencies can impact your timeline and need to be planned to avoid wasted effort and rework. Understand what needs to be finished before something else can start. Understand what needs to kick off activity before another task can start. Understand what tasks need to come together to feed another task.

Scope

Documenting out of scope is just as important as documenting in scope. Out of scope says what you are not going to do, and usually provides the most conversation with stakeholders when discussing boundaries.

Melissa Lyon, Hive Legal

We're very, very clear on the experience side of things. We want to make it easier for our clients and improve their experience. We have a project called Hive Way, where we've looked at the way we communicate with our clients and created specific advice templates, long-form and short-form. We talked to our clients; we got feedback from them. What format works for you? Do the tables work for you? What works for you in terms of how we review contracts and provide you with comments? We spent time working that out.

We stopped and thought, what do our scopes look like? We created bespoke, templated scopes that worked.

We are passionate about implementing design thinking. In short, it's about actually listening to the people you're designing for and working out what they need. Often, lawyers think we know the answer. Because we've been trained that way. You tell us you've got a problem or a question, we will jump in, and we will answer it.

Design thinking is getting all of the information from the users so that you can help solve their problem, not throw legal advice at them. It's a mindset that does not come naturally to the legal profession because we're sceptics. Lawyers are often reluctant to be creative because we think everything's serious. We want to jump to a solution, and this is why design thinking is hard for the profession.

There are a number of different mindsets that you use:

- You need to be collaborative and have multidisciplinary teams of different people to solve a problem.
- You need to have empathy. You really need to actually sit down and listen, and have the value conversation with the client from a value pricing point of view. Find out what it is that matters to them, and work out what the problem is.
- Defining what the problem is, and then ideating as to what the solution could be. And you can ideate in great, creative, fun ways, including brainstorming and role-playing.
- Once you've ideated, then you prototype. Build a quick and dirty solution. What does it look like? What does the template look like? What does the process look like?
- Then you test it and then you iterate it.
- You need to collaborate, experiment and be creative. Experiment with different processes. You give it a go, prototype it, and see how it goes. What doesn't work, you improve on.
- It is vital to trust the process.
- Value pricing allows you to do that because once you unpick the problem, it can lead to other places. For example, a client doesn't necessarily need the advice on a clause of a particular employment contract, but they might actually need to have better processes and systems to understand how the employment issues arose.

At Hive, we used our own legal design thinking framework, HiveThinkP, to design all of our pricing processes. All of our templates, all of our processes, the way the Pricing Council works, using the design process way of thinking.

We have created a system for the lawyers to brief the Pricing Council using a chatbot called Val Ewe. She is an educative tool, as well. Val Ewe provides the consistency of information and the data we need. Val Ewe assists the lawyers to work out their pricing scope and their options. She will ask them if they have had the value conversation? What does the client value? Val Ewe can help them work out the format of their pricing. And then, that's all downloaded into a document, which then goes to the Pricing Council.

We have got a library of different types of scoping options. We designed our scopes very purposefully to identify how we deliver. Our scopes set out what you are going to get, when you're going to get it, and what it's going to look like.

I think to authentically do value-based pricing in your organisation, you absolutely need to do it in your own way. You've actually got to work out why you're doing it, your vision. You've got to design it in a way which is going to work for you. Make it authentic.

Nicola Jones, Athena Professional

What's your learning strategy? That's a matter of a few short weeks to figure out what you need to achieve. Then, conduct your Gap Analysis; that doesn't have to take a long time. To be honest, you probably haven't got any data. You probably have no recorded data on your performance management. Do you do exit interviews? Do you know why people leave your business? Have you got anything that's telling you what people's current capabilities are?

You may find all you can do is identify competencies, and you can ask people how competent they feel they are, and you can either believe them or not.

The thing about learning is it takes time, so you need to allow people time. If we're on a learning journey, we want people in a position who understand enough about the business and the way it operates to be able to have intelligent contributions that can become tangible. That's what learning is. It's tangible outcomes as a result of capability. Not, 'I know more than you.'

Robin Dicks, Thriving Consultancy

The change vision has to be absolutely grounded in reality. If you are going to use a value-based pricing approach, then you have to understand what drives value. This is partly (of course) when implementing the approach with individual clients and prospects. But you should also diligently understand what value consists of for the types of clients and markets you want to serve, and this is where effective market research can ensure you don't make an expensive mistake through incorrect assumptions about what people value.

Chris Marston, Exemplar Companies Pbc

In a meritocratic world, you create your path.

We have a chief growth officer who used to be our chief human capital officer. We create executive development plans with our people. We provide business plan support so people can think about their plan and their goals and where they want to be.

As an employer, you should help them get to where they want to go. We're the enablement department for what their goals are professionally.

Simon Tupman, Simon Tupman Consulting

A firm's vision goes to the very core of its value. 'What are we here to do, and what is the value that we're creating for our clients?' 'Are we charging appropriately for it?' These are two important questions to ask. I don't think any business should exist purely to make money, but there are plenty of law firms out there who do.

Jon Whittle, Jon Whittle Consulting

The vision for me is critical because that is the piece upon which you hang everything you do. And the vision is jointly owned, jointly held, and from a marketeer's perspective, the vision is about knowing why we do what we do, again, from a market or client perspective. So, our reason for being is not to do good law. Our reason for being is to help people. And that is the vision that drives everything else.

The vision is that people come to work with a clear sense of purpose. The really important thing from a vision perspective is to check and make sure it's working. Has the firm got the right clients, in the right place? But if you're not measuring it, if you're not going back and checking that everyone's onboard, you may find you have a rogue department reverting back into its old world. You must check in terms of commitment to the cause.

It's a tough gig being a marketeer in a law firm. I would encourage a piece of education around why the marketing is not about creating leaflets or doing the website. Marketing is about engaging your client base in a sensible conversation, which you control. And so many law firms struggle conceptually with that. And it goes off on a massive tangent. I think part of that start point for the whole project is to get the law firm to understand that this isn't just about the internal mechanics; it is about the market changing, and it goes back to the cost of the iceberg melting. Nothing is not an option because everyone else will have your lunch.

Kirsty Pappin, Aries Legal Practice Management

It just seems so obvious until it's not – always have a plan. The plan will lead to process. The process to policies. But if you don't have a plan, how can you determine where the process starts? When I start any project, I start with one line, which is 'What do I want to achieve?' This is the start of my plan. Everything else evolves from here.

CRIB SHEET
READING & VIEWING

WATCH

The Power of Vision

By Simon Alexander Ong

https://youtu.be/anac6H_mObA?si=VG4MwJ7_Gg4TWbqY

READ

Questions to Ask During Your Project Kick-Off Meeting (two parts)

By Dana Brownlee, Forbes

https://www.forbes.com/sites/danabrownlee/2022/07/01/5-more-questions-to-ask-during-your-project-kickoff-meeting/?sh=5897221d29be

READ

How to Facilitate a Meeting

By Session Lab

https://www.sessionlab.com/blog/facilitate-a-meeting/

READ

Project Managing Change

Practical tools and techniques to make change happen.

By Ira Blake & Cindy Bush

TIPS/CHECKLISTS

- Ensure you have enough information for the Initiation Document to act as your anchor, yet don't get stuck in analysis paralysis.
- Spend time on the scope (in/out of scope) and explore with your Pioneers. Stress test your understanding with stakeholders. **Scope definition provides critical guidance for your Business Case and your Plan.**
- The scope needs to be that which is needed to deliver the objectives – no more and no less. Don't get distracted by other requirements people try to throw into the mix, yet don't be so restrictive that you cannot deliver the benefits.
- A Plan needs to be owned by the team responsible for delivering and endorsed by the leadership team, so make sure you run a session or sessions to talk through the Plan face-to-face. Simply sending a Plan by email doesn't cut it!
- Ignore dependencies at your peril. Dependencies can impact your timeline and need to be planned to avoid wasted effort and rework. Understand what needs to be finished before something else can start. Understand what needs to kick off activity before another task can start. Understand what tasks need to come together to feed another task.
- The Change Manager may find it useful to develop a detailed Task Plan to manage activities and tasks. Use whatever you feel comfortable with – if you don't want to use Word or Excel, you can use pens, paper and post-its, and stick the Plan up on your wall.
- Remember: Risks and Issues templates are living documents with continual review and updates required to add new issues/risks and assess impacts and progress with actions.

- Business Case Contingency: there are many unknowns at the start of a project. It is best practice to include contingency in the costs. The more uncertain you are, the higher % contingency you should include in a cost line. Often, a contingency cost line is added at the bottom of a project cost estimate: 10-15% is usually the appropriate level, although it may be higher if there is greater uncertainty at the outset.
- Make sure you can measure the benefits in your Business Case. Set up tracking mechanisms so that you can measure the success to communicate and learn from.

EXERCISES

EXERCISE 1

Kick-Off Meeting

How might people be really engaged in the kick-off meeting? Be creative!

What does good facilitation look like?

What outcomes or results are we trying to produce with our new Positioning Strategy?

A melting billable hour iceberg can be a hazard AND an opportunity.

1. What are the hazards?
2. What are the opportunities?

EXERCISE 2

Pull Together a Team: Find Your Sponsor

Identify who in the leadership team would be a suitable Project Sponsor.

Check out what you should look for in a Sponsor in the section above.

EXERCISE 3

Thirty-second elevator pitch

Create a 30-second 'elevator pitch' on the need for change in pricing and the importance of acting now.

Tip: Imagine you are in the lift with two colleagues – one senior, one junior – and you want to tell them why value-based pricing is a good thing and what the firm will look and feel like once in place.

Use the work on the Goal and the future state descriptions to craft a compelling view of the future.

EXERCISE 4

Plan

1. What would the leadership team like to see from a Plan?
2. What do you think are the key issues to this change?
3. Taking each of the key issues, how might the issue be managed?
4. What do you think are the key risks for this change?
5. Taking each of the key risks, how might the risk be mitigated?
6. What dragons are hiding?!
7. Create a Plan using the High-Level Plan template.
8. Populate the Risks and Issues Logs using the Risk template and Issues template.
9. In creating a new story about our firm, what are the primary challenges or obstacles we must overcome?

EXERCISE 5

Business Case

What cost lines will this change have?

(Some common examples include Case Management Systems changes, Finance Systems changes, updates to website design and content, updates to marketing materials, people costs if you have to backfill for a period.)

What benefits lines will this change have?

(Some common examples include conversion rate, average case charge, operational costs per case.)

With guidance and a template from your Finance team, build your Business Case with a budget.

EXERCISE 6

Create Your Own Firm Know-How

Engage with champions with regard to the design and content of templates.

Look at what you send out now. What can be sent out in the future? How is it better?

Empower whole teams to participate in the creation of assumptions and exclusions to limit scope creep.

EXERCISE 7

Recognise that change is tough for everyone – our brains resist uncertainty. The key is to understand that individuals move through the change curve (see the diagram below and reading material) at different speeds and over different timespans. As a leader, remember that although you might be at the stage where you see the change as exciting, your colleagues and those across the firm may be in denial or anger.

Plot out where you think some of your Partners/leaders and managers may be on this curve.

This version of the Kubler-Ross Change Curve is reproduced with kind permission from the World of Work Project.

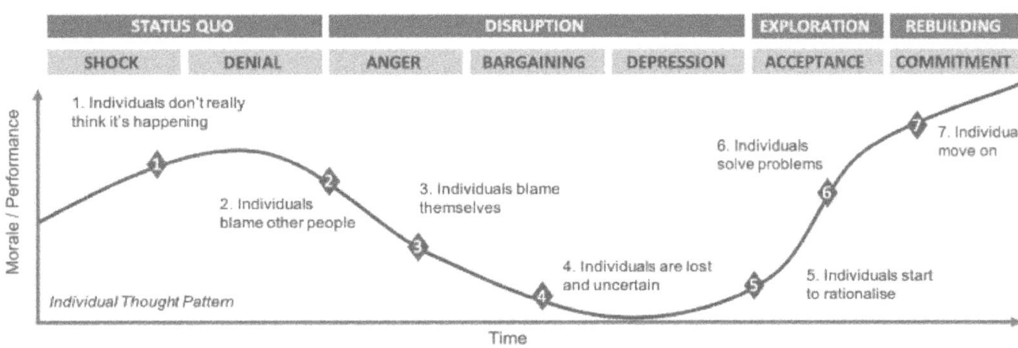

POSSIBILITY THINKING QUESTIONS TO POSE

- What can your internal agreed processes possibly look like?
- What words and descriptions can your pricing vocabulary possibly include?

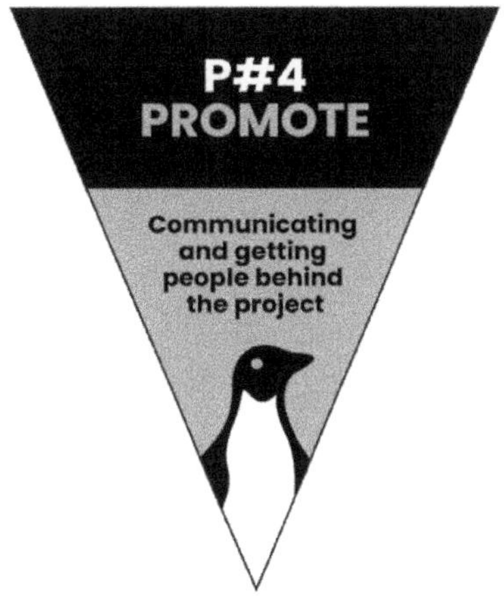

P#4 PROMOTE

COMMUNICATING AND GETTING PEOPLE BEHIND THE PROJECT

> The single biggest problem in communication is the illusion that it has taken place.
>
> **George Bernard Shaw**

DEVELOP A COMMUNICATIONS PLAN

Communication is often misunderstood and undervalued. The George Bernard Shaw quote above says it all.

To deliver change successfully, it is critical to communicate *early* to gain understanding and buy-in. Then, keep communicating over and over.

Some engagement guidelines:

- Communicate early.
- Don't wait until you have all the answers before you communicate.

- Communication is more than a broadcast – communication should include lots of engagement with a two-way dialogue.
- Avoid the 'comms vacuum'. People fill a comms vacuum with negative views. The human mind assumes you haven't communicated because there is bad news.
- Communication should be little and often. Don't wait for big news.
- Ensure consistency of messaging from the team.
- Listen and respond constructively to feedback.
- Don't just communicate what people want to hear – communicate what is needed to engage the team, and gain buy-in and support.
- DO communicate successes along the way and call out the team who are involved in delivering those successes.
- Engage your Sponsor to assist in communications to support buy-in from across the firm.

Develop a simple Communications Plan. A Communications Plan template and example are set out below. Make your Communications Plan a living document, to be continually reviewed and updated.

The Communications Plan usefully includes:

- Audience (e.g., leadership team, all staff).
- Type (e.g., broadcast, small group, 1-2-1).
- Channel (e.g., intranet, team meeting, office wall).
- Key messages to convey.
- Who is delivering the message?
- Format (e.g., presentation, poster on the wall).
- Timeline for each communication.
- Who owns the action to create the comms?

PROMOTE THE VISION

Goals, Vision, and progress should be communicated to the firm ad nauseam. If you go silent, people will assume it's gone away and is an example of yet another project which was started and not completed. You must overcome negativity, scepticism, and resistance.

The Vision you will have created will be simple, aspirational, feasible, flexible, and capable of easily being understood, communicated, and remembered. It should be communicated internally and externally. Have you created a picture people can understand and see? If you haven't, they won't get onboard. Have you clarified the future from the past and made it a reality? People have to know where the change will lead.

WORDS WITH THE WISE

Kirk Bowman, Art of Value

Kirk Bowman interviewed Andrew Barnes of the Lantern Group.

Kirk Q: What has been the reaction of younger attorneys to the practice of value pricing?

Andrew A: They are very enthusiastic when discussing the concept. The challenge is to keep the momentum going in the day-to-day practice. Those who have previously billed by the hour now call it the 'Dark Ages'.

RESISTANCE

Plan for resistance and accept that it can help clarify the issues. By addressing concerns, you can improve the change process.

You need to provide:

- Plan checkpoints to stop and recognise progress.
- Provide a mechanism for feedback/suggestions and the freedom to challenge the status quo – a forum for Naysayer penguins to communicate. Naysayers will help clarify problems and identify ones you have not thought of. They will ask tough questions which can help make the change.
- Communicate early and often, using multiple methods.
- Design and anticipate giving supportive action to deal with fear, anger, and resistance.
- Acknowledge concerns, perceived loss, and anger.
- Encourage discussions, dissent, and disagreement so that issues can be flushed out.
- Keep people talking. You need them to tell you what you know and don't know.

- Encourage consistency in senior leadership behaviours to support the Vision.

The Project Sponsor, leaders, and Pioneer penguins must model the behaviours of change.

> Be the change you want to see.
>
> **Gandhi**

The table below shows the start of a Communications Plan to help guide you both during and post-change. Consider all stakeholder groups and all levels in the business.

Consider:

- Who are your key audiences?
- How might you reach these audiences?
- How might you encourage dialogue and feedback?
- Communication is about engagement, not sermons.
- Remember to repeat key messages to ensure understanding and gain buy-in.
- Check for understanding of key messages – don't assume everyone is always on the same page.
- Your audience for change comms is everyone in the firm and all suppliers involved.
- Think about the audience and the purpose of each piece of comms – avoid a scattergun approach and ensure your comms are directed and purposeful to drive understanding and engagement.
- Use your Pioneers as your eyes and ears on the ground to assist in the continuous review of the effectiveness of the Communications Plan. Fill gaps in awareness, understanding, and buy-in across the firm.

EXPOSURE DRAFTS PRESENTS
TIME RECORDING IN HELL
BY GREG KYTE
YOU'RE A SALARIED EMPLOYEE AND WE GAVE THE CLIENT A FIXED PRICE, BUT YOU STILL MUST FILL OUT A TIMESHEET FOR ABSOLUTELY NO REASON!
GREG

Communications Plan Example

Audience	Type	Channel	Key Messages	Who delivers	Format	When	Action with
All staff	Broadcast	Town Hall	Launch: Vision. Goal. Benefits.	Sponsor	Slides	March 10th	Change Manager
All staff	Broadcast	Office walls	Vision. Goal. Benefits	n/a	A3 Posters	April	A Pioneer
All staff	Broadcast	Intranet	Progress, plans, celebrate successes	n/a	Short articles	Weekly update	Pioneers rota
Sponsor	121	F2F	Key risks & issues. Key decisions.	Change Manager	Status report	Monthly before Steering Gp	Change Manager
Operations team	Discussion group	Video call	What is changing for ops team and when. Understand fears and concerns. Answer questions. Identify potential champions. Identify sceptics.	Change Manager	Slide. Structured discussion.	End April	Change Manager
Pioneers	Meeting	F2F/Video/Hybrid	Review progress vs plan. Key plans for next week. Key risks and issues. Dependencies. Key messages	Change Manager	Status report. Plan. Risks, Issues logs.	Weekly on Tuesdays	Change Manager
Pioneers	Show & Tell	Video call	Progress on systems. Key decisions. Q&A.	IT Pioneer	Slides/demo	May	IT Pioneer
All staff	Broadcast	Town Hall	Celebrate success at key point in change	Sponsor/Change Manager	Slides	June	A Pioneer

COMMUNICATION GUIDANCE FOR EACH STAGE OF 8 PPP

Communication has to happen at each stage of the 8 PPP. Below are some communications that could be made at each stage of the process.

P#1 PARADIGM: THE FUNDAMENTAL CHANGE REQUIRED

Leaders have to lead, and that may involve defrosting the status quo at your firm.

- Clarify why change is not only required but essential for long-term survival.
- Is VBP a strategic objective? Has everyone been told?
- Define the current challenges in traditional billing methods.
- Communicate and identify industry trends and the best practices of firms that have embraced VBP.
- Highlight potential revenue, work-life balance, and the client satisfaction benefits of value-based pricing.
- Highlight the hazards and also paint a picture of the opportunities that await.

What reasons can you give in support of the change?

1. Do you have data about customer satisfaction and financial performance?
2. Is the fact that GenAI can do much of the research quicker than a lawyer the catalyst for change?
3. Feature the words and quotes of customers and authorities from the legal sector.
4. Encourage the open, honest discussion of the issues.
5. Advise Partners/directors to be honest with employees.
6. Bring to life future pricing opportunities and enhanced rewards. But be honest: the organisation has to change to create these opportunities.
7. Involve outsiders – industry commentators, analysts, or sector experts.

EXTERNAL COMMENTATORS

It may help to convince colleagues by referring them to what external commentators say about VBP. The sad thing is that many people have been saying this for years.

Law firm regulators are encouraging lawyers to embrace Value-Based Pricing. Fixing a fee upfront – based on value – is, according to the Victoria State regulator, 'innovative pricing' and is encouraged in Australia. It will be interesting to see what regulators in other jurisdictions decide to do.

The benchmarking study from the *National Westminster Bank Legal Report 2023* is worth reading. Prepared by Andrew Allen of PKF Francis Clark, it gave an interesting insight into the financial performance of law firms in the UK. The report included a section 'Questions to consider now' and asked readers to consider:

1. Do your fee-earners offer pricing choices to your clients?
2. Do your terms of engagement and time recording processes enable fee-earners to apply value billing?
3. What are you doing to identify potential new matter types for the firm to deliver in the future?

A link to obtain a copy of the NatWest report is in the Crib Sheet at the end of this section.

In the LexisNexis Bellwether Report, *The Riddle of Perception 2016*, Professor Stephen Mayson, in the foreword, wrote:

'The report provides evidence of what I once described as 'the grand delusion' – essentially, a culture that is out of tune with the market and a broken business model. The news that this delusion still persists is disappointing. Tinkering around the edges of the cost base and blaming others for the rest, rather than tackling some possibly uncomfortable home truths, will not address it and secure a sound future.

'But there is hope in these pages, too. The report also shows the correlation between growing, successful firms and other identifiable factors. The foundations lie in firms actually doing something about the fundamentals of their business through entrepreneurialism, thinking outside the legal box, focusing on client value and their experience of service delivery, specialisation, re-staffing, and the appropriate use of technology. The principal messages and lessons to be learnt are summed up in the report's title. Seeing legal services as those who pay for them would wish to see them is far more valuable than pursuing one's own pre-conceived and unchallenged notions.'

The judiciary has been commenting about the frightening levels of legal costs and complexity for years. In his speech to the Association of Cost Lawyers, Lord Neuberger identified the concept of value pricing as being worthy of further investigation as an alternative to the billable hour. Neuberger said:

'Hourly billing, at best, leads to inefficient practices; at worst, it rewards and incentivises inefficiency. Moreover, it undermines effective competition in the provision of legal services, as it penalises . . . well-run legal businesses whose systems and processes enable it to conclude matters. It also penalises the able; those with greater professional knowledge and skill, as they will tend to work at a more efficient rate. In other words, hourly billing fails to reward the diligent, the efficient, and the able: its focus on the cost of time – a truly moveable feast – simply does not reflect the value of work.'

He went on to say, 'That no-one has suggested a viable alternative is something which needs to be remedied, and the sooner the better. An approach to litigation costs based on value-pricing, rather than hourly-billing, is one which urgently needs to be worked out and applied. Rather than treating time as the commodity, which is being sold, we should be adopting an approach where skill and experience are the commodities which are sold.'

This speech from the Master of the Rolls was in 2012! Mayson was commenting on a report from 2016! Lawyers are still saying it can't be done!

Point out to colleagues and Naysayers that change is inevitable. By embracing VBP, you are getting 'ahead of the curve'.

P#2 PIONEERS: THE GROUP THAT EXPLORES THE NEW WAY OF WORKING

Pioneers need to be empowered and supported. They must not feel that the VBP project is like pushing water uphill with a fork.

There needs to be open and honest dialogue. Explain their roles and responsibilities in the project. Emphasise the importance of their leadership and support in driving change.

Stress to the Pioneers how it is not organisations but people that facilitate change.

8 PPP PENGUIN LOGIC

Who coped well at work during the pandemic?

Chances are, the global pandemic prompted a new agility inside your firm. Your people may be more able and willing to embrace new practices than you think. Choose Pioneers that worked well through the pandemic and embraced change, if you can.

P#3 PLAN: DESIGNING THE PLAN, STRATEGY AND VISION

The Vision needs to be a 'clear and compelling statement' of where your organisation is heading and – crucially – why. The 'why' is essential – it makes the status quo seem dangerous and misguided. You should seek to connect the Vision to the firm's long-term success and competitive advantage.

Be prepared to explain how the change will impact work, morale, and the daily life of the employees. Address these issues head-on. Those up for the challenge will embrace it. Those who are not at least know that it is coming.

It's important to note that the Vision is a 5-minute conversation… not a 35-page leaflet or PowerPoint.

P#4 PROMOTE: COMMUNICATING AND GETTING PEOPLE BEHIND THE PROJECT

How can you portray and promote the Vision you create? Be imaginative. Use descriptions, but keep it simple. Lay out the long-term Goal.

You will be able to point out that other law firms are doing VBP successfully.

Empower your people to spread the message and address concerns within their teams. You need to create VBP impetus in your organisation. Create momentum and spread the news.

8 PPP PENGUIN LOGIC

Leaders need to remain on message

The leaders must be onboard and must not contradict the Vision or strategic objectives. Behaviours inconsistent with the Vision will kill it. It's as simple as that.

You may need to have serious words with some Partners and Team Leaders before you go public with the project.

P#5 PERMIT: GIVING PEOPLE THE AUTHORITY TO ACT

Keep communicating the change. By the time your leadership team is getting bored of talking about the benefits of the VBP project, the penny will only just be starting to drop for some people. It's the conversations at the photocopier with a Partner, a 'well done' here and there, an anecdote, a story told that will help spread and embed the change.

Create candid and unscripted communication opportunities.

Identify potential obstacles to adopting value-based pricing, such as resistance from certain lawyers and prepare responses to them. Ensure your Pioneer penguins are briefed well.

Create opportunities for debate and questioning in the business. Ask Team Leaders to raise VBP at team meetings; it should be a standing agenda item. Ensure Team Leaders take minutes of the meetings and feed back the results to the project team.

Raise VBP often at staff meetings. Raise VBP at appraisals – what are the troops thinking and feeling? Find out. You should create Pricing Confidence Surveys. Provide staff at all levels with the information. Play the VBP message on repeat. Develop strategies to address these barriers, including clear Communications Plans to counter objections.

P#6 PRIZE: CREATING SOME QUICK WINS

Celebrate successes and link them back to the Vision. Use these wins to demonstrate the benefits of value-based pricing. Celebrate successes. Boost morale. Make public thank yous and show gratitude.

Create the opportunities!

- New customer wins.
- A client who was given three options and chose the most expensive.
- A lawyer who asked for a 'pump fist' price and received it.
- Clients who were delighted to be given a choice of options.
- Referrers who have sent clients to you because options are created.
- Clients that have been deselected!
- Notifications about the BBUs being created and where the template library is stored.
- The profitability of the pilot team members.

Tie these wins back to the Vision. Use the wins to celebrate the new behaviours in action. They will no longer be theoretical or unproven. You will need to create ways to maintain the momentum.

P#7 PERSEVERE: KEEP GOING

What established metrics can you use to track the progress of the value-based pricing project?

- Increased profit on matters?
- Reduced aged debt?
- Fewer complaints?
- Higher levels of customer satisfaction?
- A better quality of client?
- Improved work-life balance shown via HR staff surveys?

Regularly communicate updates on the key performance indicators that show VBP is working.

Continuously reinforce the importance of the VBP project and its alignment with firm Goals.

8 PPP PENGUIN LOGIC

Blow trumpets and grasp nettles

Create shared excitement about where the Vision is leading and that it is working.

Address seeming contradictions and inconsistencies head-on. Don't ignore them – you can guarantee the Naysayer penguins won't.

P#8 PASSION: CREATING THE NEW CULTURE

New principles or behaviours become part of an organisation once their worth has been proven. And we know lawyers like proof… beyond reasonable doubt. So do not declare success too soon.

Formalise the integration of value-based pricing into the firm's policies and procedures.

Your troops will need to see the new policies are working.

> For values or guiding principles to be truly effective they have to be verbs.
>
> **Simon Sinek**

Continue to develop training programmes to ensure all lawyers and staff understand and can implement the new pricing strategies.

Continuously assess and adapt the pricing methodology you create, based on client and lawyer feedback.

We know that lawyers are naturally conservative, risk-averse, and argumentative; they pay attention to detail and like to work within defined parameters (the law). That's why they are lawyers.

The change will happen, and they will see it as a new way of working that is better.

8 PPP PENGUIN LOGIC

Don't declare victory too soon

In short! Throughout the process, be acutely aware of the need to communicate well and often. Plan and emphasise the alignment of value-based pricing with the firm's values, the client-centric approach, and long-term profitability. Foster open dialogue, encourage feedback, and address concerns promptly to ensure successful implementation.

POSSIBILITY THINKING

How can we possibly communicate our value-based pricing offering to clients?

- 1-2-1s.
- Website.
- Meetings.
- Advertising.
- Workshops.
- Referrals.
- Professional organisations.
- Accountants who act for companies who refer to us.
- Email footers.
- Leaflets.
- TV advertising.
- Branded stationery.
- Videos.
- Client interviews and reviews.
- YouTube.
- WhatsApp.
- Blog.
- Marketing campaign.
- Christmas party.
- Conference.
- Shared testimonials.
- Google Ads.

- Webinar training.
- Advertisements.
- Press releases.
- Flyers.
- Mail shots.
- Branded uniform.
- Telephone calls.
- Text message.
- Billboards.
- Social media.
- Award shows.
- Contact form.
- Account managers meetings.
- Survey and thought leadership piece – how do firms charge and how would clients like to be charged?
- Video.
- Put it on a hat…
- Correspondence.
- Value-based pricing gadget.

WORDS WITH THE WISE

Dr Jacqui Rigby, Rigby Pollitt Associates

Communication is about engagement, not oration. Make it a two-way conversation, not a demonstration of PowerPoint skills.

Repeat key messages clearly and frequently. Explain the why, what, how and when.

Robin Dicks, Thriving Consultancy

I recall working with quite a big firm where there's lots of town hall stuff, where people were saying, 'This is now what we're going to do, we're going to be client-centric, we're going to do it excellently, this is important, and we're going to do this now.'

In that environment, everyone smiled and nodded and said the right thing. But what we heard from the people who were a year or two away from partnership, they said, actually, that's all well and good, but when we get back to our desks, then we're told, 'Don't worry about all that stuff. Just get on with the transaction in hand.'

You've got to have real role-modelling stuff from department heads. They're critical to success.

David Gilroy, Conscious Solutions

I think, from a marketer's view, implementing VBP is more of an internal job than an external one.

Will Whawell, Excelo Consulting

I've heard lawyers say, and it's usually men, not women, 'My billable target is 1,900 hours a year.' What does it prove? It doesn't prove anything. It could be 1,900 hours of input that created no value. Value and outcome are very important things because you could have someone now who works compressed hours and, say, works two days' work a week, but the outcome to the customer is such that they're paid for that value.

Karen Finch, Legally Yours

GenAI has democratised the ability to use technology in every aspect of our personal and professional lives. However, just because the technology can do it, it doesn't mean that people automatically trust or want the technology to do their legal work. What lawyers now must do is work doubly hard on communicating their value, promoting to their clients what their value is, and why you still need them on top of GenAI technologies.

John Chisholm, John Chisholm Consulting

The firms that have changed their business models – right from the get-go – involve and educate their whole team. The leadership continually communicates and encourages. In any change management scenario, everyone needs to be involved and everyone has a role to play. This is especially so when moving to value-based pricing. Why are we doing it? What the potential benefits are, but also the potential challenges, need to be communicated and laid bare.

In regard to pricing, for instance, most firms that made the transition did not involve many in the pricing decisions. Anecdotally, some of the best pricers I have seen are not the Partners; sometimes, they're employed lawyers, sometimes support staff in the firm, who are much better at pricing than the Partners. Why? Because, as a third party, they can be as brave as a lion pricing someone else's work because they don't have to face their clients. That is the reason artists, authors, and actors have agents. They are far better at both talking up their client's value but also their price.

Kirsty Pappin, Aries Legal Practice Management

Definitely don't say, 'This is what we're doing, and here you go, do it.' That's just opening yourself and the firm up for immediate failure.

Do let staff know the VBP pilot is taking place. Because this is part of how your change management process will start working, with people talking and saying things to others like, 'Well, hang on, why are you not time recording anymore? . . . Why are you less stressed?' Staff will become intrigued; they will want to know what the pilot is and learn about how they can get in on the action – especially if it means they are no longer clock-watching!

I would, approximately every other week, provide an update to the firm about how things are going, where we're going, where our next steps are heading. Set up an intranet page that provides key insights to staff with project progress. Guage what will be the best way to communicate with staff.

And even if some people read that and go, 'I'm not interested in this; delete the email' that's fine. But there will be some people that are sceptics and think 'Let's just see how they're going. Well, I want to see if they're failing here… oh, they're not.'

I would communicate successes; absolutely get those successes straight out there.

'By the way, guys, we've just signed up a new client using value-based pricing. They're really happy, and this is how we did it on the pilot…'

CRIB SHEET

READING & VIEWING

READ

Have You Heard About The Vacuum of Communication?

By Kelvin Kong

https://www.linkedin.com/pulse/have-you-heard-vacuum-communication-kelvin-kong/

READ

The Best Way to Develop Killer Key Messages

By Beaumont

https://talktobeaumont.com/develop-key-messages-for-effective-communication/

READ

The Difference between Communication and Engagement

By Petrina Frost

https://www.linkedin.com/pulse/difference-between-communication-engagement-petrina-frost/

READ

Law Firm Partnership: The Grand Delusion

By Stephen Mayson

https://stephenmayson.com/2012/10/09/law-firm-partnership-the-grand-delusion/

READ

NatWest Bank Legal Benchmark Report 2023

By Andrew Allen

https://www.natwestgroup.com/news-and-insights/news-room/press-releases/enterprise/2023/sep/9-in-10-small-law-firms-optimistic-about-future-despite-financia.html

READ (COMPULSORY)

Victoria State Regulator Pricing Model Summary Table

Fixing a fee upfront – based on value – is, according to the regulator, 'innovative pricing' and is encouraged in Australia.

https://lsbc.vic.gov.au/lawyers/legal-costs/innovation-pricing

WATCH

Communicating a Vision for Change

John Kotter

https://www.youtube.com/watch?v=bGVe3wRKmH0

WATCH

The Change Process – Emotions when Reacting to Change

Kim Tasso eloquently explains the emotions that people experience when dealing with change.

https://www.youtube.com/watch?v=XN5R_jePWJk

WATCH (COMPULSORY)

Dealing with Resistance to Change

John Kotter

https://www.youtube.com/watch?v=Wdroj6F3VlQ

WATCH

Your Customers Probably Aren't Paying You What You're Worth

Pricing consultant Casey Brown shares helpful stories and learnings that can help you better communicate your value and get paid for your excellence.

https://www.ted.com/talks/casey_brown_know_your_worth_and_then_ask_for_it?referrer=playlist-get_paid_what_you_re_worth&autoplay=true

WATCH

A Sixth Sense for Project Management

By Tres Roeder, TED Talk

https://www.ted.com/talks/tres_roeder_a_sixth_sense_for_project_management

WATCH

How to Know, Ask, and Get Paid What You're Worth

Freelancer Soness Stevens debunks the myths that could prevent you from earning – and knowing – your full professional value. According to Stevens, there are five myths that freelancers tell themselves about their work, their pay, and their worth.

https://youtu.be/QWCKJ9dKWjM

TIPS/CHECKLISTS

1. Communicate, communicate, communicate. Just because you believe you have communicated something doesn't mean it has landed and been understood. Repeat messages over and over. Check that the key messages have been communicated accurately by asking people to tell you what they understand.
2. Agreeing a price upfront is a competitive advantage, and clients will pay a premium for the price certainty.

EXERCISES

EXERCISE 1

At what meetings does real communication happen at your firm? Large meetings, small meetings, memos, away days, departmental meetings, etc.

Who should be communicating the Vision but maybe isn't?

Who are the Naysayers? Those who can't see their future in the new world.

Do you have these people? Identify them. Learn and understand their fears.

EXERCISE 2

Communication has to happen in many ways. Are you communicating?

Has information been disseminated through team meetings? How do you know?

What happens when a new staff member joins? Is the Vision and pricing policy part of the induction process?

How can you keep pricing at the forefront of the firm's mind as a whole?

Is there a mechanism to collate feedback and collect hindering thoughts? Are your staff being able to voice concerns?

Are you and the project team, and those initially involved, still leading by example?

Is there a Plan to deal with resistance?

EXERCISE 3

You can use the Communications Plan template to develop your comms plan. Check out the Tips section, below, for a partially completed example.

Consider:

Who are your key audiences?

How might you reach these audiences?

How might you encourage dialogue and feedback?

Communications Plan Template

Audience	Type	Channel	Key Messages

	Who delivers	Format	When	Action with

EXERCISE 4

Website

Critically compare your website with those of your competitors. Is it all about you? Does it deal with customers' pain and the outcomes they seek? What should your website contain?

EXERCISE 5

Have you a Plan to:

1. Tell customers.
2. Burn timesheets.
3. Publicise your USP.
4. Rewrite your induction training.
5. Redesign team training.
6. Create a Team Skills Matrix, which includes VBP.
7. Create a Value Council.
8. Amend your values, if required.
9. Created a VBP Succession Plan – who will take it forward and drive it? Are leaders trained and still onboard?

POSSIBILITY THINKING QUESTIONS TO POSE

1. How can we possibly communicate with the whole firm?
2. Who are our possible audiences?
3. How might we possibly communicate with our audiences?
4. How can we possibly empower our people more?
5. How can we possibly create opportunities to maintain the VBP momentum?
6. How can we possibly encourage dialogue and feedback during and post-change?

EXPOSURE DRAFTS
BY GREG KYTE
LET'S SEE... TWELVE HOURS OF LABOR... LOOKS LIKE THIS LITTLE GUY OWES ME £3,060 PLUS EXPENSES.
LAWYER CHILDBIRTH

P#5 PERMIT

GIVING PEOPLE THE AUTHORITY TO ACT

> 'Sometimes, you have to get far enough down the path alone to convince everyone else there is one. You have to lead long before anyone else starts to follow you.'
>
> **Jon Cobb, Jon Cobb Consulting**
>
> Nothing is easy; it requires practice.
>
> **Professor Brian Cox**

EMPOWER YOUR PEOPLE

Remove barriers. Allow those who want to make the Vision a reality to go about their work.

EMPOWER THE TEAM

Being a leader is not about knowing all the answers or giving the impression you do. Leadership is not about seniority – the most junior person in your firm can be a leader.

Leadership is a set of behaviours that helps people align collectively, and – in business – deliver against a common purpose and goal.

Leadership is about followership. Watch the *First Follower Dancing Guy* video (see Reading section) for a fun view of what followership is all about. In the Reading section, there are several articles, books, and videos about leadership, followership, and empowerment.

To empower a team, ask them questions so that they think more deeply, and come to a solution. Try to use thought-provoking and open questions – encouraging thoughts from others. A good leader doesn't want to make all the decisions but wants decision-making to be a collective team effort. This adds more 'brain power' to decision-making and includes deliberations from different perspectives and experiences.

Empowering people to act will not come naturally to many lawyers; there are understandable reasons why. Firstly, we operate in a highly regulated environment; as lawyers, we are subject to immense scrutiny, regulations, codes of conduct and common law. It's a hard gig!

Our lawyers know the law. They will be concerned. By their very nature, lawyers are naturally conservative, risk-averse, and don't like change. So, the empowering element will require careful communication and explanation. The psychological safety net will need a detailed explanation… it must not be career-limiting for people to help and participate on this journey.

To implement value-based pricing, we need to develop a new way of thinking and also accept that pricing is an art, not a science (I've said it once, I'll say it again!). We need to be prepared to give things a go and also be prepared to fail. Lawyers don't like things that are not certain, and they don't like to fail!

So, it's incumbent on you to look at any individual organisation and identify the barriers to change. Quite often, the solutions will come from the employees themselves. Remember, if you get stuck, you can turn the problem into a question using Possibility Thinking. Your people will know what frustrates them in the workplace. The leader's job is to find out what those frustrations are and work out how to resolve them. This isn't anything new in the world outside of the law; it's called process improvement. However, that isn't a phrase that is often used in the legal industry.

Innovation involves generating new ideas. Again, innovation is not most lawyers' default happy place. However, the new ideas to implement in your firm may often be available in other industry sectors. Part of your role should be to look at what they are and how you can muscle in, mercilessly rip them off, and introduce them into your organisation.

Do not forget to look at other change management projects you've introduced in your organisation. Why were they successful, or why did they fail? They might not have got off the ground at all. Look at what didn't work and work out why. Similarly, look at what worked and why, and try to replicate some of those good practices.

As with all change management projects, it is important to adopt the KISS principle. Keep It Simple, Stupid. It will be necessary to strip away processes that slow things down. You will need to create your own set of golden rules and ensure that you do not get bogged down in developing long and complicated processes. Perfection should not become the enemy of good.

REMOVING OBSTACLES AND ROADBLOCKS

As more people come onboard with the project, more roadblocks will be identified and will fall.

It will be necessary to resolve opposition and facilitate reconciliation with Naysayer penguins if required. Anticipate and plan how you will deal with resistance. Some people will be genuinely apprehensive; others will be active saboteurs. You will need to bring out your tools of persuasion!

It is crucial that the strategic promotion of the VBP project is kept on track. The leadership must actively support the Vision, the processes created, and the new way of pricing.

Ensure the methodology you create is regularly reviewed, developed, and improved.

The rollout will need to celebrate success. Reward those who are actively contributing to the success of the project. The Pioneers must be celebrated.

Empowering others includes:

- Giving people freedom and direction.
- Permission to find team-led solutions.
- Encourage people to speak up and seek differing views.
- Encourage people to take risks.
- Affirm and refine the Vision.
- Be honest and tell people what you know and what you don't know.
- Encourage teamwork and collaboration.
- Provide training and support.
- Set short-term goals.
- Identify clients for deselection.

Common barriers that will be put in your way will include:

- Pressures of work whereby people are too busy to try anything new.
- Partner patronage. Someone may be promoted because they are favoured but don't do the right things.
- A silo mentality where the head of the silo doesn't want to change.

- Naysayer penguins will be concerned.
- Existing structures and policies that people may not want to change.
- Unwillingness to engage or a lack of team skills to manage and facilitate change.

In the appendices, I have listed over 50 reasons your colleagues will tell you why you shouldn't embark on the VBP journey. You can probably think of a further 50. The person leading the project must have answers to all of these 50+ reasons, plus any others thrown at them.

Looking at your organisation, its structure skills, and supervisors, have you got the right structure and skills for the right people running the teams? Where are the Naysayer penguins? How are you going to engage with them?

As I've stated already, pricing is a skill that must be learnt. You will never stop learning. And failing to embark upon the training and continuing to train is one of the biggest single points of failure.

As the project proceeds, you will need to start identifying *future* Pioneer penguins, those who are enthused and interested in becoming involved. These are people you can work with in the future. There may be cautious enthusiasts; people who are interested but who have lots of hindering thoughts. That's okay; you can work with those people later.

There may be, however, people who simply refuse to change. At some time in the future, these individuals will have to be dealt with. It won't come as a surprise to learn that your HR team – if you have one – is likely to play an important role in this process. The HR team may already know who they are, as some of these people may have voiced concerns about this project.

Changes and conversations may well be underway in different parts of the business.

- Partners/Shareholders
  - Should be seeking information and updates regarding progress.
  - Asking questions about the training programme rollout.
  - Asking questions about the financial implications.
- Operations
  - Identifying policies which need to be designed/amended/scrapped.
- Finance
  - Will be looking at the information/data they need to track and report on progress.
  - Files opened.
  - Bills delivered.
  - Aged debt.

- Allocating fee splits on matters where time has been recorded (assuming your lawyers continue to time record for a while). What work created the value?
  - Team and individual lawyer gross profitability.
  - Increases in individual client spend/average prices.
  - Will be actively requesting data from teams… what prices have been given?
- IT
  - May be updating and creating fields in CRM systems to collect data.
  - Be considering how training materials/BBUs can be created and made available throughout the firm.
  - Be actively designing Fixed-Price Agreement master templates for Practice Areas.
  - Creating tools and templates to help create and calculate base costs.
- HR
  - Looking at how VBP impacts appraisals and performance reviews.
  - Revisiting bonus schemes to see if they need amending.
  - Creating questions to ask candidates at interviews about their pricing knowledge.
  - Be considering how to roll out firm-wide training and induction programmes.
  - Be coaching individuals who are concerned about the changes, especially if their clients have been identified as candidates for deselection.
  - Be identifying possible candidates for the second wave of Pioneers.
- The Marketing team/BD
  - Designing eye-catching templates for your Fixed-Price Agreements.
  - Creating case studies where clients report how delighted they were in being given a choice of options.
  - Drafting elevator pitches for staff to use when discussing the new pricing methodology.
  - Planning a recruitment advertising campaign to promote the new ways that you work at your organisation.
  - Updating website pages and other marketing collateral to promote your VBP policy.

- Analysing source codes of new matters. Looking at new clients already onboarded.
- Looking at opportunities created and conversion statistics.
- Identifying clients to deselect.

PRICING CONFIDENCE

- The next subject, to be honest, is a tricky one. It deals with a lawyer's lack of confidence, and lawyers rarely admit that they lack confidence to each other. However, many have admitted it to me in my surveys.
- It's natural for recent graduates or inexperienced lawyers to have a low opinion of the value they can create for clients. But it can last for far too long. Some of the most experienced and expert lawyers I have met, who are specialists in their fields, lack Pricing Confidence – Lawyers who have worked in the sector for years and have had numerous successful outcomes.
- This is why taking control of pricing and creating a system, process, and framework will help boost confidence levels at all levels in the business.
- It is not uncommon for many British people to feel uncomfortable when talking about money. I remember having one training session with a group of wills and probate lawyers via Zoom. I pointed out the natural British hesitancy when discussing the subject of money and pointed out that this is something we would have to address. The whole group were shocked when a junior lawyer piped up to contradict my assumption. She said, 'I have no difficulty discussing the subject of money at all – but then again, I am Polish.' And believe me, she didn't. She was very confident talking about the value she created and why she felt she was worth every penny.
- Historically, lawyers have managed to hide behind Engagement Letters and estimates of hours and huge ranges of costs, which are meaningless on so many occasions. I remember when I started my career in the 1980s, and you would have to give a range of costs for a litigation case, and you could indicate that it would be between £1,000 and £100,000 because – if the case went to the House of Lords – that was indicative of the costs that might be incurred. Totally meaningless for the client, who may have had no intention of going to trial, let alone the Supreme Court.
- Lawyers need to grow in confidence and see themselves as problem-solvers, businesspeople, business owners, entrepreneurs and opportunity-generators. That's what they are. Our lawyers generate value and outcomes. They are not 'order takers' participating in a process.

DITCHERVILLE
by Jonathan Stark
We need a proposal from you!
The project should be pretty easy!
It'll only take a few hours!
What's your hourly rate so we can get started?
No.
What do you mean "No"?
No, the project isn't going to be easy or you wouldn't be talking to an expert like me.
No, it's not only going to take a few hours because you're not qualified to diagnose that.
And no, I'm not going to give you my hourly rate because I don't have one.
So... are you going to give us a proposal?
No.

I don't describe myself as a lawyer; I describe myself as a problem-solver and risk adviser.

Steve Brown, Lynne & Brown, Perth

Let's make the future so bright you have got to wear shades.

Shaun Jardine

What determines the level of self-esteem is what the individual does.

Nathaniel Branden, The Six Pillars of Self-Esteem

Customers prefer to associate with successful professionals. Customers want their professionals to be successful because they want to be successful. Do not be afraid to show opulence in front of your customers.

Ron Baker, Professional's Guide to Value Pricing

Take new clients slowly, show them your intent to take care of them and give them a wonderful experience. Deeply consider where you have developed your thinking on the creative profession and its worth, and then step out with some guts to charge your clients for your true value. Strategic pricing comes with practice, and your skill will grow over time. Pricing is a learned discipline that anyone can learn. Start practising! Do your clients a favour, charge them what you're worth. You will both be happy as a result.

Tim Williams

When broaching pricing with your people, I strongly recommend that you do not talk about low self-esteem. Refer to *Pricing Confidence.* That, after all, is the confidence that this book is seeking to address.

Nathaniel Branden, in his book, *The Six Pillars of Self-Esteem*, (I wish he had called it something else), defines self-esteem as:

1. Confidence in our ability to think.
2. Confidence in our ability to cope with the basic challenges of life.
3. Confidence in our right to be successful and happy, the feeling of being worthy, deserving, entitled to assert our needs and wants, achieve our values, and enjoy the fruits of our efforts.

So, the good news here is that it is all about confidence!

PRICE SENSITIVITY METER

The Dutch Economist Peter Van Westendorp introduced what he called a Price Sensitivity Meter (PSM) in 1976. You can be forgiven for not knowing about it until now, although you will readily understand the principles.

The PSM incorporates four key questions that lawyers can use to gather valuable insights into Pricing Confidence for their legal services:

1. At what price would you consider [the legal service] to be too expensive that you would not consider purchasing it?

This question helps lawyers identify the upper price threshold at which potential clients would be discouraged from seeking their legal services. It provides a clear understanding of the pricing ceiling clients are willing to accept.

2. At what price would you consider [legal service] to be priced so low that you would question its quality or expertise?

This question reveals the lower price limit at which potential clients may perceive the legal services as lacking quality or expertise. Lawyers can use this insight to avoid pricing their services too low and potentially undervaluing their expertise.

Questions 1 and 2 create a range for your services.

3. At what price would you consider [legal service] to be starting to get expensive, but you would still consider purchasing it?

This question identifies the range within which potential clients feel the legal services are moderately expensive but still within an acceptable range. This is the question we are interested in.

4. At what price would you consider [legal service] to be a bargain – a great deal for the quality and expertise offered?

This question reveals the price point at which potential clients perceive the legal services as great value, considering the quality and expertise provided. This is the price you should not go below.

By incorporating these four questions into team meetings, surveys, or interviews, you can gather comprehensive data for your Pricing Strategy.

You may also (when trying to gather information) ask clients a slight variation of the question, which is, 'How much do you think other people will pay for this service?' If you frame the question in this way, you may get more honest feedback as they are not on the defensive; you are not asking how much they would pay… it is others.

In my view, a good starting point for any information gathering is to ask your own lawyers to answer these questions. I am often astounded by the range of prices I am given for a defined service from the members of the same firm.

IF YOUR LAW FIRM WERE A SHOP

We must take control of the way pricing is dealt with and operated. Think of your firm as a shop.

If you went into your local supermarket, picked out a basket of goods, and went to seven different checkouts in the same shop, you would be given seven identical prices.

If clients approach your lawyers for legal work, let's say seven lawyers, are you confident that they will get seven identical prices? I have tested this with law firms that I consult with. One law firm gave me seven different prices for the same conveyancing transaction. The price differential between the lowest and the highest was nearly 300%.

LACK OF CONFIDENCE: SURVEY RESULTS

In the summer of 2023, I was invited to speak at a large legal conference in London. I thought it would be a good idea to do a survey of the delegates before the event, as it would give me something to discuss at the conference itself. The survey sought to take the temperature of the residential conveyancing market with an emphasis on pricing and financial know-how. The survey of 80 firms was totally anonymous. Extracts of the survey are set out below.

BIG SURVEY QUESTIONS

Q: I am confident that the work we do helps and benefits our clients.

To some extent: 3.75%.

Always/Yes: 93.75%.

Q: Which of these are issues within your firm?

Work-life balance challenges: 63.29%.

Risk of burn-out for some individuals: 60.76%.

Significant resources spent on time recording: 10.13%.

Significant resources spent on chasing unpaid bills: 16.46%.

Lack of confidence in negotiating fees at the outset of a matter: 25.32%.

Lack of confidence when asking for an increased fee when a matter is progressing: 62.03%.

Q: I believe my firm tends to reduce prices based on what our competitors may charge.

Not at all: 38.75%.

To some extent: 43.75%.

Always/Yes: 5.00%.

Q: My colleagues and I know how to confidently deal with price objections from clients when we receive them.

Not at all: 3.75%.

To some extent: 56.25%.

Always: 32.50%.

Comments: 'Some members of staff are better than others. Those in supervisory positions tend to provide wording to use with clients who challenge our fees.'

Q: Would you be happy for someone else to price work initially at the outset (seeking input from you regarding complexity, etc.) and then onboard the

client, and then leave you to get on and deliver the service to the client?

Not at all: 37.50%.

To some extent: 32.50%.

Always: 20.00%.

Q: Which of these do you think would be materially helpful inputs to help the firm improve its profitability?

More pricing training, including value-based pricing: 41.89%.

Better training explaining the data extracted from the firm's management systems: 25.68%.

Better training about how law firms operate, including on costs and profitability: 47.30%.

Sacking some of the existing clients: 29.73%.

Creating, documenting, and distributing details of our pricing policy: 21.62%.

Having a consistent pricing policy: 35.14%.

Moving major pricing decisions away from individuals: 21.62%.

Ceasing copying competitor pricing: 24.32%.

The firm starting to operate as a price setter: 29.73%.

Reducing or stopping the use of the billable hour: 10.81%.

Comments from participants:

'Charging fees that are worthy of you.'

'Some lawyers need to build their confidence and value themselves.'

'Educating the public on what we do to justify our fee.'

'Coaching to increase confidence in securing better pricing.'

Q: What prevents your firm from charging more for your services?

'Nothing.'

'The local market/competition.'

'Quality of service for clients.'

'Concern about profitability, losing clients/fear.'

'Referrers fee scales.'

'The customers we service can ill afford higher fees.'

'Management decisions.'

'Clients will leave.'

'We will be too expensive.'

'They will think we are ripping them off.'

Q: Do you think your firm should increase your fees? If so, by what amount?

10% of current fee: 15.19%.

20% of current fee: 24.05%.

30% of current fee: 5.06%.

40% of current fee: 1.27%.

50% of current fee: 5.06%.

More than 50% of current fee: 2.53%.

They are fine as they are: 17.72%.

In surveys with other firms, I have asked identical questions of other Practice Area teams. The answers are usually not very different.

The surveys show that confidence is an issue, and it is one which I hope can be addressed by pursuing this project.

WORDS WITH THE WISE

Tim Williams, Ignition Consulting

We are quick to lay the blame at the feet of the client, but is it possible that the problem really starts with us? For starters, we constantly refer to our business as a 'service business'. Some firms – like advertising agencies – have 'client service' departments. We call ourselves a 'professional service firm'. Consider how this creates our self-perception.

Many firms lament that they have become 'order-takers'. But why? Who turned your firm into an order-taker? You did – not your clients. You did it by forgetting what it is you're really selling. You're not selling service. You're selling important business outcomes. The firms that understand this invest in better people who can produce a better product. They resist hiring an army of junior people who are good at service but fail to add the value that clients are ultimately paying for. They realise that the way to deal with demanding clients isn't to give them exactly what they want, but rather to counsel clients on what they really need. You only get treated like a servant if you act like a servant.

The fact is that we shouldn't be regarded as professional service firms, but rather professional knowledge firms. Clients don't just hire us for what we do, but rather what we know.

> We, as a profession, are terrible at pricing. Awful. Lost. Clueless. Atrocious. Self-immolatory. I could go on, but only to hammer home the point, so that we can come to accept it more easily. The shoe fits, so we might as well wear it. We're useless at pricing — and that's okay. It's understandable. No one ever trained us in pricing, either in law school or during our bar admissions procedure. Even if a senior lawyer took us under her wing when we first started out, we only learned the same scattershot substitutes for pricing that lawyers have been relying upon for decades.
>
> **Jordan Furlong**

BELIEVE IN YOUR PRICE

To price for value, we must have confidence in the fact we can create value.

We need to have confidence in our judgment and confidence in our intellectual capacity.

STOP AVOIDING THE CONVERSATION

Lawyers have a number of fears when it comes to pricing.

1. Lawyers fear giving a fixed price. They regard the hourly rate as a security blanket. They will ask, 'What if it goes wrong and I have to do more work?' We have dealt with that. We suck it up and learn from it.

2. They fear having a structured value-based price conversation with the client.
3. They fear having to present their price in a new way and create options.
4. They fear having to work in a way that is different.
5. They fear rejection.

HOW CAN YOU INCREASE A LAWYER'S PRICING CONFIDENCE?

Boosting someone's confidence takes time and effort. Again, a disclaimer: a detailed analysis of coaching techniques is way beyond the scope of this book. I have spoken with a number of coaches, and they have all told me the silver bullet I was hoping for (to improve Pricing Confidence) does not exist.

Coaching and support are key. It may well be the case that the coaching and support needs to come from a counsellor.

Some things you may be able to try yourself include:

- Encourage your lawyers to focus on their achievements, strengths, and skills that led to them becoming the lawyers they are.
- Offer constructive feedback, provide support, and remind them of their past successes.
- Set achievable goals to build their confidence gradually. Can they increase prices by 10% at a time rather than go for a doubling of the price straight away?

Remember, progress may be gradual, and consistent effort is key.

You can say things that show support and appreciation to help improve a lawyer's confidence. Here are some examples:

1. **Recognition of Effort:** 'I want you to know that your hard work and perseverance haven't gone unnoticed. Your contributions are valuable to the team.'
2. **Specific Praise:** 'The way you designed and produced that proposal demonstrated your scoping skills and attention to detail. Your expertise is crucial to our success.'
3. **Encouragement:** 'I believe in your abilities and am confident in your potential. Keep pushing yourself and know you have the skills to overcome challenges.'
4. **Affirmation of Value:** 'Your input during team discussions is always insightful and helps us think differently. Your perspective is important to our decision-making.'
5. **Feedback Balance:** 'While there's always room for growth, please don't underestimate your current achievements. Your progress is commendable.'

6. **Inclusion:** 'We value your ideas and opinions. Your presence enriches our team dynamic and contributes to a positive work environment.'
7. **Highlighting Growth:** 'I've noticed how you've tackled new responsibilities and stepped out of your comfort zone. Your willingness to learn and adapt is impressive.'
8. **Reminding Past Successes:** 'Remember that successful project you landed last month where you played a crucial role? Your ability to handle challenges was evident, and I have confidence in your abilities.'
9. **Personal Support:** 'If you ever doubt yourself, know that I'm here to support you. Don't hesitate to reach out if you need guidance or reassurance. You are on the right track.'
10. **Emphasising Team Effort:** 'All members' contributions are vital to our success. You are an integral part of our team, and your efforts make a difference.'

Tailor your words to the individual's situation and personality. Consistent encouragement, sincere feedback, and recognition can go a long way in boosting an employee's confidence. Remember, communication is key to the success of this project.

WORDS WITH THE WISE

Nicola Jones, Athena Professional

Confidence can be generated when we have evidence of success. We've gone on this journey, we've done our strategy, we've got our Gap Analysis, we've discovered need, our people have had the opportunity to learn over time in applied ways.

All the time, we're gathering evidence of success. We're trying something new out and we're gathering evidence of success. Or we may find evidence of failure from which we can learn.

But the question always is, what have we learned? What would we do differently next time?

We're gaining momentum, a snowball effect, where we're creating a new narrative that it's possible for me to do this thing differently and when I do it differently, this is what happens, and I get this. It's not just about the objective facts. There will be empirical information;

there will be data that we can look at and say, well, we value these things accurately and repeatedly, but there will also be sentiment.

There will also be qualitative stuff that is hugely valuable, which you should gather, too. Our clients felt that they were getting a valued service. That we'd served their needs. Our clients felt that they were understood. We felt that we had been close to the client, that we'd served their needs. We personally felt positive about the contribution we made.

8 PPP PENGUIN LOGIC

Coaching Questions

Sometimes, the right question at the right time can work wonders. Listed below are some powerful coaching questions which may help. You will see that one or two are already 'possibility' thinking questions.

- What do you want to achieve?
- What exact date will you achieve this by?
- What resources could possibly help you?
- What possible help could benefit you?
- Who could possibly help you?
- Who else could possibly help?
- What could you possibly gain from involving others?
- What might be the best way of persuading them?
- What else?
- What is your top priority?
- Who will you choose to involve?
- By when?
- How strong is your self-belief that you could achieve this (1-10)?

- Are you going to take responsibility for this?
- How will you review and measure your results?
- When are you going to start to take action?
- What could you learn from others that would possibly help you achieve your goal?
- What possible obstacles might you face?
- How could you overcome these?
- What are the options?
- How can you obtain the buy-in of others?
- If you could select any person to help you, who would it be?
- What possible skills are required?
- What else?
- How else?
- Who else?
- What concerns do you have?
- What is causing you to feel/react in this way?
- How confident are you in your abilities?
- What additional knowledge, skills, or experience do you believe you need to develop?
- What could you do to develop greater self-belief?
- How will you act in order to inspire others?
- What will you do to maintain your momentum?

PROFESSIONAL ADVISORS WANT TO BE MAGICAL AND ARE SUPERHEROES!

Now, you may think this is a corny heading and something you might expect someone from California to shout out at a conference. To be fair, it was at the conference in Dallas in 2017 that I heard someone from California actually shout this out. Although he did add the 'F' word before saying he was magical!

The man doing the shouting was Chris Marston of concentric circles fame. He is 100% right. He was then, and if he is shouting about it now, he still is, in my view. Law is hard; it is complicated. Lawyers are bad at saying well done to each other and celebrating success.

In 2023, when I led a Possibility Thinking session at a national conference in the UK, one of the things that younger lawyers mentioned that might encourage them to stay with a law firm was being told occasionally that they had done a good job! How sad is that!

Lawyers need to understand three things:

1. They create tremendous value for clients when they get the job done for them, and they do this every day.
2. The lawyers' skills provide the client with a competitive advantage. The problem facing the client will be solved.
3. The client gets a great benefit from the work the lawyer undertakes. The clients get their outcomes.

When you consider the outcomes that lawyers deliver day-in day-out – the outcomes clients want from us – we are superheroes!

1. We save and preserve relationships.
2. We enable people to start new lives.
3. We create new businesses.
4. We help fulfil retirement dreams.
5. We help protect people, their families and property, and their wealth.
6. We protect them from injustice.

That's not a bad list, and I know I have left lots out.

Pricing Confidence comes from:

- Knowing what to do.
- Training on how to do it.
- Following a structured framework.
- Practising again and again.

DEALING WITH OBJECTIONS

> The important thing to remember here is, for hourly billing, you need a calculator.
>
> For value pricing, you require courage!
>
> **Ron Baker, VeraSage Conference 2017**

Dealing with objections is never easy. What do we say when a client doesn't accept the price – or options that have been lovingly crafted – and pushes back?

It is probably a sweeping generalisation, but I will make it anyway: many people simply do not like haggling. Some, however, absolutely love it. Whenever we go on holiday and end up in a marketplace or bazaar where there aren't any prices on the goods, we know that we are going to have to ask the price and then be given a price that we have to haggle about. That's the game.

Now, I'm not for one moment suggesting that we become market traders (we will never get that good at it), but we do have to become better at negotiating our own fees and prices.

One of the first things to consider is this. If the customer is asking about the price, after we have presented our FPA, have we done a good enough job explaining the value we create?

A few thoughts:

- Don't take objections personally.
- Don't panic.
- An objection is a sign of interest.
- Regard objections as signals that the client wants to buy and a sign that the client requires more clarity and information.
- Anticipate possible objections and pre-prepare your responses.
- Prepare questions that show you have thought about their situation.
- Don't provide the 'My firm is 100 years old, and we are specialists…' speech instead of answering a specific question.
- Price is usually only ever an objection in the absence of value. If a client is saying it's price, they may be saying:
    - I don't understand your proposal.
    - Maybe they have not listened correctly to what you have told them. Maybe you haven't explained it well.
    - Maybe you didn't listen properly when taking instructions.

If clients say you are too expensive, ask, 'Compared to who… what firm?' Ask to see the proposal, as you will need to check whether the same grade of lawyers is being offered. Are the scopes the same? Is it more expensive than doing nothing? Is it more expensive than losing the case? Is it more expensive than damage to reputation?

Are there any creative options that you can add to your proposal? It may be extending payment terms. It may be aligning payments with clients' cash flow cycles. Can you accelerate payment terms to offer a reduced fee?

If the customer is only interested in price, and a rock bottom price at that, you need to consider whether they are the right clients for your firm and whether they are in the right place. The correct pricing decision may be to let the opportunity pass.

If a client decides that they are going to work with a competitor, it is important that you're not defensive. Take the opportunity to find out who that competitor is, and why they decided to choose them. And always leave the door open and point out that if the project doesn't go as they had hoped with the alternative firm, you would welcome the opportunity to speak to them again. If you leave the door open, you will be surprised how many clients take the opportunity to come back.

The important thing when facing objections is to maintain your pricing integrity. If you immediately knock 10% off your price, or tell the client you will do the same work for the fee quoted by the competitor, the client will immediately think you were trying to rip them off when you sent your original proposal.

Here are some thoughts about profitability and some steps lawyers could take to preserve their integrity while reducing price.

1. **Can you delegate something?** Can the work be undertaken by another member of staff at your firm? Could part of the work be undertaken by someone at the customer's office? Think about creating a list of documents in a litigation case. The first draft could be undertaken by a customer in accordance with a guidance sheet that you create for them. It takes a task away from you and puts the onus on the client.
2. **Can you recycle documents**? Is this a matter that's been dealt with before? Can an old file be taken out of storage so that wheels don't have to be reinvented? Can we utilise a barrister who has dealt with similar legal issues while representing other clients?
3. **Can you recycle any people**? Staff who helped on previous matters and who can now bring their learning to this matter.
4. **Can the customer do more**? Could the client create the first draft of witness statements, or collate documents, or take photographs and obtain plans?
5. **Can other people do more**? It may be that you can get an expert witness to do something.
6. **Control the idiots**. It's important to realise that other idiots may be on the scene. An idiot may even be your customer or possibly your opponent. It is important they are controlled and understand the parameters as far as you're able to communicate them.
7. **Get better at saying no**. To price for value, you have to set a baseline price and be prepared to walk away. Remember Baker's Law? 'Bad customers drive out good customers.' You don't need every bit of work that comes into your organisation; you need more than your fair share of the good stuff.

8. **Become a better negotiator.** If you're going to start offering discounts, start small at 1 or 2%. You know a discount of 10% can result in a reduction of 33% of the net profit. So, if a discount is going to be offered, start small. But then only offer a discount if the customer is going to do something or give something up.

   If the price is £2,000 and the client wants to pay £1,500, focus on the £500 difference; it's the smaller amount.

8 PPP PENGUIN LOGIC

Beware discounts

Remember that once you give a discount, expect to get further and increasingly outrageous demands for more! You started it!

One other thought on negotiation. Lawyers need to get better at having conversations with clients when they start demanding gold service but have only paid for bronze.

SERVICE GUARANTEE

Another thing to consider is the inclusion of a Service Guarantee. In this case, you are not guaranteeing the outcome of a particular matter (you obviously can't do that, especially in a litigation case), but you are offering a guarantee that your client will receive great service. You back yourself.

Many law firms offer Service Guarantees and put the pen in their client's hands, letting them write a price up or down by a specified percentage. I realise this will, of course, cause palpitations for many people reading this book.

Questions that will arise will be:

1. 'What are we going to do if they start reducing our bill?'

   If clients have had an awful service, chances are you will always reduce bills anyway. Look at your complaint/compliance files.

2. 'How often are the Guarantees called in?'

   In reality, extremely rarely. Clients, in fact, forget you even offered it. You may have to remind them. I know of one firm that had the Guarantee called in on three occasions. On two occasions, the price was reduced. On one, the price was increased! In all three cases, the law firm learned from it.

8 PPP PENGUIN LOGIC

The question you always ask

When a client tells you a price is too high, ask the following question.

'Can you tell me more…?'

It puts the onus on the client to explain what the issue is. If, for example, the client then says, 'I am not sure that this proposal will work and get the result I want,' you know the objection is not price-related. You can then ask the client more questions about what their concerns are and address them.

WHAT IS YOUR HOURLY RATE?

Clients believe that all lawyers bill by the hour. Why do they think this? Because most do. What will you say when a client asks how you arrived at a cost?

How you actually arrived at your client's price is – with respect to them – none of their business. Remember that value is subjective and it's a feeling, that it's contextual and it's complicated, and that you haven't calculated it by hours and inputs. It's been calculated based on the perceived value that you generate for your client and based on your experience of dealing with matters like this in the past.

When you consider it, where else do we get asked about time?

Tim Williams, like practically everyone else mentioned in this book (apart from Richard Branson and Confucius), was at the Dallas Conference in 2017. Tim wrote a brilliant blog post which dealt with the hourly rate question. Do we know the number of hours that it took to build our car? Do we know how many hours it took to build a smartphone? Of course, we don't. We have no idea. We drive the cars we have because we like them, and they have the features that we want from a car. The same goes for our smartphones.

Tim's article concluded, 'Costs and profits are the seller's business. Transparency is for windows, not for pricing professional services.'

NOT WINNING WORK IDENTIFIES A TRAINING NEED

As indicated above, the reason that clients won't immediately say yes is because the lawyer has failed to educate them about the value. It's a sign we must get better at pricing conversations. We must get better at demonstrating expertise and the value that we create for our clients. We must get better at explaining how using our services will create the better future that the client seeks and create the results that they want.

Learning these new skills is not about turning lawyers into salespeople. Reminder: avoid the 'S' word here. We just want lawyers to become better at explaining what we do; it's better for them because they want to do the work… that's why they created the proposal in the first place.

When we create options, we can give clients a choice of service levels, and they can choose the ones that they want. Price sensitivity can be eliminated if we find and discuss what is important to clients.

By asking good questions of clients, even at the objection stage, we can unlock and understand what is important to them and discover what the desired outcomes are. It will allow us to talk about what their futures are going to be. Discuss what the consequences of not retaining us are likely to be. We can match the service lines to what our clients want.

It is important that we show empathy and that we have a caring and curious side. We want to find out what the problems are and assist. When you ask most lawyers why they chose to go into the law, you will typically hear, 'So I could help people.' Let's start helping.

CAPTURE THE KNOW-HOW

Understanding and dealing with objections is crucial to the success of a VBP project. This is why the objections need to be captured, written down in the BBU, and have answers prepared, practised, and rehearsed. You need to upskill your lawyers to deal with objections. So they can say the right thing at the right time, and deliver the right response in their own style and personality. If answers are practised, lawyers will say them more naturally. Your teams should brainstorm common objections. What comes up the most?

MAKE THE VBP VISION A PRIORITY

What you do with your Vision after you create it will determine your success. Your VBP project will likely have strong competition from other day-to-day activities and communications within the business, so you need to communicate it frequently and powerfully and embed it within everything you do.

Don't just call special meetings to communicate your Vision. Instead, talk about it every chance you get. Use the Vision daily. When you keep it fresh in everyone's minds, they'll remember it and respond to it.

WORDS WITH THE WISE

Dr Jacqui Rigby, Rigby Pollitt Associates

Avoid the blame game. People need to know you have their back. Mistakes and failures are an opportunity to learn. Instil a culture of regular reviews of what has gone well, and less well, and what you will do differently as a team.

Nicola Jones, Athena Professional

We want to get people capable, motivated, and give them the opportunity to do things differently. That's not always the case in the legal sector.

We know that learning can be killed with a look or a sigh. You can come back full of zeal and joy, and you've learned something and then someone goes, 'Really?' and you may then think, 'Well, no, maybe not. Maybe I won't risk doing something differently.'

We're going to have to risk doing things differently if we're going to live in this new world where things are done with systems that we can hardly conceive of now. We need to think about how people are going to deploy that learning, and find opportunities for *applied learning* so that people can practise what they've learned. It might be that we have to construct scenarios to give people opportunities to learn in various different creative ways.

David Gilroy, Conscious Solutions

Permitting others to act is vital in any business if you want to grow it. In my business, we have levels of authority about pricing. If it's a one-hour job, I don't even know what's being quoted. But if it's a £25,000 website, I absolutely want to see the quote before it goes out. Empowerment is important so people know where their authority level starts and stops.

Chris Marston, Exemplar Companies Pbc

We don't tell people what to price. There are a lot of factors in value-based pricing. You give lawyers the tools, but you let them screw up here and there.

Kirsty Pappin, Aries Legal Practice Management

If a lawyer on the pilot underbills a client or they overbill, and then you lose the client, it's okay. There's no implication for the disciplinary policy and there's no HR involvement. It's made very clear that this is going to take a period of time and they are okay to make mistakes. We need to understand the mistakes so we learn from them. The Managing Partner must make it clear that it's okay to make mistakes and there will be mistakes on a pilot.

Simon Tupman, Simon Tupman Consulting

One of my professional frustrations is that, often, when a client leaves a planning retreat with a list of things that they want to do and action, things slip and initiatives fail to get implemented. Someone needs to be in charge. Does that person have the mandate and the authority to actually take tough decisions? Is he or she able to confront a fellow Partner and say, 'We all signed up to behave in this way or agreed to action a certain number of things'?

To overcome this problem, I believe it would help law firms if their leaders created, and adhered to, a Leadership Charter. (Quite different from a partnership deed.) A leadership charter requires its leaders to sign up to certain agreed standards and behaviours, with everyone being a signatory; it helps to facilitate change.

Matthew Burgess, View Legal

While we're timeless and we've got no timesheets, velocity is critical. And so, one of the requirements is that people do their timesheets in advance. They're not recording time as such, but they need to be thinking about project management. That's a promise that they make to themselves and to the business. The timelines are all ultimately set by getting a promise to the customer. So, we begin with the end in mind, and we're going to work back from that.

John Chisholm, John Chisholm Consulting

One firm I worked with had a vision and a helicopter view of their framework, but they didn't have all the answers. They didn't know exactly what was going to happen, where the successes, the challenges, and the failures were going to come from. But once they communicated and engaged with everyone in the firm, empowered them to not only make decisions themselves but empowered them to fail, the transition to a value-based pricing practice was far easier.

That firm didn't get it all right from the beginning – no firm does. For instance, they regularly changed the format and the structure of their Value Council meetings until they got it to how it best suited their firm, their people, their culture, and their clients.

CRIB SHEET
READING & VIEWING

WATCH (COMPULSORY)

First Follower Dancing Guy

Spoiler alert… you (in some way) feature in this film!

By Derek Sivers

https://www.youtube.com/watch?v=fW8amMCVAJQ

WATCH

How To Find Your Place In The Universe

Professor Brian Cox

By High Performance

https://youtu.be/lsCC_G5G9YE?si=0EGhxYgqOpbAESkH

WATCH

Why Do You Want To Know My Hourly Rate?

https://www.youtube.com/shorts/TxeEzZvVGUc

WATCH

How Can Leaders Encourage Employees To Take Action?

By Russell Raath and John Kotter

https://youtu.be/UsDd7tawa88?si=cpj5gentgR5Jq-o0

WATCH

The Best Leaders Are The Best Followers

By Simon Sinek

https://www.youtube.com/watch?v=V5wtzze9L_M

WATCH

The Heart of Change

By John Kotter

https://www.youtube.com/watch?v=1NKti9MyAAw&t=53s

WATCH

How JFK and a Janitor Put Man on The Moon

By Karen Eber

https://www.youtube.com/watch?v=7zLWGGZQQVw

WATCH

Learning About the Power of Empowerment

By David Hughes, TED talk

https://www.ted.com/talks/david_hughes_learning_about_the_power_of_empowerment

READ

The Nobility in Being Paid What You Are Worth

By Ron Baker

https://www.verasage.com/verasage-institute/blog/pricing-on-purpose/the_nobility_in_being_paid_what_you_are_worth

READ

Simple Truths of Leadership: 52 Ways To Be a Servant Leader and Build Trust

By Ken Blanchard & Randy Conley

READ

6 Ways to Empower People To Be Their Best

By Laura Garnett, Inc

https://www.inc.com/laura-garnett/6-ways-to-empower-people-to-be-their-best.html

READ

Top 6 Ways To Empower Employees

By Ronald E Reggio, Psychology Today

https://www.psychologytoday.com/us/blog/cutting-edge-leadership/202011/top-6-ways-to-empower-employees?eml

READ

Followership: A Valuable Skill No One Teaches

By Sandra Slager, Forbes

https://www.forbes.com/sites/forbesbostoncouncil/2019/05/16/followership-a-valuable-skill-no-one-teaches/?sh=e50b0b34695d

READ

For Smarter Decisions, Empower Your Employees

By Aaron De Smet, Caitlin Hewes and Leigh Weiss, McKinsey

https://www.mckinsey.com/capabilities/people-and-organizational-performance/our-insights/for-smarter-decisions-empower-your-employees

READ

Getting Unstuck in Pricing Discussions

By Tim Williams

In this article, Tim looks at some of the issues that arise when discussing pricing.

https://www.ignitiongroup.com/propulsion-blog/getting-unstuck-in-pricing-discussions

TIPS/CHECKLISTS

1. Remember: if you negotiate once on price, you set the template for your relationship.
2. Don't give free advice. Preserve your pricing integrity.
3. You are worth it! Remember the 'I am billing time' song from the Reading and Watching section of P#1? It had a line in it: 'My mind and my time are my merchandise.' Don't give it all away.
4. When you signpost prospects away who can't afford your fees, keep track of the referrals.
5. Believe in your price. Do not project *your* price sensitivity onto the client.
6. When you discount, you train customers to expect a discount. Don't do it.
7. Train staff to appreciate they sell intellectual capital, NOT time.

EXERCISES

EXERCISE 1 (COMPULSORY)

Meet with your team. Collect details of common objections and discuss how, in the future, you might deal with them.

Objections are finite. Write them down. Have answers ready for when one is raised.

EXERCISE 2

What closing questions can your lawyers create to ask for the work?

EXERCISE 3

1. Write an HR recruitment advertisement/brief to a legal recruiter promoting your firm's new way of working.
2. What would a performance review look like in the brave new world?
3. What additional skill-based questions could you ask a prospective staff member at interview?

EXERCISE 4

Looking at the Skills Matrix in the Appendices:

- Can you add to them?
- Do you agree with them?
- Can you deliver them?

EXERCISE 5

Write a page for your company website explaining your new pricing policy.

EXERCISE 6

Review any Pricing Confidence questions asked at the beginning of this process.

- What do they tell you?
- Where are you currently with your pricing?
- What is your firm-wide pricing knowledge level?
- What is good in the pricing space, and where are you doing poorly?
- What parts of the firm are doing well on pricing, and which areas are struggling? Why?

EXERCISE 7

Design a teambuilding exercise. Ask your Practice Areas to develop a detailed list of FAQs and typical answers. You want team members to be fully aware of your policies and how they should implement pricing.

EXERCISE 8

The following paragraph is taken from the website of a legal practice in suburban Melbourne:

'We develop strategy, manage projects, and create value for you and your business. We also share knowledge and work with people to develop their skills. And all this at a pre-agreed price. No estimates. No ranges. No hourly rates.'

What is your service promise? Is it unique and compelling?

POSSIBILITY THINKING QUESTIONS TO POSE

1. What are the possible thought-provoking questions we need to ask?
2. What rules/procedures/policies possibly need to be kicked out?
3. How might we possibly encourage an introvert to contribute their thoughts and ideas?
4. How can we possibly deal with a lack of commitment or resistance?
5. What possibly distinguishes our business model from that of our competitors?
6. How can we possibly incentivise people to try VBP?
7. Where can we possibly store the knowledge we have in our business?

P#6 PRIZES

CREATING SOME QUICK WINS

> 'It is better to lead from behind and to put others in front, especially when you celebrate victory when nice things occur. You take the front line when there is danger. Then, people will appreciate your leadership.'
>
> **Nelson Mandela**

CELEBRATE SUCCESS

Delivering change can take time. So don't wait until the end to celebrate success – make sure you celebrate the milestones and achievements as you go along. Celebrations can be simple and low or zero-cost.

Build celebrations into your Communications Plan and let everyone know what has been achieved and who has been part of it.

When you go live, have a bigger celebration with the whole firm. Maybe a themed lunch or branded cupcakes or a fun quiz (which works well virtually, as well as in person). You could take pictures of the team and activities throughout the change journey and create a slideshow to show the journey.

One of the most important steps of the 8PPP is to create visible, unambiguous successes and celebrate them ASAP. Let's face it, everybody wants to be associated with a winner. Everybody likes the feeling of winning. We all want to be admired, celebrated, and told we have done a great job. It's a vital element of building long-term success.

Celebrating the wins and communicating this to the wider firm will demonstrate that the change management project is on track and succeeding. It will show that the Vision and the Strategy are working. It will build enthusiasm and bring with it the desire to continue with the change. It also challenges the cynics – the Naysayer penguins in the organisation.

Those who were perhaps unsure whether the change was a good thing will lean towards the Strategy and the Vision.

Wins will drive change in the second wave of Pioneer penguins and create enthusiasm in other Practice Areas. Celebrating wins does not need to be expensive. When I train lawyers, I give out toy penguin figures and give each penguin a name. Those penguins don't go in the bin. They sit on desks as a reminder of a job well done.

Remember to tailor the celebration to the team's preferences and culture. The goal is to make team members feel valued, motivated, and proud of their accomplishments.

Here are some other ways to celebrate the wins:

1. **In meetings:** on a flip chart, capture and build a record of the journey. Bring sweets and chocolates into a team meeting. Start the day with breakfast sandwiches for the Pioneer penguin team.
2. **Public Acknowledgment:** Use other company communication channels to publicly recognise the team's achievements and improvements. It could be something as simple as highlighting the fact that there is a 'Penguin of the Week' or that someone has done something so brilliant they get mentioned in the newsletter feature called 'Kudos Corner'. This validates their efforts and boosts their confidence.
3. **Rewards and Incentives:** Offer tangible rewards such as gift cards, bonuses, or other incentives for achieving specific performance goals. If you want to continue the penguin theme, purchase small penguin figures. No one will throw away a toy penguin! This not only acknowledges success but also provides a direct benefit to team members.
4. **Team Outings or Lunches:** Arrange a team breakfast, lunch, picnic, or outing to celebrate accomplishments. It's a more relaxed setting to show appreciation and encourage team bonding.

5. **Certificates or Awards:** Create certificates or awards highlighting specific achievements or improvements. Present these awards in a team setting to emphasise the significance of the accomplishments.
6. **Personalised Notes:** A win could be as simple as sending a 'Cheers to Peers' thank you card of some description. Write a handwritten note to a colleague saying what a great job they have done.
7. **Professional Development Opportunities:** Offer opportunities for skill development or additional training as a reward for improved performance. This not only acknowledges success but also invests in the team's growth.
8. **Wall of Fame:** Create a physical or digital 'Wall of Fame' showcasing the team's achievements and improvements. This serves as a constant reminder of their success.
9. **Flexibility or Time Off:** Grant the team members some flexibility in their work schedule or offer them an additional day off as a reward for their hard work and improved performance.
10. **Peer Recognition:** Allow team members to recognise and commend each other's achievements. This can foster a positive and supportive team culture.
11. **Guest Speakers or Workshops:** Organise guest speakers or workshops related to the team's field of expertise. This can be both educational and celebratory, highlighting the team's growth.
12. **Company-wide Communication:** Share the team's achievements through company newsletters, internal social media, or other communication channels to ensure their success is known throughout the organisation.
13. **Case Studies:** It is also important to create more formal case studies of the successes. These can be used and recycled and demonstrate the value to new clients.

> Life is too short not to celebrate nice moments.
>
> **Jurgen Klopp**

MEASURES OF SUCCESS

The management team should be looking at the metrics that were put in place when the project was taken on. How will the lessons learned integrate into your processes?

These metrics will show:

- A reduction in write-offs.
- A reduction in aged debt.
- Improved profit margins.
- Fewer complaints.
- Clients that have been won.
- Clients that have been deselected.
- There may well even be other soft HR measures – such as improvements in employee absence figures and improvements in employee satisfaction.

> To help people believe they can achieve victory, put them in a position to experience small successes.
>
> **John C. Maxwell**

RESISTORS AND NAYSAYERS

Helping people learn new skills is not easy. In meetings, there will be Naysayers and Resistors. Plan for this.

People don't always learn when you tell them something.

They don't always learn by doing.

Some learn when they recall what has previously happened and why.

This is why your quick wins need to identify and document:

- What happened.
- Why it happened.
- The result.

Try to ensure that team meetings start with questions like:

1. Has anyone got any stories they can share about the project?
2. What was the most useful thing you have learned?
3. What have we learned since the last time we met?
    - Successes?
    - Learnings from things which did not go well.

> It's quite remarkable; the changes in behaviour that you start to see when lawyers are not getting paid by the hour.
>
> The profitability of their matter is going to depend on how much they can get done in a short period of time and how efficiently they can operate.
>
> Those lawyers have become incredibly efficient.
>
> **Jim Hassett, Client Value and Law Firm Profitability**

WORDS WITH THE WISE

Dr Jacqui Rigby, Rigby Pollitt Associates

Celebrate the little things, like when someone has presented to a small group despite being nervous.

Celebrations don't have to cost lots of money. Simple acts of recognition have a huge impact. Use low-cost celebrations like a box of doughnuts, finishing an hour early, or a fun quiz over lunchtime.

Robin Dicks, Thriving Consultancy

Definitely use case studies and real-life examples of those within the firm who are successfully using VBP and have won/maintained relationships.

This helps boost the kudos of early adopters and interest from those who are more cautious in adopting.

Independent feedback from satisfied clients can be gained to help do this and be visible. Interview transcripts, online feedback, or live feedback can all be used.

Bring 'the change to life'.

John Chisholm, John Chisholm Consulting

I have never really thought that individual financial bonuses work with professionals. I think they have very limited ability to foster and incentivise genuine long-term change because a bonus glorifies an individual's success over a team's success, and over time – instead of being seen as a bonus – it becomes an expectation. Team bonuses can work exceptionally well, however.

I think what really can work, though, is your professionals feeling wanted, being valued, and leaders saying, 'Thank you.'

Nicola Jones, Athena Professional

Your Naysayer penguin can be quite a handy penguin to have. And being risk-averse has its place and has value. Bring them into the tent. When you hear what the Naysayers have got to say, it could well be valid. It could nudge you in a different direction.

Kirsty Pappin, Aries Legal Practice Management

Trumpeting the successes of the pilot and the wins for the law firm – these are great for morale, and they should be presented as case studies and advertised. These initial wins will help the change process. As the year moves forward, and as there are more wins under the belt, these will provide management with information indicators that can be used to make strategic growth decisions.

For example, compare the position to last year when the law firm had one fewer person and 20 fewer matters, but they are now more profitable. Better work, life balance, et cetera. So, we've got to make sure that we do celebrate those successes and keep retesting the model to make sure it works.

Melissa Lyon, Hive Legal

We have weekly staff meetings. One week, it will be a short, sharp 20-minute meeting. These always include a pricing tip. And then, once a month, we have a longer form meeting where people will, for example, do an activity that involves the whole firm. That sometimes involves sharing a pricing story or tip.

We've been very careful about how we design the agenda for that meeting. We start with HiveFives and HiveStars, which celebrate successes and/or contributions.

CRIB SHEET
READING & VIEWING

READ

Master of the Rolls Speech: Association of Costs Lawyers 2012

By Lord Neuberger of Abbotsbury

https://www.judiciary.uk/wp-content/uploads/JCO/Documents/Speeches/mr-speech-acl-lecture-may-2012.pdf

READ

In An Uncertain World, How Do Leaders Resist The Gravitational Pull of Certainty?

A list of tips to help business leaders to deal with uncertainty.

By Dr Jacqui Rigby

https://www.linkedin.com/pulse/uncertain-world-how-do-leaders-resist-gravitational-pull-jacqui-rigby/

READ

Celebrating Achievement

By Mind Tools

Celebrating Achievement – Recognize Success to Increase Motivation (mindtools.com)

https://www.mindtools.com/ax3c2aw/celebrating-achievement

WATCH

Celebrate Good Times

Kool & The Gang/Ziggy Mack

Celebrate Good Times

https://youtu.be/3GwjfUFyY6M?si=dZEXEuvI8Ga9Qwym

TIPS/CHECKLISTS

1. Make sure your Plan identifies milestones and check if any are appropriate to celebrate.
2. Celebrate the little things, like when someone has presented to a small group despite being nervous.
3. If you have phased your change and have a quick win, make sure you celebrate.
4. Celebrate learnings to build a positive, engaged team.
5. Pricing is a process that is reliant on people, strategy, and systems.

EXERCISES

EXERCISE 1

How Can You Celebrate Success?

- Create rewards/certificates/vouchers/penguin cards.
- Penguin of the Week – inflatable penguin on a desk?
- Dress up as a penguin in a suit?
- Desktop homescreen to feature Quick Win champion?
- Small gifts? Vouchers? Experiences?
- Penguin chocolate bars.

POSSIBILITY THINKING QUESTIONS TO POSE

1. How can we possibly celebrate success?
2. How can we possibly reward people at the end of the change?
3. How can we possibly record and track our VBP activities?
4. How can we possibly deal with objections?

P#7 PERSEVERE
KEEP GOING

> 'If everyone is moving forward together, then success takes care of itself.'
>
> **Henry Ford**

EMBEDDING CHANGE

Embedding change is hard. One reason it can feel so tough is that even though people can see the benefits of change, the effort to make the changes is so great that it feels like an unfair deal.

In their book *Uncommon Sense, Common Nonsense,* Jules Goddard and Tony Eccles listed 12 tips to 'strengthen people's understanding, commitment and willpower.' They are:

1. **Rules rather than goals.** As with following a diet, success is best assured by adhering to a small number of strict everyday rules, rather than by simply signing up to a general principle.
2. **'On the job' change rather than a free-standing initiative.** Change is not something done alongside 'work as usual' but is a different way of doing the everyday things.
3. **Different measures.** If none of the performance measures is changed, no amount of proselytising will alter anything.

4. **Different motives.** Change is motivated more by the fear of social embarrassment than by feelings of personal guilt.
5. **Actions rather than words.** People take more notice of what their bosses do than of what they say.
6. **Commitment rather than imposition.** People do not like being changed, but they will support changes they have helped to create.
7. **Skin in the game.** If senior executives put their careers on the line – for example, by making their jobs and rewards contingent upon the success of the change programme – they will earn the trust of their people. Otherwise, it is just posturing.
8. **A matter of principle more than an expedient tactic.** People will sign up to change only if it possesses moral force – and is widely believed to be the right thing to do.
9. **Loyalty to colleagues.** People will commit more because they don't want to let other people down than because it will help the bottom line.
10. **Volunteers not conscripts.** People must join because they want to, not because they are coerced into doing so or because they fear the consequences of not doing so. They have to be part of the choice, made on their terms.
11. **Choice of consequence.** Change is less about converting people and more about offering a choice and respecting the choice – of whether to commit or to leave – of every employee.
12. **Little by little does the trick.** The principles driving the need for change may be long term, but the incentives and measures for tracking performance will need to be short term. Tracking daily progress, however modest, is the art of longer-term achievement.

This extract from *Uncommon Sense, Common Nonsense,* is reproduced with the kind permission of the authors: Jules Goddard and Tony Eccles.

> A hero is an ordinary individual
> who finds the strength
> to persevere and endure in spite of
> overwhelming obstacles.
>
> **Christopher Reeve**

ORGANISATIONAL CHANGES

The journey you and the Pioneer penguins have undertaken is likely to have identified business areas that need to undergo organisational changes.

As I mentioned at the beginning of this book, there is no one-size-fits-all when rolling out a VBP project in a law firm. How it will work in practice depends on the size of your organisation and the willingness of the people within it to change.

Various operational functions have realised that to support the VBP implementation, some of their processes have had to change.

The Board will have appreciated that for VBP to become a reality across the whole business, these operational changes need to be built into the operational side of the business. A failure to do so will leave VBP as a 'hobby project' tried by some lawyers but ignored by many.

However, it is likely that pricing is now owned in the organisation and has a champion.

PRICING STEERING GROUP

A Pricing Steering Group may exist which has proved, in the pilot project, that the principles of VBP can work.

The purpose of the Steering Group is to support the Pioneers and oversee the change, to help resolve key issues and risks, and to take decisions that are beyond the remit of the Pioneers and the manager leading the change.

The Pricing Steering Group has a Board-level Sponsor and also key senior members of the firm who will be impacted by the change, including legal, IT, finance, HR, and operations representatives.

The Pricing Steering Group is visible, respected, and enthusiastic about its role in helping others embrace VBP.

An outline Pricing Steering Group agenda should be looking at:

1. Progress versus Plan.
2. Forward Plan view.
3. Key risks and issues.
4. Key decisions.
5. Key actions.

Decisions the Group may be considering include:

1. How do you ensure all staff understand the reasons for the changes and continue to bring them towards the Vision?
2. How to prepare people for the next wave of change.
3. What tools and training are required to reinforce new behaviours?
4. How to reinforce and reward new behaviours.
5. How do you raise the bar for the second wave of Pioneer penguins?
6. How do you acknowledge what people have left behind and bring them forward?

7. How to ensure senior management and Partners continue to 'walk the talk'.
8. What systems and structures must be put in place to reinforce the new behaviours?
9. How to recalibrate success metrics once improvements have been made.
10. A commitment to seek to hire people when vacancies arise who can buy into the Vision and help implement it.
11. Conduct structured 'lessons learned' sessions and be willing to discuss the good, bad, and ugly of the change effort and document them. Reflect as a team on the following and document:
    a. What went well.
    b. What went less well.
    c. What you would do differently next time, with clear actions.

The Pricing Steering Group should prepare regular updates on the change using a concise visual of each element of the change using a red/amber/green (RAG) status to show – at a glance – the areas that need attention. Remember that communication is still key.

The Pricing Group should issue a status report weekly to the Pioneers and any other stakeholders that need to be kept aware of the activities. Not only is a status report useful for communication, but it also builds great discipline for the Change Manager to review progress, Plans, and issues on a weekly basis.

> Success is no accident. It is hard work, perseverance, learning, studying, sacrifice and most of all, love of what you are doing or learning to do.
>
> **Pele**

PIONEER PENGUIN GROUP

The Pioneer Penguin Group meets regularly and reviews progress against the Plan.

1. Discuss risks and issues (using the Risk and Issues templates).
2. Manage dependencies.
3. Take decisions.
4. Agree communication messages.

Decisions they may be considering include:

1. How they can sustain and build momentum.

2. Capitalise on wins and gains to produce bigger results.
3. What projects and policies need to be abandoned?
4. What meetings do you no longer need to attend?
5. What resources do you divert?
6. What habits do you need to break?

There will be Pioneer penguins in a wider number of Practice Areas who are embracing VBP. Others will be looking on and asking, 'How are they doing it? How do I get involved?'

A BBU pricing methodology and process has been created and is being developed as part of your pricing Knowledge Management know-how. People will be enquiring, 'When will the training be rolled out in our team?'

SALARIES AND BONUSES

Pioneers and VBP champions will be required at all levels of the business. Pricing Confidence can become infectious.

Those lawyers who have embraced VBP and started asking for 'pump fist' prices will achieve more revenue for the business. Inevitably, they will seek greater remuneration and benefits. The best practices must be celebrated and rewarded. As a business, you will need to explore and design what incentives you are prepared to offer these individuals who have embraced the way you want to work.

Your HR team and Pricing Group will have reviewed Role Profiles/job descriptions and created a framework which incentivises those who have engaged and embraced VBP, not just lawyers who may have had the initial contact with clients but other team members who have assisted in the creation of the know-how and followed the processes you have created.

To ensure the process becomes embedded, consider how the best pricers will be identified and recognised and make sure you are rewarding the right things.

The HR team will have considered how staff in other business areas – such as business development, marketing, finance operations, and legal support functions – can be rewarded and motivated.

Employment Role Profiles may be amended and KPI measures adjusted.

8 PPP PENGUIN LOGIC

People do what they are paid to do

Make sure that you pay your people to do the right things

- Consider making a percentage of bonus schemes dependent on achieving and supporting VBP initiatives.
- Naysayer penguins may still opt out, but ensure if they do, they can't achieve 100% of a bonus.
- Consider a revenue split of a percentage of the income achieved over and above a base cost with the lawyer who did the work.
- Failure to attend VBP training and abide by VBP processes should exclude staff from any bonus scheme.
- Remember, some pay is emotional. Employee of the month, for example. Public recognition is currency as well.

TRAINING

Giving someone a briefcase, a copy of Halsbury's statutes, and a suit does not make a lawyer. The VBP tools you will have created in your business will not turn your lawyers into pricing experts.

Training your people will take time, and training will need to eventually be rolled out in all Practice Areas; that will involve all levels of the business, including the Board, Partners, Heads of Departments, and senior lawyers down to legal assistance and support staff.

Sources of relevant knowledge:

- Baseline price data.
- Disseminating knowledge.
- External training.

- Webinars.
- Podcasts.
- Blogs.
- Workshops.
- Exercises.
- TED Talks.
- Possibility Thinking exercises.
- Role-playing.
- Partner/team awaydays.
- Departmental BBUs.
- Reading books. (This one, for example!)

The crib sheets set out in this book have many ideas for reading, viewing, and doing.

Teams should be enthusiastic about creating and sharing the knowledge they learn. Those who didn't participate in the Pioneer Penguin Groups will be excited to learn when and how VBP will be introduced into their Practice Areas.

The psychological safety of those participating in VBP is important. I have mentioned it many times. There should be no recriminations for anyone embracing value-based pricing and making mistakes. Your staff will know this.

There will need to be a conscious effort when recruiting new talent into your business to ask questions regarding their pricing experience and how they view VBP.

Those in the management roles of legal teams will need to embrace VBP as a concept and deliver it within their teams. Skills will need to be developed. Appraisal and performance reviews should ensure that individual performances and commitments to VBP are reviewed and discussed. Are people embracing VBP, creating options for clients, and adhering to the policies, procedures and processes you have designed?

Skills can either be taught via training or brought into teams by actively recruiting lawyers who already have VBP experience.

The best pricers in your organisation need to be developed further and have the skills they have developed recognised. As you do so, others will follow, and whole teams will get onboard.

Senior managers must buy into VBP and should be prepared to step down from their positions if they are not prepared to engage with the process.

Those unwilling to engage with the process, who are unable or unwilling to manage and implement the changes required in their teams, may well have to be moved on.

> Leadership isn't what you say when things are easy. Leadership is what you do when things are hard.
>
> **Jon Cobb, Jon Cobb Consulting**

ROLE MODELS

Walking the walk and adapting to the new ways is fundamental.

Remember golden rule number one.

GOLDEN RULE #1

The management of your business must be 100% onboard with this project. Otherwise, it won't be fully implemented.

- They must become engaged and be involved in championing the change in culture that needs to happen.
- They must help define the objectives and then implement them.
- Resources must be made available.
- Staff must be made available to participate in the project.
- Obstacles will need to be removed.
- Funds and expertise will need to be made available.
- It will need to be made clear – across the business – that this is a serious initiative and vital for the firm's success.

Lots of carefully considered communications will be required.

Managers must be passionate advocates of the benefits for clients, lawyers, and the firm. They must actively and regularly commit to creating and storing knowledge within the BBUs and adhere to and promote the golden rules.

Managers must be prepared to let clients go if they are the wrong fit or if the price the client wants to pay is lower than the base cost.

The CEO/Managing Partner should be told of individual successes so that they can make personal commendation calls or private one-to-ones with members of staff and congratulate them on the work and the price achieved. The confidential conversations will not remain confidential for long.

> It always seems impossible
> until it is done.
>
> **Nelson Mandela**

Pricing needs to become a subject that is discussed often. It needs to feature visibly at Board and team meeting agendas. Activity needs to be recorded in the minutes.

The Board should actively seek monthly reports from Practice Areas regarding their pricing processes, successes, and improvements. This will demonstrate its importance and identify those managers/teams that may be seeking to opt out of the process.

Pricing should be reviewed and discussed in quarterly management meetings and staff conferences, showing that the Board is totally committed to the project.

The After-Action Reviews that are conducted will result in new revisions of BBUs/Processes and these results will be discussed in team meetings.

The Board, Heads of Departments, and senior lawyers must keep the dialogue going and remain in touch with each other and what is happening in the legal pricing world at large. News should be circulated.

HR reports should be submitted to Practice Areas and marketing BD teams, identifying what information has been learned about their competitors' pricing policies. This information will have been collated whilst HR have been interviewing other prospective members of staff from other law firms.

Partners and those aspiring to partnership must demonstrate that they are passionate about VBP.

If Naysayer penguins are not engaging with the process and cannot be turned around, they will need to leave the business. You will not be able to promote them as they don't buy into your Vision. You will need to replace them with those who do.

Your staff will know if you take no action. That will speak volumes about your own commitment. You will be the ones who have opened the door to complacency.

> Make Nudgery the centrepiece of your change strategy. Study the Art of Nudgery! Practise Nudgery! Become a Professional Nudgist!
>
> **Tom Peters**

CAREER DEVELOPMENT

Creating and recruiting pricing talent is important. How will those who embrace VBP progress through your organisation?

When appointing new Heads of Departments, pricing excellence should be a major reason for career progression. A recently promoted Head of Department should be a champion of your Vision and be instrumental in making it a reality. The message to staff needs to be that embracing VBP is a good way to advance your career. Attend the training.

An example of a Role Profile with pricing skills as KPIs is set out in the Appendices.

FINANCIAL DATA

You cannot manage what you cannot measure. It is vital that the right financial data is available to the relevant decision-makers at the right time.

The data must be accurate enough to help guide the decisions that need to be made. The data must be supported by facts and examples that make it easier for the Board and stakeholders to understand and digest.

Examples of successes achieved in all Practice Areas should identify price increases achieved since the 'Dark Ages'. Examples of base costs for services should be listed.

KPIs must be established to allow the business to monitor progress and demonstrate it is able to achieve pricing goals. Things you can measure include:

- The opportunities that are coming into the business.
- Conversion of the opportunities.
- Complaints.
- Staff happiness via employee pulse surveys.
- Deselection of clients.
- Lawyer performance/team performance comparing the new processes against the Dark Ages.
- Goals achieved.
- Better quality of customer identified through the CRM system.

- Teams hitting targets will create competition and success in other teams.
- Lawyers' individual VBP efforts. The increase in fees generated will show who has increased their Pricing Confidence.

You should also seek to measure progress by looking at leading indicators as evidence of your success. These could be:

- Number of staff trained.
- Number of FPAs created with clearly defined scope.
- Commercial clients where audits have been conducted.
- Number of suggested clients to deselect.
- Number of clients deselected.
- Training courses lawyers attended.
- Agendas/meetings/minutes being prepared and mentioning VBP.
- Interviews and questions regarding prices being asked of prospective candidates.
- Client feedback demonstrating positive comments.
- Projected increased income based on fees agreed.
- The number of cases where change orders were issued when scope creep was identified.

LEGAL PAPERWORK

As you have progressed on your VBP journey, it will have dawned on you that some of your own legal paperwork may need amending to reflect the changes you are making in your organisation.

EMPLOYMENT DOCUMENTATION

1. Employment contracts.
2. Role Profiles.
3. Staff Handbooks.
4. Compensation models and bonus schemes.
5. Performance review documentation.
6. Recruitment advertisements for new staff.
7. Recruitment pages on your website.
8. Instructions to recruiters.
9. Template interview questionnaires/scoring templates.
10. Job offer letters.

8 PPP PENGUIN LOGIC

Ask VBP questions in interviews

Develop a culture of asking questions about pricing when you interview prospective employees.

1. What have they seen?
2. What have they experienced?
3. What training have they had?

Create a list of standard questions to be used at interviews.

CLIENT DOCUMENTATION

Your clients need to know things have changed.

1. Conversations with lawyers.
2. FPAs/Retainer letters/Engagement packs.
3. Pages on your website regarding your pricing methodology.
4. Client feedback forms.
5. AARs.

MARKETING COLLATERAL

1. Brochures.
2. Case studies.
3. The FPAs and options you create may even be the result of a creative legal design process.
4. Elevator pitches and presentation skills training will mention VBP.
5. Social media posts will mention your USP.
6. Awards will be won for customer service and excellence.

PARTNERSHIP/SHAREHOLDERS' AGREEMENTS

1. Your commitment to VBP processes may even feature in your shareholders/members/partnership agreements.
2. Will it become a requirement to practise the skill in your organisation?
3. Will it become part of your Partners/owners' bonus/incentive schemes?

4. Would it become a disciplinary matter if a Partner refused to practise VBP?

Here are some law firm websites to visit. These are businesses that have completed the journey:

Lynn & Brown

'We provide our clients with a fixed price proposal and obtain our client's agreement with that before we commence work.'

https://www.lynnandbrown.com.au/pricing/

View Legal

'Offers service guaranteed upfront fixed pricing on an agreed scope of work.'

https://viewlegal.com.au/

Timeless Counsel, Plc

'Invaluable Advice at a Pre-Agreed Price.'

https://www.timelesscounsel.com/

Legally Yours

'Guaranteed agreed upfront fees.'

https://legallyyours.com.au/

Hive Legal

'Hive value our work based on the outcomes we achieve for our clients.'

https://hivelegal.com.au/

Exemplar

'Relationship as a service. Exemplar never bills by the hour.'

https://exemplarcompanies.com/

Moores

'With Moores Agreed Pricing (MAP) you know exactly what you're getting and what it will cost. No estimates. No ranges. No hourly rates.'

https://www.moores.com.au/here-for-good/#moores-agreed-pricing

James Legal

'We believe legal costs can be fixed.'

https://www.jameslegal.co.uk/

Peer Legal

'Aligning our pricing to your objectives and desired outcomes.'

https://www.peerlegal.com.au/

Law Squared

'Our model is built around giving you transparency and control.'

https://www.lawsquared.com/our-difference

Bartlit Beck

'We believe our interests should be aligned with our clients' interests.'

https://www.bartlit-beck.com

Bowers Law

'The independent Hong Kong law firm with no hourly rates.'

https://bowers.law/

WORDS WITH THE WISE

Melissa Lyon, Hive Legal

One of the things that we learned early on, and we continue to do now, is to appreciate that you have to continue to evolve your approaches and processes – it's never going to be perfect. In fact, we are continually looking for ways to improve what we do and the way we do it, and we've been doing it for ten years.

When you are building a culture, you need to appreciate that people who join you may still have their old firm cultures and mindsets. That's why mindset and legal design are so important to this. Even though people may say they have bought into the whole idea of value pricing – when they start actually doing it – they may think this is a little bit hard, clients will find it different, how do I measure our team's performance now? People may revert to muscle memory.

Value-based pricing provides flexibility because you're not accounting for every minute of your day.

It also makes people feel more valued because they're contributing to the outcomes that are given to the client. This provides an alignment of expectations and outcomes. Our lawyers can really build great relationships with the clients because they're really invested in providing value and outcomes and aligning those expectations. Everyone knows what they're going to do, how they're going to do it, and why they're going to do it, because those conversations have occurred right from the start.

Adopting Value-based pricing gives you the opportunity to revisit how you measure performance. We created a career growth program called Thrive@Hive, which focuses on strengths and takes a more holistic point of view. What are your technical skills? What are your business skills? What are your human skills? And what are your contributions? It's looking at it more from a contribution and strengths perspective rather than always defaulting to the billables.

The Thrive@Hive program provides Hivesters with the opportunity to meet regularly and also includes a mentoring and a 'wellbeing' focus. It includes goal setting, check-ins and transparency on salary review information.

One of the biggest tips that you can give people is persist, persist, persist, because – especially in the early days of adopting Value-based pricing – there are times when it's very tempting to say, oh, we'll just do time-based pricing on this one. We have resisted that temptation. And I think that's been the making of us, being able to confidently go ahead with value pricing in the way that we've done it. One of my tips is just don't go backwards. There are always ways where you can re-scope or change the way that you're looking at the pricing or talk to the client more. There's always a way to bring it back to value, always.

Dr Jacqui Rigby, Rigby Pollitt Associates

Make sure your Plan has included activities post-go-live that are designed to ensure the change is embedded.

Graham Moore, Katchr

There are three obstacles I see to achieving VBP.

1. People. There is a lack of awareness of the need to change.
2. Data. People just don't have the data to actually see what the problem is, and where the problem is. They don't know what the profitability is on individual matters because of all the issues around time recording and accounting.
3. The partnership model. In many multi-disciplinary law firms, you've effectively got a mishmash of different businesses with different business models, different priorities, and no common process.

Sometimes, law firms even measure the wrong things. They decide the measures independently of the objectives they're trying to achieve. It tends to be they decide the measures based on what's easy to measure and what's obvious to measure (e.g., time and billing), as opposed to what clearly demonstrates that they're achieving those objectives.

David Gilroy, Conscious Solutions

Implementation and sustaining change. That's the hard bit.

In my business, the first slide in every team meeting is about our culture code. It's called The Conscious Code. Our vision is 'To help make law firms more successful online.' I have been known to ask people to repeat it in the meeting! Our five values are Generous,

Transparent, Inquisitive, Collaborative, and Empowering. Every time we do an individual catch-up every 4-6 weeks, each person is asked to describe behaviours they have exhibited since the last meeting that support at least two of our five values. Our five values are: Generous, Transparent, Inquisitive, Collaborative, and Empowering, and talk to those points.

Imagine doing something like that in a value-based pricing world. How have you demonstrated value to people to explain why you charged what you did? It's a constant battle. I use the word battle deliberately. What we started to see is we would 'try' and use those words in our language patterns, and at some point, they became the norm. I knew they were embedded when my team stopped 'tittering' after they had used one of the values in their usual conversation!

Robin Dicks, Thriving Consultancy

The ability to track performance, results, and effectiveness is important. You must track results and gain feedback for what we're doing – scoring how well you are delivering value. Where have you fallen short? What are the correct performance indicators directly related to VBP? KPIs and measures to track individual performance can include:

- Average client satisfaction.
- Average likelihood to recommend.
- Average value for money score.
- Number of accepted introductions to other Practice Areas (if collaborative working is an issue).

It's really important to ensure the measures are tracked at firm-wide, practice-specific and (for appropriate measures) the individual level. This helps ensure that the Heads of Departments, who are so critical for any new approach to work, are focused and motivated around that approach. Otherwise, it becomes more theoretical than real, and people pull in different directions.

New joiner induction programmes are also a vital way to sustain change and explain this is how we do things around here. HR and marketing people shouldn't be an afterthought as they can really help reinforce the change through the right language and processes.

Chris Marston, Exemplar Companies Pbc

Nobody's allowed to track anything hourly at Exemplar. We don't permit intellectual urine samples in our firm; I don't care about them, I don't want to see them. I don't want our clients to see them. So, it's a hiring requirement that they're onboard with value-based pricing, and we just don't tolerate any form of Marxist pricing activity.

From a KPI standpoint, we have a lot of values. We have a no-assholes rule. We have net giver KPIs that are really focused on being a net giver as opposed to a net taker, meaning for every thousand dollars of work they do, we're expecting them to cross-sell, share, and identify new opportunities. So, our lawyers genuinely care about what the customer needs, rather than thinking only about what they're here to do in this moment.

Our recruitment ads are very explicit and bold. I mean, we're very clear about value-based pricing, about no assholes, and everything we stand for as a firm. It attracts a large number of candidates. The problem that we have – relative to most firms – is getting candidates to stop thinking about time. If you have people who are counting time and who think in terms of time, they're not going to manufacture value because the only thing they understand how to manufacture is time. It's not their fault. It's just how they've been trained.

Our model is an entirely value-based meritocracy model. We are pure in our execution of value theory, both inside, in terms of how we price a customer, but also how we compensate our team. In a meritocratic model, there's no limit to what you could make. Exemplar is a firm where you can shape your own destiny. But it might not be for everybody.

Paul Roberts, My Customer Lens

If you're trying to change talent development from an HR perspective, you need details, including the voice of the client. Because we've got a whole bunch of clients going, 'You know what? The mix of your team just isn't right anymore.'; 'You're not getting the right people.'; 'They haven't got it right.'; 'I keep having to go back to the senior people because the juniors just aren't cutting it.' HR need to know this and fit it into their talent development.

John Chisholm, John Chisholm Consulting

Staying the course can be so hard, especially when you hit an obstacle, or you get a price wrong and leave too much money on the table, or a client says I will only pay you by time, etc. It is easy to fall back into old habits, many of which were successful in the past, but a transition to a value-based pricing firm is more about the unlearning than the learning. We have to forget many of what we were taught in the past.

That is where the better firms have been more sustainably successfully. They were disciplined and learned to say no more often, even if it meant some loss of short-term gain (both financial and otherwise).

I would love to tell you the journey ends sometime and somewhere. It doesn't. That is what makes this both so challenging but so exciting and rewarding at the same time.

Kirsty Pappin, Aries Legal Practice Management

To persist with the project and its development, pull together a dedicated VBP section on your intranet. Produce videos on value-based training, discussing it and successful case studies; in short, two or three-minute videos – include how things work and have worked so far for the firm, and the associated case study. All processes and policies should be there and easily accessible. Have an open section for frequently asked questions and a place to submit questions for answering, because that allows for change discussion. Put in place a strong Learning and Development game, as this will assist with success.

CRIB SHEET
READING & VIEWING

WATCH

Why Do Change Efforts Lose Momentum?
By John Kotter
https://youtu.be/u1417S5AolU?si=cbbjq_cXPF3tHzwP

WATCH

TEDx Perth – Embracing Change

By Jason Clarke

An interesting insight into how people deal with change.

https://youtu.be/vPhM8lxibSU?si=7FSDiG7Pe5Y9MB-k

READ

Let Me Nudge You to Be a Nudge

By Tom Peters

https://tompeters.com/pdfs/TLBT_section1.pdf

READ

Project Team Meeting: Don't Let Yours Be Boring

By Project Manager Success

https://projectmanagersuccess.com/communication/project-team-meeting/

READ

RIP Hourly Rates

A lawyer celebrating the success of their VBP project.

https://www.hk-lawyer.org/content/rip-hourly-rates

TIPS/CHECKLISTS

Frequency Of Meetings

The point of meetings is to manage the Plan and address issues and risks as a team, as early as possible. The frequency of these meetings may change throughout the lifetime of the change. So, at the start, you may need meetings of two hours once a week. As you approach the launch, you may need daily meetings of 10 minutes. Don't be afraid to adapt as you go along.

Keep having meetings post-launch and check the agendas of Practice Area meetings to make sure VBP is still on the agenda.

EXERCISES

EXERCISE 1

Establish regular Pioneer Team meetings

- The Change Lead should drive Pioneer Team meetings with an agenda and specific points to discuss. They should engage with the team and ask open questions to inform the change.
- Use Pioneer Team meetings to review Risks, Issues and Dependencies as well as the Plan.
- Be well prepared for the Steering Group to discuss the key actions and decisions you have identified. Make it an active group with skin in the game, not a show-and-tell session.

EXERCISE 2

Set up a Steering Group, including the Sponsor

Who should be on your Steering Group?

Create a standard agenda and pack structure and check with members in advance when you chat to them individually.

EXERCISE 3

Complete a Change Status Report

A Change Status template is provided below with the Red/Amber/Green (RAG) boxes and Blue Complete. You can simply delete or copy the status boxes as required.

big yellow penguin

Status Report

Overall Status RED AMBER GREEN COMPLETE

Summary

- *Summarise achievements, key risks, issues and key plans for next week in a few bullets*

Key Milestone	Progress	Key plans for next week	RAG status
			RED
			AMBER
			GREEN
			COMPLETE

Key Risks and Issues

Include top risks and issues with actions

EXERCISE 4

Set up a list of recipients of the Change Status Report

On your list should be Pioneers, Steering Group members, and any other stakeholders who need to be kept aware of the activities. Issue the Change Status Report at the end of every week.

EXERCISE 5

What internal programmes have you created?

Who could you now bring on to lead/deliver these programmes?

Who are the candidates to be the next wave of Pioneer penguins?

EXERCISE 6

How can you demonstrate that you have publicly abandoned old ways and routines?

1. Avoid doing things which are exhausting and pointless.
2. How have you dealt with pricing failures?
3. Have you developed a culture of psychological safety/no blame? Give examples for and against.

EXERCISE 7

Feedback

Design a mechanism for feedback/suggestions and the freedom to challenge the status quo.

POSSIBILITY THINKING QUESTIONS TO POSE

1. How can we possibly capture knowledge before it is lost from our firm?
2. How can we possibly document and store the knowledge we retain?
3. How could we possibly produce a second/third wave of change?
4. How can each team possibly keep the momentum going?

EXPOSURE DRAFTS
BY GREG KYTE
I HEARD YOU CAUGHT KEVIN SLEEPING WITH YOUR WIFE.
I FEEL SO BETRAYED HE WAS SUPPOSED TO BE WORKING ON A BRIEF TO COUNSEL.
MANAGING PARTNER

P#8 PASSION

CREATING THE NEW CULTURE

> Changing the culture where you work starts with not letting negative people and circumstances change you.
>
> **Jon Cobb**
>
> No Moment of Truth should ever be taken for granted, for no matter how small it may be, in the long run, each one determines the destiny of your firm.
>
> **Ron Baker**

Anyone who has been involved in a cultural change project will know it takes time… lots of time. It is hard work, but the work becomes easier if it is shared by many hands.

This section – P#8 Passion – aims to project you into the future, where the change from your hard work and effort is embedded.

CREATING A NEW CULTURE

So, at this point, where are you in the planning and implementation process? What have you got? Hopefully…

- You will have a documented Plan outlining the steps required to reinforce and sustain the change required.
- You will have given people time to mourn their losses. Remember the change curve graph. Remember, you will always be further along the graph and in front of many who will still be feeling upset.
- You will be providing skills, knowledge, and habits training.
- You will routinely recognise accomplishments.
- You will have developed performance measures to continually monitor the results and identify future improvements.
- You will be making adjustments to your Change Vision and Strategy to reflect new learnings and insights. You know VBP is an art, not a science.
- You will encourage people to be open to new challenges and aware of the work required for the next changes.
- You will be measuring the benefits of the VBP change and communicating them across the firm. Make sure you continue celebrating success.
- Communications will continue so your troops understand the change and the benefits.
- New people will have joined the business, and VBP will be new to them. They will have been inducted into your VBP procedures.
- You will not let have let communication become a form of osmosis.
- You will continue to create and recruit Pioneer penguins who work in the key areas of the business; candidates who can engage with people in their team to support them and answer questions or concerns.
- You will seek customer feedback through carefully designed surveys and interviews.
- You will build feedback into continuous improvement and celebrate and publicise the successes.

CULTURE CHANGE COMES LAST, NOT FIRST

It is important to recognise and appreciate that changing culture comes last. Only after people have changed their actions can there be a change in culture. Again, this is why creating a system and process is so important. We need people to change.

Most alterations in cultural norms and shared values will come at the end of the process.

The change you want will be results-driven. New approaches will sink in and become practice after success has been shown. The new ways will be demonstrably better than the old.

You will have been communicating lots. Not just at team and firm meetings but also by giving feedback, creating case studies, internal memos, cheers to peers' cards, one-to-one meetings, etc. Communication – you know – is vital.

Some of your people may still be reluctant to acknowledge and try the new practices; they will need encouragement. You ultimately may need to part company with some of your people.

Change management is hard, and many projects fail. Yours should not be one of them.

Listed below are some of the areas to keep an eye on, to ensure your project succeeds.

- Not making the VBP project a strategic priority. It needs to be. Believing that just because the CEO says 'Make it so' is not enough.
- Leaders/Partners/Stakeholders not supporting the project, losing enthusiasm, and allowing complacency to become the norm will kill your project.
- Neglecting to make some of the tough decisions, which can include taking on the Resistors and Naysayer penguins.
- Not truly integrating the Vision into the way your business works.
- Failing to create a sufficiently powerful Pioneer Penguin Group.
- Allowing obstacles to block change.
- Not celebrating wins enough.
- Lack of training, coaching, and mentoring.
- Poor communication – not repeating messaging often enough.
- Inadequately rewarding those who have engaged with VBP and increased revenue is also to be avoided. Celebrate their achievements.
- Openly rewarding lawyers who have not engaged in VBP. Avoid Partner patronage.
- Believing that implementing VBP is a technological solution. Technology can help, but lawyers must be trained so they can learn how to implement VBP and then use the technology provided.
- Not creating Plans to replace key leaders of change as they move on. You must ensure that their legacy is not lost or forgotten.

CLIENTS WILL BE THE MEASURE OF YOUR SUCCESS

As the change becomes embedded, you will find that you come across examples of VBP happening magically… you will find that people just get it and do it. It becomes second nature. Karl Albrecht, the modern founder of Total Quality Service ('TQS'), calls these moments of truth.

> Any episode in which the customer comes into contact with the organisation and gets an impression of its service.
>
> When moments of truth go unmanaged, the quality of service regresses to mediocrity.
>
> **Karl Albrecht**

What is interesting about Albrecht's definition is its 'any episode' of the service you offer. Think about it. This could be:

- A client who received a warm welcome when they contacted your business.
- A client who feels they are at the centre of your services.
- A client who appreciated being given a choice of service levels and price options so they could choose what they wanted.
- A client who was asked searching questions in an empathetic way by a lawyer who really seemed interested in their issue and how it might be resolved.
- A client who really does feel that you are the trusted advisor.
- A client who really knows that you understood their case.
- A client who knows that you achieved the outcome they wanted.

If you started to map out every potential moment of truth with a customer, the list could look something like this:

- How easy it was to get in contact with your firm?
- Are the profiles on websites up-to-date?
- Are email addresses and contact numbers clearly displayed?
- How accessible is parking at your office?
- Do your lawyers return calls within a reasonable time?
- Do clients comment that 'Shaun is a very busy lawyer…' What they're saying is he doesn't get back to them.
- Are clients kept waiting in reception for too long?

- Are clients' names being misspelt in draft documents? Are their addresses correct?
- Do you have awful coffee? Do you offer any coffee at all?
- What are your toilet facilities like?
- Is your reception area adorned with magazines that are two years old?
- When your lawyers go on holiday, do they notify the clients well in advance?
- Do your lawyers notify clients when they are about to leave the firm? Some management teams don't allow their lawyers to tell clients until a week or two before they leave. Not exactly client-centric!
- Do you keep clients informed about their cases and deadlines?
- Do your lawyers ring clients and speak to them rather than hide behind emails?
- Do they ring clients even if they don't have a transaction on the go?

I'm sure that you've read many articles about the seven touchpoints that prospective purchasers typically need to have with an organisation before they decide to buy.

> If we aren't customer driven,
> our cars won't be either.
>
> **Donald E. Petersen,**
> **Ford Motor Company**

Again, think about those touch points – they are part of the customer journey.

- Your marketing/advertising material.
- How your staff conduct themselves at networking events.
- Your website.
- The way your reception team handled the initial call. Answered in two rings? Recorded voicemail and put on hold?
- How was the call transferred from reception to an assistant?
- The conversations had with the assistant.
- The transfer of the call to the lawyer. The information that gets to the lawyer before they ring them back. Are all of the same questions asked?
- How the first meeting is conducted.

Referrals from existing and former clients of the firm are a great indicator that your service is valued. I stress here that it is referrals from existing or former clients.

Sometimes, referrals from third-party professionals may only be coming to you because you are cheap or because you pay for them. There is a distinction here.

Client satisfaction is obviously important. Some firms regularly conduct client listening exercises. These could be undertaken by senior lawyers, retired Partners, or an independent third party. The advantage of conducting listening exercises is that clients get the opportunity to give honest and open feedback. You will learn lots if you carry out this exercise. Just don't let your lawyers select the clients you should contact.

In the section dealing with After-Action Reviews, I highlighted that some firms involve the clients in the AAR process. Questions asked of clients could be along the following lines:

- Whether they felt they got value for money.
- Whether they thought the work was of a high quality.
- Was the service delivered in a timely way?
- Do they consider your firm a trusted advisor to the business, or was this just a one-off transaction?
- Will they come back to you at some time in the future?
- Will they recommend you? If not, why not?
- How did they feel your staff treated them?
- Were they kept up-to-date and fully informed?

But how do you measure client satisfaction? The answer is the same way as most businesses do, we look at the Net Promoter Score (NPS) numbers. NPS is a management tool used to gauge the loyalty of a firm's customer relationships.

In short, an NPS is nothing more than a question which asks.

'On a scale of 0-10, how likely are you to recommend our business to a friend or colleague?'

It's the scoring brackets that are interesting.

- Scores of 9 or 10 are promoters.
- Scores of 7 or 8 are passives.
- Scores of 6 or below are detractors.

The NPS is calculated when the number of detractors is subtracted from the number of promoters. Passives are neutral.

> We believe people with passion can change the world for the better. That's what we believe. And we believe that those people who are crazy enough to think they can change the world are the ones that actually do.
>
> **Steve Jobs**

In my experience, law firms think anything above 6 is a result. In reality, you need lots of 9/10s as the 6s and below will dramatically impact your score and drag it down. So be careful about believing some of your own propaganda from the client feedback forms you receive. To calculate the overall NPS value, you subtract the % of detractors from the % of promoters.

As mentioned in P#3 Plan, in 2021, an organisation called Insight 6, in their report, *The Professional Services Client Journey Report 2021,* measured the NPS from a sample of 256 businesses in the UK spread across the legal, financial, accountancy and property sectors. To put this in context, the NPSs at the time of the report saw Amazon on 53, Netflix on 55, and Apple on 56.

The Insight 6 report found that the NPSs of the following sectors were… (Drum roll please…)

- Property: -30
- Financial: -32
- Accountancy: -47
- Legal: -54

Now, before you think great – Legal got the highest number – it's a **MINUS!** The businesses that were sampled in the report intensely disliked the way that the law firms treated them. Read the report. I wonder if some law firms were answering the phone and just telling the callers to 'bog off and leave us alone!' There were many moments of truth experienced by the researchers in this survey.

We know when some of our clients are desperately unhappy and feel ripped off, they make formal complaints. As we work in a regulated environment, we log the complaints according to the appropriate level and move on. But what about the clients we don't hear from… the silent majority? Many will be unhappy. They just don't tell us and don't come back.

> However beautiful the strategy, you should occasionally look back at the results.
>
> **Winston Churchill**

POSSIBILITY THINKING

What are the moments of truth that will possibly negatively impact your brand?

- Not returning calls.
- Kept waiting in reception.
- Typos.
- Wrong name.
- Coffee is either bad or good.
- Our toilets.
- Chipped crockery.
- Lawyer on holiday – not telling client.
- Lawyer leaves – client not told.
- Missing deadlines.
- Telling the client something is needed with zero notice.
- The way we keep them informed.
- The way we answer the phone.

POSSIBILITY THINKING

Why should clients possibly use our firm?

- Because we are experts.
- We specialise in this area.
- We have done it all before.
- We have a supportive team.

- Our people.
- We are friendly.
- We are informative.
- We will communicate with you the way you want.
- We value price.
- We agree a price upfront, and there will be no surprises or extras.
- We have got your back.
- We are quick.
- We have great coffee.
- We are good at communicating.
- We understand your needs.
- We are relaxed.
- We will adhere to deadlines.
- We will take away your stress.
- We are confident in our ability.
- We have great client reviews.
- We have people who refer to us.
- We understand your challenges.
- We have won awards.
- We have case studies that show we understand your issues.
- We are committed to your success.
- We allow dogs in our reception.

WORDS WITH THE WISE

Kirsty Pappin, Aries LPM

Culture is a feeling.

You will know when it is changing. You will feel it.

Melissa Lyon, Hive Legal

We believe it is essential that our team understand the business of the firm. You don't create completely technically brilliant people and then expect them to suddenly understand the business, manage people, and understand the processes and systems of the firm. You've got to help them learn how to do it, be part of its development, and you've got to do it from the start. Our grads and our paralegals all have exposure to our operations and how we do things, not just pricing.

When we talk about value, it's not just the value that you give to the client. It's also about the team feeling valued. And when you've got your entire firm contributing to a client or a team outcome (rather than on the time it is taking them), it shifts the focus to providing a better experience and, ultimately, a better outcome.

We've got people now who started with the firm as juniors who are now senior associates and they've never done timesheets. They've only ever valued price.

It's a different way of thinking, it's a different way of working, it's a different way of delivering the services, and you need to have people who understand not just why we do it, but also the way we do it. That takes a different mindset, and it is essential for people to understand how that works.

Dr Jacqui Rigby, Rigby Pollitt Associates

Gather customer feedback post-go-live to see how the change has impacted your customers. Understand what works well for customers and how things might be improved further.

Ensure your customer satisfaction survey is capturing feedback on pricing. Benchmark the results prior to the change, then track over time. Monitor Net Promoter Scores (NPS). Report the results across the firm as everyone plays a part in customer satisfaction.

Will Whawell, Excelo Consulting

Changing culture is hard. It's a change in management style; it's a change in your billing habits. And the word empowering is used quite a lot, but it is an empowering thing. I've seen people have a weight drop off their shoulders when they've been told they're no longer going to bill by the hour.

Chris Marston, Exemplar Companies Pbc

Our culture is candid, irreverent and team-oriented. We're diversified. Everybody here is expected to think bigger than just Practice Areas and one domain.

We're much more explicit about our values. If the clients don't want a relationship, we don't want them. We further extend the no assholes rule to our clients.

Paul Roberts, My Customer Lens

Having values on the wall is pointless. Having values when everything's going well is not pointless, but it's not helpful. The point of values, and whether you really live them, is when it's hard. When you have to start making hard decisions as a result of your values.

If we value the health and wellness of our teams, and making sure they enjoy coming to work, are you prepared to fire a client because they're a nightmare to work with? And they might be worth hundreds of thousands to your firm, but your people are worth more. That's where values come into play; it is when you make hard decisions to live by the values, not when everything's going well.

Simon Tupman, Simon Tupman Consulting

Culture is intangible. When I go into a law office, I can sense it. It may be the smile that you get from the Director of First Impressions, it may be the decor, it may be the care and attention that's being given while I'm sitting in the reception. In one firm I know, clients and guests receive a muffin with a smiley face on it with their tea or coffee! It's the small things that can make a big difference. I think culture is self-defining and comes from all levels of the firm; it is a combination of how people feel, how they act, and how they react to each other.

Karen Finch, Legally Yours

The key will be re-skilling and up-skilling everyone within the law firm whilst fostering a culture of innovation, collaboration, and positivity around change. Experimentation and imagining new ways of doing everything within a law firm will be vital to the legal profession's survival.

John Chisholm, John Chisholm Consulting

Pricing can and must be absolutely embedded in a firm's culture, but it is not pricing alone that makes these firms different and better. Once you move away from the 'we sell time mantra', a whole new world opens to these firms. They have a flatter structure, are much more collegiate, the wellbeing of their people improves, they have a sense of purpose and empowerment, and they have better and more lasting relationships with better clients, for starters. They are more profitable, have better cash flow, and little or no cost complaints.

If you stood in reception at such a firm, would it feel much different than going into another law firm? Maybe, maybe not, but as soon as you engage their professionals, you experience a big difference. They have a genuine customer-centricity. You can tell by the questions they ask and how much they listen to you. I think it was Voltaire who said that you should judge someone 'not by the answers they give, but the questions they ask.' A true professional anywhere is much more judged by the questions they ask. Value-based pricing professionals ask and listen – we call it having a value conversation. They will consider whether they can or cannot assist; if they can, they will agree on a scope of work and prices after first offering you three options. They concentrate more on increasing your profit so theirs will follow.

CRIB SHEET

READING & VIEWING

READ

Oh, We Forgot About Change Management!

By Tim Creasy

https://pmhappyhour.com/ep084/

READ

Five Steps to Making Business Change Stick

By Jenna Phillips, Edward Wallace, PA Consulting

https://www.paconsulting.com/insights/five-steps-to-making-business-change-stick/

READ

How Professional Are The Professionals?

By Insight 6

https://www.insight6.com/how-professional-are-the-professionals/

READ

Secrets for Making Change Stick

By Ann Latham, Forbes

https://www.forbes.com/sites/annlatham/2016/05/29/5-secrets-for-making-change-stick/

TIPS/CHECKLISTS

1. Always have some post-go-live activity in your Plan to ensure the change is embedded.
2. Gather customer feedback. Understand what works well for customers and how things might be improved.

EXERCISES

EXERCISE 1

Metrics of success

Set the metrics, track the benefits of the change, and communicate across the firm.

EXERCISE 2

Communications Plan

Ensure your Comms Plan has post-go-live activity, and if not, update the Plan now.

EXERCISE 3

Internal feedback

Set up mechanism(s) for internal feedback.

You can use surveys, run group sessions, and talk to individuals.

EXERCISE 4

Identify advocates/champions

Identify people who will act as champions across the business – this should be done during the change itself and these people can be involved in communications and training as well as to engage people on the ground at the time of go-live.

EXERCISE 5

Lessons Learnt

Run a Lessons Learnt workshop.

EXERCISE 6

External Feedback

Gather customer feedback.

Set up surveys and structured interviews with customers to seek feedback.

Ensure your customer satisfaction survey is capturing feedback on pricing as a benchmark prior to the change, then track it over time. Monitor NPS. Report the results across the firm.

EXERCISE 7

Impact on complaints

Ask your compliance officer to give details on how many complaints originate from disputes over costs and a failure to keep clients advised about fee levels.

Look at:

- Client satisfaction reports.
- Complaints from clients.
- Complaints to the Legal Ombudsman and your Regulator.

EXERCISE 8

Moment of truth award?

Does the firm have an award for team members for delivering outstanding customer service or going above and beyond the call of duty for a customer? Should it do so?

EXERCISE 9

Training Needs

How could we benefit from Training Needs Analysis?

What leadership training is required to make this stick long term?

POSSIBILITY THINKING QUESTIONS TO POSE

1. What type of culture workshops would possibly help make this change stick?
2. What questions might we possibly ask employees post-launch?
3. What possible topics should we seek customer feedback on?
4. What are the best ways we can possibly use to reinforce the new ways of working?
5. How do we possibly broadcast VBP as our USP?

THE FINAL PART

SO, WHAT NOW? AND FAQS

So, as we near the end of the book, I imagine you will be thinking – How do I actually implement VBP? I imagine you have many questions.

What I have sought to do in this section is to set out some of the FAQs that you may have. Some of them have been covered in earlier parts of the book; some are new.

Q: What do we do now?

A: Plan a project. Follow the eight steps and the 8P Point Plan, and then just do something. You will not have to get everybody onboard from day one. Follow the steps in P#3 Part 4 Plan to create a Plan. Work out your own sense of urgency. Pull together a team and then create a Vision that works for you.

Q: Will our clients like it?

A: My view is they will, but – of course – I would say that, wouldn't I?! If you don't believe me, next time you have the opportunity to talk about lawyers and the way we price, ask a customer if they would like to be offered, say, three price points and a choice when it comes to buying legal services. The answers you get will convince you that this is a project worth pursuing.

Q: What do we say to clients who ask us, 'Why the change'?

A: Some clients may pose this question. You could respond with something along the following lines.

'The billable hour did not align with what our clients wanted.'

'We only wanted to be paid if we created value for our clients.'

'We wanted to turn off the billable hour meter and give clients a choice of options.'

Q: How do I select clients to try VBP with?

Answer the following questions with a yes/maybe/doubtful.

1. Is the client strategically important?
2. Do they value what you do?
3. Do they accept your fees without quibbling?
4. Do you know the management well?
5. Would you be upset to lose their work?

6. Do you have a strong relationship with the buyer/decision-maker?
7. Is the client a potential reference for similar-quality clients?

If you have answered with lots of 'yeses' – they are probably ideal candidates!

Q: How do I implement VBP?

A: If you create a pilot project in one or two work areas, you can practise the processes you've created before going live. Look at some of your old cases. Look at the complaints files. What would have happened if those matters had been value-priced? All training is a product of knowledge and practice. The sooner you start, the better you will get at value-based pricing. You and your troops *will* become more confident.

Q: Do I go Big Bang or Practice Area by Practice Area?

A: This really depends on the size of your firm. If you are an organisation with six people, you could seek to roll out VBP once you have created your policies and proved the concept. If you are an organisation with 100 people, then perhaps roll it out with a few pilot teams first. Much will depend on where your pilot teams are selected from and the level of enthusiasm that they have.

Projects usually work best with one or two evangelical teams that decide they want to embrace VBP and do things in a different way.

When these teams prove the concept and start gaining success (which will be promoted as you celebrate the quick wins), other teams will become interested, and other Practice Areas will start looking at what is going on and requesting the training.

Some firms will test the process on new customers to the firm. They are happy to try the process on these clients because if they don't win the work, they haven't damaged a long-term existing relationship. But, sooner or later, you will have to try out the process on existing customers and have confidence in your offering. You may think it is worth doing it the sooner, the better.

There's absolutely no harm in explaining to customers that this is a new process. The clients will likely enjoy the experience and appreciate the choices you offer.

Q: Do I abandon hourly rates altogether? What about those clients that I have to bill by time?

A: I appreciate there will be some areas of work where time recording rules, such as Legal Aid and Court of Protection work. There are complex conditional fee work areas where cost judges want to see the hours listed… usually so they can start marking them down and disallowing items.

There are areas where time recording is, in my view, irrelevant. Residential conveyancing is one such Practice Area. Let's face it, most firms offer conveyancing on a fixed fee. Many firms, of course, don't actually fix the fee at all but give a base fee of £X and then add on lots of extra prices that only serve to shock and annoy clients. As mentioned earlier in the book, in 2023, I did some research into the conveyancing sector and came across over 120 additional menu-based additions to the initial cost of buying a property.

You may find it's worth occasionally testing time recording matters, almost as a 'time and motion study', to ensure that your base costs are still accurate.

Q. Is value-based pricing a technological project?

A: No, sorry. Technology will have a role to play in the creation of FPAs. At this stage, you are seeking to change the way people work.

Think about your CRM system and how well it is utilised. I suspect it's not utilised to its full potential. It may not be used at all. Why? In many law firms, it's not valued, and lawyers have not been trained to use it nor understand why it's so important. VBP is the same. You must get hearts and minds onboard. Technology is an enabler, not a solution.

> The only app you need to Price Value is the one between your right and left ears.
>
> **Rhondalynn Korolak, Pricing Value**

Q: What if customers still want to be billed by time?

A: This very much depends on the customer and how important they are to you. You may want to carry on. However, you have to be alive to the fact that if you carry on the hourly rate, you are continuing to endorse the artificial cap on your earnings and will be leaving value on the table. In the fullness of time, you may want to redirect your lawyers' efforts to act for VBP clients who are more profitable.

Q: When should we stop time recording?

A: This is a common question. The answer is very much up to you. The finance team may decide that they want to carry on looking at these figures. Eventually, once the metrics used are embedded, you may find that time isn't important anymore. After all, it's an input.

Those firms that do get to ditch the hourly rate completely often ask themselves what took them so long. Read the section where I interview Jacqui Brown of Lynn & Brown again. The benefits her firm received were significant.

Q: What if we get it wrong?

A: You will. Pricing is an art, not a science. It is hard to know the exact amount someone will pay for a job. In fact, it's impossible to know that. Keep referring back to the amount of work in progress that you write off every year and set yourself a target of not making mistakes of that magnitude. You won't.

I make no bones about it, VBP is a significant change in your business model. However, you are in the process of preparing a Plan and outline as to how this can work. Clients like it, lawyers like it, and it's a benefit to the owners of the law firm. It's probably costing you a significant amount every day when you don't implement value-based pricing.

Q: This sounds like it's a large training project?

A: It is. But actually, some of the skills your lawyers may already have. You don't know as you haven't asked them yet. By following the 8PPP, I'm asking you to carry out a Gap Analysis regarding training needs, document them, and then create new skills. Put them in a format that can be learned, captured, and developed. In this way, any new lawyer joining your firm knows how you go about doing things. This becomes your BBU, your operating manual.

You will need to train your lawyers to have detailed conversations with customers so you can ascertain what the value is. You need to know what their outcomes are. You need to move away from your preconceived solutions, listen to clients, and understand what they want to achieve. You will then design an FPA which shows the customer that they have made the right choice in contacting your firm.

You will start recruiting lawyers against a Skills Matrix you design. You may find that some lawyers have already used value-based pricing at their former firms. You will promote lawyers who have VBP skills to managerial roles.

Q: Will we have to adopt a new mindset when pricing customers?

A: Absolutely. If there is one thing I hope you take away from this book, it is that law is not a commodity product. No two clients are the same. No sets of circumstances are the same. The lawyers on the transactions are not the same. Clients want different things as far as service levels are concerned, and their attitude towards risk and value is different.

Q: Will we need to produce scoped, Fixed-Price Agreements and deal with assumptions and exclusions?

A: Yes, you will. But you're probably doing something like that already in your client Engagement Letters. The problem with client Engagement Letters is they have become so unwieldy that clients don't even bother reading them. Even worse, some lawyers don't even bother filling them in correctly at the outset.

You will have to get better at defining a project scope, identifying what you will do, what you will not do, and the assumptions made in the process. Taking time at the beginning to get these detailed and accurate will save time later when the templates are used repeatedly and honed and refined.

Q: Will we need to create options?

A: You will. It never ceases to amaze me how often people tell me that you can't give different versions of their service. Quite often, 30 minutes later, we can develop two or three versions on their own. Half the problem is the way lawyers are wired. We are naturally conservative, risk-averse, and pay attention to detail. Lawyers are professional sceptics. Creative thinking about our own services is not something that comes naturally.

Embrace Possibility Thinking. The easiest way to start the option creation process is to ask, 'What could a gold service for (insert work area) possibly look like?' You will come up with a long list of features. Use this list to create another two options by stripping out some of the features.

Keep working on the options that you create for clients. Save them in your PMS in your BBUs/department manual. Remember to always start with the highest price first. You'll be surprised how many clients decide they want the more expensive service options.

Q: Will we have to stop pricing our own work?

A: Yes, you most certainly will. This is one of the golden rules. At the risk of repeating myself, why do barristers have clerks, and footballers and actors have agents? It's because the clerks and agents get a better price than their footballers/actors would negotiate.

You may need a pricing buddy or you may need a Value Council. Much depends on the nature of your firm and the type of work you do. As long as there is another pair of eyes on every price, you will find that you will start making more money. Your pricing buddy will be more bullish about the value you create than you do.

Q: Will we have to get used to telling a client that we can't provide a price immediately?

A: Yes, you will. Speed is bad for pricing. Remember the builder analogy. Nobody is impressed by a builder who will give us a fixed price for a house extension within 20 minutes of meeting a customer.

If a client is insisting on a price, go in very high. If you get pushback on the high price, then you can explain that you're being pushed into a situation, so you're deliberately going high.

Q: Will we have to stop being afraid of objection handling?

A: Yes, you will. The more experience you get in handling the objections, the better you will become. Document the objections you receive. Discuss them regularly and refine the answers. Remember, it is important to protect your pricing integrity. Do not offer a discount without trading something for it. This means that the client might have to do something themselves, or you might take away one aspect of the service.

Q: Are you recommending we get more bullish when it comes to pricing?

A: I am. Stand your ground. Don't be nervous. When you protect pricing integrity, it makes clients want you more. Remember, you are selling intellectual capital.

Clients always want a lower price… but they also want value.

Q: Will we have to get better at discovery calls, value conversations, and interviews?

A: Yes, you will. It is far better to invest some time into preparation before a meeting as it gives you a better chance of securing the work. You may also realise that the client is not the right fit for your firm. Remember, it's better to find out that the client is not suitable before you do the work, rather than at the end when they're not paying.

Q: I'm worried about giving a Service Guarantee.

A: Don't be. It always amazes me that people get hung up on this. You are giving a Service Guarantee anyway, every time you open a file. Most clients who feel they received a poor service probably tell their friends about how poor you were; they vote with their feet, and you never see them again.

With the Service Guarantee, you and your legal team are committing to providing a service at a level you and the client have agreed to. They know and expect what they will get. It's much better to find out that the service is not being delivered as you go along, rather than at the end. Remember, you're not guaranteeing an outcome – you are guaranteeing a service delivery.

Q: Might we miss out on work from existing customers?

A: Yes, you may. In fact, you might actually be getting rid of some of those customers. If clients are in the wrong place, not profitable, and difficult to deal with, I suggest you gently ease them out of your organisation and towards your competition. Chances are that 50% of your lawyers are already acting for clients they dislike. Weeding out those difficult clients will only make your lawyers grateful.

Q: We need to get better at saying no to clients?

A: Yes, you do. We have to believe we are worth the prices we charge. We then have to accept that we are not going to do work at any cost, and be prepared to walk away.

Q: Will we need to agree systems for undertaking After-Action Reviews?

Yes, you do. And these can happen at all kinds of levels within Practice Area teams. The important thing is to learn when things go right and also learn if things go wrong and ensure that the learning is disseminated throughout the organisation.

Q: Who else needs to be told about our VBP journey?

A: Believe it or not, quite a few people. You will find your bank managers and other advisors will need to know that you are adopting a different method when you can no longer show them huge WIP figures.

You will also need to have conversations with referrers and explain your new method of pricing.

Q: This VBP project sounds complex?

A: It's not. But it is a change management project, and you have to treat it as such. This is not a project where an email is sent by the Board or you listen to a webinar, and that's it.

You need to break this project down into a series of stages. The 8PPP Plan will help you do that. Adopt the KISS method and keep it simple. Sometimes, lawyers are guilty of overcomplicating matters. Do not let perfection be the enemy of good.

8 PPP PENGUIN LOGIC

Don't get confused

The 8PPP should not be confused with the military's adage of the 7Ps, although it is worth mentioning it here for completeness!

Proper Planning and Preparation Prevents Piss-Poor Performance.

EPILOGUE

Star date 428.65 … Hang on, that's a different type of log.

8 PPP PENGUIN LOGIC

What goes around comes around

Pricing success will create more pricing success.

I do hope that after reading this book, you have decided to embark on a VBP journey and embrace a pricing methodology that is new to you and your people.

It will take effort to create the tools and processes, obtain the historical pricing information, design your procedures, train your people, create and develop role models, and keep the project going.

You know there are Golden Rules!

GOLDEN RULE #1

The management of your business must be 100% onboard with this project. Otherwise, it won't be fully implemented.

- They must become engaged and be involved in championing the change in culture that needs to happen.
- They must help define the objectives and then implement them.
- Resources must be made available.
- Staff must be made available to participate in the project.

- Obstacles will need to be removed.
- Funds and expertise will need to be made available.
- It will need to be made clear – across the business – that this is a serious initiative and vital for the firm's success.

Lots of carefully considered communications will be required.

GOLDEN RULE #2

If complacency is allowed to settle in, then the change won't happen.

GOLDEN RULE #3

Every lawyer knows that real, meaningful relationships with clients are not built on charging for time.

GOLDEN RULE #4

One of the golden rules of VBP that you have to accept is that it is an art, not a science.

GOLDEN RULE #5

Bad clients drive out good clients AND good lawyers.

GOLDEN RULE #6

Be a price setter, not a price chaser.

Do not follow your competitors' pricing.

GOLDEN RULE #7

The response to scope creep is
'I will speak to the client and agree a revised price.'

GOLDEN RULE #8

No one prices their own work in isolation.

You will always get two pairs of eyes on every price.

GOLDEN RULE #9

Present your most expensive option first
and be proud of it.

GOLDEN RULE #10

Create an AAR Process.

Let's learn from our mistakes… lawyers are human!

Hopefully, you will decide to make VBP and the benefits it brings your clients, your lawyers, and your firm a cornerstone of your Strategy.

You will commit to understanding your customers and learning what is important to them, giving choices and satisfying their needs. Become an advisor that they recommend to others.

You will understand your competitors and gather data about them, but be a price setter not a price chaser.

You will look at your business, the areas of work you want to do, and those you can actually profit from. You will actively seek better clients and develop better client relationships.

You will be fully committed to training your people and embark on continuous learning programmes to improve their Pricing Confidence.

You will have taken back control of pricing in your organisation and elevated it to the position where it is now recognised as vitally important. You and all your employees know that nothing impacts your profits more than pricing.

> No single management lever available to you, can boost profitability more quickly than even a slight improvement in average price levels.
>
> **Michael Marn, Eric Roegner, and Craig Zawada**
>
> **The Price Advantage**

As Melissa Lyon of Hive Legal told me as we wrapped up our Words With The Wise interview, 'You have to have passion, understanding, commitment and the drive to implement value-based pricing. I always talk about purpose as being purpose beyond profit. But if you get purpose right, then the profit will follow. And that's the case with value pricing. If you purposefully value price and you do it for the right reasons, then the profit will follow.'

She is 100% right.

A FINAL THOUGHT

Value-based pricing is not new to the legal industry. There are firms out there doing value-based pricing day-in and day-out. They have happier clients. They are making more money. Their lawyers are experiencing a better work-life balance.

Implementing value-based pricing is a challenge. Some may even say it is difficult. You should be relieved about that… because if it was easy, your competitors would have already done it. They probably haven't, and they may never do so. Go for it!

Good luck!

APPENDICES

PEOPLE TO FOLLOW

Name	Web details	Linked In
Ron Baker Radio Talk-Show Host, The Soul of Enterprise at VoiceAmerica Talk Radio	verasage.com	linkedin.com/in/ronbaker1/
Mitch Kowalski European/Canadian, Head of Legal and Legal Operations Advisor	kowalski.ca	linkedin.com/in/mitchkowalski/
Tim Williams Business model and pricing strategist for professional services firms	ignitiongroup.com	linkedin.com/in/timwilliamsicg/
Kirk Bowman Pricing & Performance Consultant	artofvalue.com	linkedin.com/in/kirkbowman/
John Chisholm Thinking Differently In Your Shoes. Talks about #auslaw, #lawyers, #pricing, #lawfirms, and #valuepricing	chisconsult.com	linkedin.com/in/chisholmjohn/

Dr Jacqui Rigby Accelerating Strategic Change with SMEs | 5-Dimensional Thinking		linkedin.com/in/jacquirigby/
Matt Homann Founder of Filament and inventor of Thinksgiving. I help smart people think together better, and I've got 'Idea Surplus Disorder' real bad.	nonbillablehour.com MeetFilament.com	linkedin.com/in/homann/
Jacqui Brown Problem-Solver and Director	lynnandbrown.com.au	linkedin.com/in/jacquelineabrown
Steven Brown Founding Director | Commercial Lawyer (Dispute & Transactions) | Problem-Solver and Risk Advisor	lynnandbrown.com.au	linkedin.com/in/stevenbrown perthlawyer/
Matthew Burgess Viewlegal.director.author. speaker. entrepreneur. fellowverasage	viewlegal.com.au	linkedin.com/in/ matthew-burgess-101/

Thomas Bowden Founder of Timeless Counsel, Plc	timelesscounsel.com	linkedin.com/in/ venturelawyer/
Ed Kless Meta-Consultant, Business Iconoclast, Radio Talk-Show Host	thesoulofenterprise.com	linkedin.com/in/edkless/
Simon Tupman Legal business consultant Leadership mentor Author. Keynote speaker – Helping law firms thrive	simontupman.com	linkedin.com/in/simontupman/
Nicola Jones Helping Legal to Overcome the Status Quo: Developing the cultural & individual conditions to drive innovation	athenaprofessional.co.uk	linkedin.com/in/ nicolajoneslearningexpert/
Will Whawell Projects. Pricing. Process. Legal Costs Management. Legal Pricing. Legal Process.	excelo.co.uk	linkedin.com/in/willwhawell
Paul Roberts Customer Experience. Client Listening. Feedback Intelligence. SaaS. Customer Insight | CEO MyCustomerLens – future-proofing firms to compete on experience	mycustomerlens.com	linkedin.com/in/paul-j-roberts/

Graham Moore Helping law firms improve performance and make better decisions using data. Founder of Katchr	katchr.com	linkedin.com/in/grahamnmoore
Kirsty Pappin Award-winning Legal Practice Manager supporting law firms to effectively manage business operations. Trainer & Writer at the ILFM. The Lady in the Blue Trousers™	arieslpm.com	linkedin.com/in/kirsty-pappin-legal-practice-manager/
Jon Whittle Helping law firms drive commercial growth and win in a changing legal world	jonwhittleconsulting.co.uk	linkedin.com/in/jonwhittle
Robin Dicks Director, The Thriving Company	thrivingcompany.co.uk	linkedin.com/in/robin-dicks-0b00a82/
Katherine Thomas Growth and strategy for legal businesses. Adviser, consultant, speaker and lecturer. Owner – Free Range Lawyers.	freerangelawyers.com	linkedin.com/in/katherinethomas75/
Greg Kyte Cartoonist, Emcee, CPE Presenter, Stand Up Comedian & Co-Host of the Oh My Fraud Podcast	X | @gregkyte	linkedin.com/in/gregkyte/

Karen Finch CEO @Legally Yours Pty Ltd. President @ ALTA. Legal Technology. Legal Innovation	legallyyours.com.au	linkedin.com/in/karen-finch-1b1568124/
Jordan Furlong Legal Sector Analyst and Forecaster	law21.ca	linkedin.com/in/jordanfurlong/
Melissa Lyons Purpose Driven Legal Design Thinker | Executive Director & Experience Designer at Hive Legal	hivelegal.com.au/	linkedin.com/in/melissa-lyon-1a68b618/
Terri Mottershead Generative AI enthusiast, Innovation strategist, Legal ecosystem podcaster and blogger	cli.collaw.com	linkedin.com/in/terri-mottershead/
Leanne Bentley-French Microsoft Training for Lawyers and Secretaries Training Consultancy	wonderwordtraining.co.uk	linkedin.com/in/leannebentley/
Heather Suttie Legal Market Strategy and Management Consulting. Global to Solo. BigLaw to NewLaw	heathersuttie.ca	linkedin.com/in/heathersuttie/

Jon Cobb Leadership Coach and Speaker – I help leaders reach their full potential in life and business	endeavorlab. joncobbcoaching.com	linkedin.com/in/jondcobb/
Jonathan Stark The Ditching Hourly Guy For freelancers, consultants, and other independent professionals who want to make more money without working more hours	jonathanstark.com	linkedin.com/in/jonathanstark/
Andy Gilbert Founder & Managing Director at Go M.A.D. Thinking. Challenging leaders and teams to solve problems, manage change, and transform results using 7 proven principles	gomadthinking.com	linkedin.com/in/andygomad/
David Gilroy A marketing agency that specialises in helping law firms make more money from their website.	conscious.co.uk	linkedin.com/in/davidgilroybs8/
Christopher Marston Chief Executive Officer at Exemplar Companies, Inc.	exemplarcompanies.com/	linkedin.com/in/christopher-marston-esq-125a121/
Alice Stephenson CEO of Plume Group and author of *(Out)Law: From Teenage Mum to Legal Trailblazer*	alicestephenson.com/	linkedin.com/in/alicestephenson/

FURTHER READING

1. Our Iceberg Is Melting – John Kotter and Holger Rathgeber (Macmillan 2017)
2. Avoiding Extinction: Reimagining Legal Services For the 21st Century – Mitch Kowalski (iUniverse 2012)
3. Positioning For Professionals – Tim Williams (Wiley 2010)
4. Professionals Guide To Value Pricing – Ron Baker (Aspen Law and Business 2001)
5. Dialogues on Business in the Knowledge Economy – Ron Baker and Ed Kless (VeraSage Press 2015)
6. Pricing On Purpose – Ron Baker (Wiley 2006)
7. Smarter Pricing – Tony Cram (FT Prentice Hall 2006)
8. Implementing Value Pricing – Ron Baker (Wiley 2011)
9. Pricing Value – Rhondalynn Korolak (2019)
10. Value-Based Pricing – Harry Macdivitt and Mike Wilkinson (McGraw Hill 2012)
11. Double Your Price – David Falzani (Pearson 2023)
12. The Heart of Practice – Simon Tupman (Lawyers with a Life Ltd 2023)
13. The Price Advantage – Michael Marn, Eric Roegner, and Craig Zawada (Wiley 2004)
14. The Six Pillars of Self-Esteem – Nathaniel Branden (Bantam 1995)
15. The Coaching Habit – Michael Bungay Stanier (Box of Crayons Press 2016)
16. Client Value and Law Firm Profitability – Jim Hassett (LegalBizDev 2014)
17. Billing Innovations: New Win-Win Ways to End Hourly Billing – Richard C Reed (American Bar Association 1996)
18. Switch: When Change is Hard – Chip and Dan Heath (Random House 2010)
19. Uncommon Sense, Common Nonsense – Jules Goddard and Tony Eccles (Profile Books 2013)
20. How To Lead Smart People – Arun Singh and Mike Mister (Profile Books 2019)
21. (Out)Law: From Teenage Mum to Legal Trailblazer – Alice Stephenson (Hawksmoor Publishing 2023)

FURTHER LISTENING

Art of Value

Kirk Bowman

www.artofvalue.com

Kirk is not a lawyer, but he has interviewed lots of them on the Art of Value.

Soul Of Enterprise

Ron Baker and Ed Kless

www.thesoulofenterprise.com

Ron and Ed's weekly show interviews guests from all over the world, including lawyers and other professionals who have views about VBP.

Ditching Hourly

Jonathan Stark

www.podcast.ditchinghourly.com

Lots of different guests from many industry sectors. The podcast with Mitch Kowalski is well worth a listen.

Accounting Influencers

Rob Brown and Martin Bissett

www.accountinginfluencers.com

Aimed at accountants but lots of transferable information.

The Value Pricing Podcast

Mark Wickersham

www.wickersham.co.uk

Also aimed at accountants. Mark reinforces lots of VBP basics.

Legally Speaking

Robert Hanna

www.legallyspeakingpodcast.com

Aimed at inspiring and educating those in the legal sector.

50 REASONS NOT TO CHANGE (COURTESY OF FACEBOOK POST)

1. It's too expensive.
2. That's someone else's responsibility.
3. We've always done it this way.
4. It's too political.
5. We're doing OK as it is.
6. We don't have the staff.
7. We tried that before.
8. This is just a fad.
9. Maybe, maybe not.
10. We've never done that before.
11. It needs committee study.
12. There's not enough time.
13. It's against tradition.
14. It's not my job.
15. It can't be done.
16. We don't have consensus yet.
17. It's too complicated.
18. It's contrary to policy.
19. It won't fly.
20. Will catch flack for that.
21. I'm not sure the boss will like it.
22. It's too ambitious.
23. No one asked me.
24. What's in it for me?
25. It will take too long.
26. We didn't budget for it.
27. We don't have the equipment.
28. It's impossible.
29. I don't have the authority.
30. It's hopeless.
31. We can't take the chance.

32. They won't fund it.
33. It's too radical.
34. We have too many layers.
35. There's too much red tape.
36. It needs more thought.
37. They're too entrenched.
38. There's no clear mandate.
39. I'm all for it but...
40. It will never fly upstairs.
41. They don't really want to change.
42. It's too visionary.
43. It won't work in this department.
44. It's not our problem.
45. Another department tried that.
46. Another firm tried that.
47. We are waiting for guidance on that.
48. It won't be chargeable work.
49. There may be GDPR issues.
50. CBA.

ANSWER TO THE MATHS OF DISCOUNTING

FEE	LAST TIME	10% DISCOUNT
	100	90
Costs	70	70
Profit	30	20
		33% off the profit!

NB: If you found the calculation difficult, it's because many do not automatically think to put in the cost figure of £70, which remains the same.

SKILLS MATRIX/ KEY PERFORMANCE INDICATORS

KPI 1 **Professional Expertise**	• Understands the business's strategic objectives and the role that VBP can play. • Understands customer fit and the importance of customer selection and deselection. • Supports Practice Area in pricing, adheres to golden rules, and is a second pair of eyes on colleague's work. • Understands the importance of, and can create and ask value-based questions. • Can understand how to ask questions to establish client value. • Creates clear scopes of work. • Delivers high-quality service. • Communicates clearly with the client on the scope of work and throughout the project. • Is committed to understanding and improving the client's experience. • Demonstrates a knowledge of the importance of customer journey mapping. • Supports and contributes to the gathering of know-how to expand the Knowledge Management database. • Actively seeks out and circulates examples of VBP best practice.
KPI 2 **Operations and Strategy**	• Raises Change Orders when matters go out of scope. • Ensures consistent service delivery. • Ensures deadlines and constraints are met. • Conducts and participates in the After-Action Review process.
KPI 3 **Customer and BD**	• Is able to confidently communicate value to clients. • Manages client matters within the framework and scope of the FPA. • Communicates empathetically and clearly with clients at all times and shows a genuine interest in the matter and achieving the outcome. • Develops close relationships with clients and referrers.

	• Ensures that data on the CRM system is kept up-to-date. • Engages with and supports the business's marketing activities.
KPI 4 **Finance & Risk**	• Is a pricing enthusiast and supporter of VBP. • Is aware of how decisions made may impact profitability. • Complies with pricing processes. • Helps define and refine the pricing processes. • Achieves both individual and team targets by utilising VBP principles.
KPI 5 **People and Teams**	• Helps others understand the importance of VBP and engages with the process. • Complies with the documents and agreed pricing processes. • Encourages and acts as a mentor to others on their VBP journeys. • Delivers feedback sensitively and in a supportive way. • Is prepared to call out bad pricing behaviours. • Leads and supports client deselection. • Creates and shares knowledge with Practice Area members and Pricing Groups. • Participates in and leads training sessions.

8 P POINT PLAN RACI (RESPONSIBLE, ACCOUNTABLE, CONSULTED AND INFORMED) TASK LIST

Decisions

Primary Responsibility ❸ | Some Responsibility ❶

Key

KM =Knowledge Management

SME = Subject Matter Experts

IT = Information Technology

Practice Manager includes COO and Compliance responsibilities.

Set out below are what I have identified as some of the typical tasks that may have to be undertaken as part of a VBP implementation project. The list is only a starting point. Depending on the nature and size of your business, the task list will alter, as will the responsibility for carrying them out.

	TASK											
	PRELIMINARIES	**Project Manager**	**Pioneer Penguins**	**Project Sponsor**	**EXCO/ Board**	**Partners HODS Team Leaders**	**Practice Manager**	**Finance**	**Marketing BD Comms PR**	**HR**	**Lawyers/ Teams**	**IT**
1.	Buy and read *Our Iceberg Is Melting*.			❸	❶	❶	❶	❶	❶	❶	❶	❶
2.	Register with the VBP Colony website.	❶		❸								
3.	Appoint Project Sponsor.				❸							
	P#1 PARADIGM	**Project Manager**	**Pioneer Penguins**	**Project Sponsor**	**EXCO/ Board**	**Partners HODS Team Leaders**	**COO COLP**	**Finance**	**Marketing BD Comms PR**	**HR**	**Lawyers/ Teams**	**IT**
4.	Ensure there is commitment from EXCO.	❶		❸	❶							
5.	Collate and review financial MI.	❶		❸				❶				
6.	Appoint Project Manager.	❶		❶	❸							
7.	Investigate how pricing is currently undertaken.	❸	❶			❶		❶				
8.	What is current pricing strategy and policy?	❸	❶		❶	❶						
9.	Establish how base costs are calculated.	❸	❶			❶		❶				
10.	Gather in and review practice area pricing materials.	❸	❶			❶						
11.	Establish how practice areas generate fixed prices.	❸	❶			❶						
12.	Identify what financial training is undertaken and/or required.	❸	❶					❶		❶		
13.	Design pricing confidence survey.	❸				❶		❶		❶		

14.	Ask clients' views about options and fixed prices.	1	1			3			1			
15.	Collate and review customer feedback NPS data.	3				1			1			
16.	Collate and review complaints data.	1	1			1	3					1
17.	Create and communicate the psychological safety net for Pioneers.	1	1	3	1	1				1		
18.	Reason for paradigm shift - Define the goal.	1		1	3							
19.	Create possibility thinking questions to solve problems.	3										
20.	Communications.	3										
	P#2 PIONEERS	**Project Manager**	**Pioneer Penguins**	**Project Sponsor**	**EXCO/ Board**	**Partners HODS Team Leaders**	**Practice Manager**	**Finance**	**Marketing BD Comms PR**	**HR**	**Lawyers/ Teams**	**IT**
21.	Ensure EXCO/Board support for Pioneers is made public.	1		3	1	1			1	1		
22.	Ask who in the business already has VBP experience.	3		1	1	1	1	1	1	1	1	1
23.	Selection and recruitment of Pioneers.	3		1		1						
24.	Create Pioneer Group measurable objectives.	3		1								
25.	Ensure practice area leaders free up time for Pioneers to participate.	1		3		1						
26.	Meeting launch agenda and preparation.	3	1			1						
27.	Meeting launch kick-off.	3	1	1	1	1	1	1	1	1	1	
28.	Undertake confidence surveys with Pioneer Group.	3	1	1						1		1
29.	Conduct "What do clients want?" exercise - LexisNexis Report.	3	1			1						

30.	Anticipate Resistors/Naysayer penguins.	1	1	3		1				1		
31.	Create possibility thinking questions to solve problems.	3										
32.	Communications.	3										
	P#3 PLAN											
33.	**Knowledge**	**Project Manager**	**Pioneer Penguins**	**Project Sponsor**	**EXCO/ Board**	**Partners HODS Team Leaders**	**Practice Manager**	**Finance**	**Marketing BD Comms PR**	**HR**	**Lawyers/ Teams**	**OIT**
34.	What do we do in our business? Review levels of awareness.	3	1								1	
35.	What do our clients buy? List outcomes we sell/create.	1	1						3		1	
36.	Active listening and empathy training. What is available?	1								3		
37.	Design and implement client journey mapping exercise.	1	3			1			1		1	1
38.	Define and plan customer segmentation exercise.	3	1			1	1	1	1		1	1
39.	Create parameters and rules for client deselection.	3		1	1	1	1	1				
40.	Create rules of engagement regarding CRM system.	1	3			1	1		1			1
41.	Create and complete competitor analysis table.		1			1			3		1	1
42.	Create onboarding scripts /discovery calls.		3			1			1		1	
43.	Discovery call training. What is available?	1							1	3		
44.	Speed of quoting. What happens now? How can it be slowed down?	3	1			1						
45.	Review/create free work/pro bono policy.	3			1	1		1				

	Tools	Project Manager	Pioneer Penguins	Project Sponsor	EXCO/ Board	Partners HODS Team Leaders	Practice Manager	Finance	Marketing BD Comms PR	HR	Lawyers/ Teams	IT
46.	Create a lawyer scoring matrix.	3				1	1		1			1
47.	Review/introduce/create guidance for Farmer mentality.	1		3		1				1		
48.	Creation of VBP questions for practice areas.	3	1			1			1		1	
49.	Creation of internal resourcing questions to be asked.	3				1	1	1		1	1	1
50.	Create value proposition worksheets.	3	1								1	1
51.	Create commercial client audit.	1				1	1		3			1
52.	Establish a methodology for base price calculations.	3	1			1		1				1
53.	Create Fixed Price Agreement (FPA) template.	3	1			1	1		1		1	1
54.	Create practice area assumptions list.	1	1			3						
55.	Create practice area exclusions list.	1	1			3						
56.	Create practice area scopes list.	1	1			3					1	
57.	Create practice area versions/options examples.	1	1			3			1		1	
58.	Create pebble in pond scoping matrix.	1				3					1	
59.	Define and create change order process.	3	1	1				1			1	
60.	Create practice area Value Council/ two pairs of eyes processes. Rules of engagement.	3	1	1		1					1	
61.	Create and define AAR process for each practice area.	3		1		1					1	1

	Vision	Project Manager	Pioneer Penguins	Project Sponsor	EXCO/ Board	Partners HODS Team Leaders	Practice Manager	Finance	Marketing BD Comms PR	HR	Lawyers/ Teams	IT
62.	Create draft vision.	❶		❸		❶	❶	❶				
63.	Obtain Board/EXCO approval of vision.	❸		❶	❶							
64.	Design vision communications.	❸		❶					❶	❶		
65.	Publish and promote vision.	❶	❶	❸	❶	❶	❶	❶	❶	❶	❶	❶
	Plan	Project Manager	Pioneer Penguins	Project Sponsor	EXCO/ Board	Partners HODS Team Leaders	Practice Manager	Finance	Marketing BD Comms PR	HR	Lawyers/ Teams	IT
66.	Set change goal.	❶	❶	❸	❶							
67.	Conduct GAP analysis.	❸	❶	❶	❶	❶	❶	❶	❶	❶	❶	❶
68.	Define future state.	❸	❶	❶	❶	❶	❶	❶	❶	❶	❶	❶
69.	Identify hurdles and blockers.	❸	❶	❶		❶		❶	❶	❶	❶	❶
70.	Develop initiation document.	❸	❶	❶	❶	❶	❶	❶	❶	❶	❶	❶
71.	Draft business case.	❸		❶		❶		❶		❶		
72.	Create high-level plan.	❸	❶	❶	❶	❶	❶	❶	❶	❶	❶	❶
73.	Create project issues template.	❸		❶								
74.	Create project risk template.	❸		❶								
75.	Design pricing process/BBU.	❸	❶	❶		❶	❶	❶	❶	❶	❶	❶
76.	Analyse where your firm is on any financial benchmarking studies.	❶		❶	❶	❶		❸				
77.	Conduct HR training gap analysis.	❶				❶				❸	❶	❶
78.	Create HR training induction plans.	❶				❶				❸		❶
79.	Create possibility thinking questions to solve problems.	❸										
80.	Communications.	❸										

	P#4 PROMOTE	Project Manager	Pioneer Penguins	Project Sponsor	EXCO/ Board	Partners HODS Team Leaders	Practice Manager	Finance	Marketing BD Comms PR	HR	Lawyers/ Teams	IT
81.	Create communications plan for 8 P Point Plan.	3		1					1			
82.	Plans for celebrations - list.	3		1					1	1		
83.	Role profile amendment.	1		1	1	1				3		
84.	Agendas for pricing discussion and feedback with practice areas.	3	1	1		1				1		
85.	Financial metrics for pilot project.	3		1				1				
86.	Create possibility thinking questions to solve problems.	3										
87.	Communications.	3							3			
	P#5 PERMIT	**Project Manager**	**Pioneer Penguins**	**Project Sponsor**	**EXCO/ Board**	**Partners HODS Team Leaders**	**Practice Manager**	**Finance**	**Marketing BD Comms PR**	**HR**	**Lawyers/ Teams**	**IT**
88.	Identify obstacles to vision. How can they be overcome?	3	1	1	1	1	1	1	1	1	1	1
89.	Review existing policies. Which should be retired or amended?	3	1	1		1	1	1	1	1	1	1
90.	Conduct firm-wide pricing confidence surveys.	3		1						1		1
91.	Identify training needs arising from firm-wide pricing confidence surveys.	1		1		1	1	1		3		
92.	Conduct price sensitivity meter (Van Westendorp) exercise in each practice area.	3	1			1		1			1	1
93.	Conduct skills matrix review.	1				1				3	1	1
94.	Identify typical customer objections by practice area.	1	3			1	1		1			

95.	Create practice area examples of answers to handle objections.	1	3			1					1	
96.	Create practice area service guarantee.	1	3	1		1			1			
97.	Review AAR's minutes and feedback.	3		1		1	1		1		1	
98.	Marketing/BD update report - what are their findings?	1	1	1	1	1		1	3	1	1	1
99.	IT update report - what are their findings?	1	1	1	1	1		1		1		3
100.	HR Report updates - what are their findings?	1	1	1	1	1		1		3		
101.	Operation updates - what are their findings?	1	1	1	1	1	3	1		1		
102.	Create pricing group steering committee.	1		3	1			1		1		1
103.	Define and measure lagging indicators.	3		1			1	1	1	1		1
104.	Create possibility thinking questions to solve problems.	3										
105.	Communications	3										
	P#6 PRIZE	**Project Manager**	**Pioneer Penguins**	**Project Sponsor**	**EXCO/ Board**	**Partners HODS Team Leaders**	**Practice Manager**	**Finance**	**Marketing BD Comms PR**	**HR**	**Lawyers/ Teams**	**IT**
106.	Secure celebrating success budget.	1		3				1				
107.	Remuneration/compensation for staff implementing VBP.	1		3	1					1		
108.	VBP annual award approval.	1		3	1					1		
109.	Create list of ways to celebrate success.	3	1	1					1	1		
110.	Create possibility thinking questions to solve problems.	3										

111.	Communications.	3										
	P#7 PERSIST	**Project Manager**	**Pioneer Penguins**	**Project Sponsor**	**EXCO/ Board**	**Partners HODS Team Leaders**	**Practice Manager**	**Finance**	**Marketing BD Comms PR**	**HR**	**Lawyers/ Teams**	**IT**
112.	Pricing steering group - create terms of reference and template agendas. Set meeting dates.	1		3				1	1	1		1
113.	Pioneer Penguin Group - second wave. What is required?	3	1	1						1		
114.	Define and create career development pathways for VBP champions.	1		3	1					1		
115.	Amend role profiles to identify VBP requirements.			1	1					3		
116.	Update employment contracts and bonus/compensation schemes.			1	1					3		
117.	Review, report on, and (if necessary) amend financial data measurements and lagging indicators.	1		3				1	1	1		1
118.	Review client engagement packs/retainer letters to see evidence of VBP.	3	1			1						1
119.	Review marketing collateral to see evidence of VBP.	1		1					3			
120.	Review if LLP/shareholder/ partnership agreement documentation requires amending to embed VBP.			1	3							
121.	Review client complaint/NPS data.	1		1			1		3			
122.	Design and issue change status reports.	3	1	1								

123.	Create and publish AAR annual report.	1		1		1	1		3			
124.	Create possibility thinking questions to solve problems.	3										
125.	Communications.	3										
	P#8 PASSION	**Project Manager**	**Pioneer Penguins**	**Project Sponsor**	**EXCO/ Board**	**Partners HODS Team Leaders**	**Practice Manager**	**Finance**	**Marketing BD Comms PR**	**HR**	**Lawyers/ Teams**	**IT**
126.	Conduct lessons learned workshop.	3	1	1	1	1	1	1	1	1	1	1
127.	Analyse customer feedback. Moments of truth.	1	1	1		1	1		3			
128.	Review Net Promoter Score analysis.	1	1	1		1	1		3			
129.	Review Strategy. Is the VBP vision embedded?	1		1	3	1						
130.	Culture change - has it happened?		1	3		1				1		
131.	Create possibility thinking questions to solve problems.	3										
132.	Communications.	3										

Other Books from the Publisher

The Secret Magistrate

Every criminal case starts in a magistrates' court, and most end there. Last year, the 14,000 magistrates of England & Wales dealt with almost 1.4 million cases.

But what exactly does a magistrate do, who are they, and how are they recruited and trained? Are they out-of-touch and unrepresentative, or still fit for purpose with a role to play in today's increasingly sophisticated and complex judicial system?

The Secret Magistrate takes the reader on an eye-opening, behind-the-scenes tour of a year in the life of an inner-city magistrate. Chapters cover a variety of cases, including the disqualified driver who drove away from court, the Sunbed Pervert, and Fifi the Attack Chihuahua.

(Out)Law: From Teenage Mum to Legal Trailblazer

(Out)Law is a powerful and inspiring journey of survival and resourcefulness, exploring the remarkable life of Alice Stephenson, who defied adversity to become a beacon of change in the legal world. At just 18, Alice faced the challenges of teenage motherhood and homelessness, yet refused to be defined by her circumstances. Determined and focused, she embarked on a path of education, navigating the complexities of university while juggling her responsibilities as a young mother.

Togetherness: How to Build a Winning Team

Togetherness is a powerful state of connection between individuals that can lead to amazing triumphs. In sport, teams win matches, but teams with togetherness win championships and make history.

If you want the individuals on your team to develop their skills and reach their potential, get them 'together'. The key to this, is to understand your players' group memberships and how to harness them, to create a unique team identity that is special to "us".

This concise and practical book – from Dr. Matt Slater, a world authority on togetherness – shows you how you can develop togetherness in your sporting and business teams. The journey starts with an understanding of what underpins togetherness and how it can drive high performance and well-being simultaneously. It then moves onto practical tips and activities based on the 3R model (Reflect, Represent, Realise) that you can learn and complete with your team to unlock their togetherness.

What Business Can Learn From Sport Psychology: Ten Lessons for Peak Professional Performance

This book is about getting into a winning state of body and mind for your performance – whatever that might be – sales pitches, presentations, leadership, strategic thinking, delivery, and more.

In *What Business Can Learn From Sport Psychology*, you will develop the most important weapon you need to succeed in business: your mental approach to performance. This book reveals the secrets of the winning mind by exploring the strategies and techniques used by the most successful athletes and professionals on the planet.

As you read this book, you will learn about practical and powerful techniques and refine your mental approach to business performance.

Based on decades of scientific research, the authors' professional experiences, and the experiences of winning athletes and business professionals, this book is a practical and evidence-driven resource that will teach you how to deal with pressure, break through adversity, embrace challenges, project business confidence, and much more.

www.ingramcontent.com/pod-product-compliance
Lightning Source LLC
LaVergne TN
LVHW070906210926
848482LV00017B/1009